A Concise Guide to Market Research

Erik Mooi • Marko Sarstedt

A Concise Guide
to Market Research

The Process, Data, and Methods
Using IBM SPSS Statistics

 Springer

Prof. Erik Mooi
VU University Amsterdam
Marketing Department
De Boelelaan 1105
1081 HV Amsterdam
Netherlands
emooi@feweb.vu.nl

Prof. Marko Sarstedt
Ludwig-Maximilians-University
Institute for Market-based Management
Kaulbachstr. 45
80539 Munich
Germany
sarstedt@bwl.lmu.de

ISBN 978-3-642-12540-9   e-ISBN 978-3-642-12541-6
DOI 10.1007/978-3-642-12541-6
Springer Heidelberg Dordrecht London New York

Cover design: WMXDesign GmbH, Heidelberg, Germany

Printed on acid-free paper

Springer is part of Springer Science+Business Media (www.springer.com)

To Irma and Alexandra

Preface

Charmin is a 70-year-old brand of toilet paper that made Procter & Gamble the undisputed leader in the US toilet paper market. In Germany, however, Charmin was unknown to consumers, something Procter & Gamble decided to change in the early 2000s. Acknowledging that European consumers have different needs and wants than their US counterparts, the company conducted massive market research efforts with hundreds of potential customers. The research included focus group interviews, observational studies, and large-scale surveys. These revealed considerable differences in usage habits. For example, 60% of Germans also use toilet paper to clean their noses, 7% to clean mirrors, 3% to clean children's faces and hands, and 8% use it to remove make-up. Further research led Procter & Gamble to believe that the optimal tissue color is blue/yellow and that the package needed to be cubic. Advertising tests showed that the Charmin bear worked well, giving the product an emotional appeal. In the end, Procter & Gamble launched Charmin successfully in an already saturated market.

In order to gain useful consumer insights, which allowed the company to optimize the product and position it successfully in the market, Procter & Gamble had to plan a market research process. This included asking market research question(s), collecting data, and analyzing these using quantitative methods.

This book provides an introduction to the skills necessary for conducting or commissioning such market research projects. It is written for two audiences. First, it is aimed at undergraduate as well as postgraduate students in business and market research. Second, it is aimed at practitioners wishing to know more about market research, or those who need a practical, yet theoretically sound, reference. If you search for market(ing) research books on Google or Amazon, you will find that there is no shortage of such books. However, this book differs in many important ways:

- This book is a bridge between the theory of conducting quantitative research and its execution, using the market research process as a framework. We discuss market research, starting with identifying the research question, designing the data collection process, collecting, and describing data. We also introduce essential data analysis techniques, and the basics of communicating the results, including a discussion on ethics. Each chapter on quantitative methods describes key theoretical choices and how these are executed in IBM SPSS Statistics. Unlike most other books, we do not discuss theory *or* SPSS, but link the two.

- This is a book for non-technical readers! All chapters are written in an accessible and comprehensive way so that non-technical readers can also easily grasp the data analysis methods. Each chapter on research methods includes simple examples to help the reader get a hands-on feel for the technique. Each chapter concludes with an illustrated real-life case, demonstrating the application of a quantitative method. We also provide a second, real-life case with an accompanying dataset, thus allowing readers to practice what they have learnt. Other pedagogical features such as key words, examples, and end-of-chapter questions support the contents.

- This book is concise, focusing on the most important aspects that a market researcher, or manager interpreting market research, should know.

- Many chapters provide links to further readings and other websites besides that of the book. Several mobile tags in the text allow readers to quickly browse related web content using a mobile device (see section "How to Use Mobile Tags"). This unique merger of offline and online content offers readers a broad spectrum of additional and readily accessible information. A comprehensive Web Appendix with further analysis techniques, datasets, video files, and case studies is included.

Chapter 9 - Cluster Analysis

Grouping similar customers and products is a fundamental marketing concept. It is used, for example, in market segmentation. As companies cannot connect with all their customers, they have to divide markets into groups of consumers, customers, or clients (called segments) with similar needs and wants. Each of these segments can then be targeted by firms who can position themselves in a unique segment (such as Ferrari in the high-end sports car market). While market researchers often form market segments based on theoretical or practical grounds, cluster analysis allows segments to be formed on the basis of data. The segmentation of customers constitutes a standard application of cluster analysis, but it may also be used in different, sometimes rather exotic contexts such as evaluating typical supermarket shopping paths or deriving employer branding strategies.

This chapter introduces the basic principles of and steps associated with cluster analysis. Special emphasis is paid to hierarchical and k-means clustering but the chapter also introduces the more recent two-step clustering approach.

Clustering variables ... hierarchical methods ... partitioning methods ... k-means ... two-step clustering ... agglomerative clustering ... divisive clustering ... distance matrix ... Euclidean distance ... city-block distance ... Chebychev distance ... matching coefficients ... dendrogram ... profiling clusters ... icicle diagram

- Lastly, we have set up a Facebook community page labeled "A Concise Guide to Market Research." This page provides a platform for discussions and the exchange of market research ideas. Just look for our book in the Facebook groups and join.

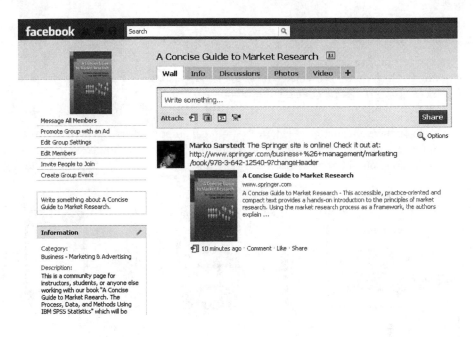

How to Use Mobile Tags

In this book, you will find numerous two-dimensional barcodes (so-called mobile tags) which enable you to gather digital information immediately. Using your mobile phone's integrated camera plus a mobile tag reader, you can call up a website directly on your mobile phone without having to enter it via the keypad. For example, the following mobile tag links to this book's website at http://www. guide-market-research.com.

Several mobile phones have a mobile tag reader readily installed but you can also download a reader for free. In this book, we use QR (quick response) codes which can be accessed by means of the readers below. Note that the reader you need to install will depend on the type of mobile phone you use.

- Kaywa: http://reader.kaywa.com/
- i-Nigma: http://www.i-nigma.com/or iPhone App store
- Upcode: http://www.upcode.com/or iPhone App store
- Optiscan: iPhone App store

Once you have a reader installed, just start it and point your camera at the mobile tag and take a picture (with some readers, you don't even have to take a picture). This will open your mobile phone browser and direct you to the associated website.

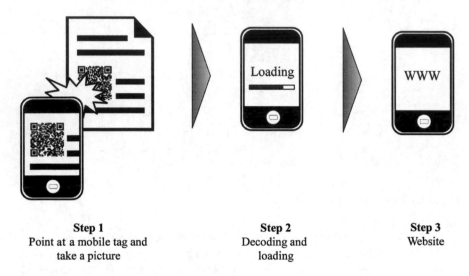

Step 1
Point at a mobile tag and
take a picture

Step 2
Decoding and
loading

Step 3
Website

Several of these mobile tags direct you to interesting sites containing additional descriptions of the concepts we discuss, case studies or videos.

For Instructors

Besides those benefits described above, this book is also designed to make teaching using this book as easy as possible. Each chapter comes with a set of detailed and professionally designed instructors' Microsoft PowerPoint slides tailored for this book which can be easily adjusted to fit the specific course's needs. These are available on the website's instructor resources page at http://www.guide-market-research.com. You can gain access to the instructor's page by requesting login information under Service ▶ Instructor Support.

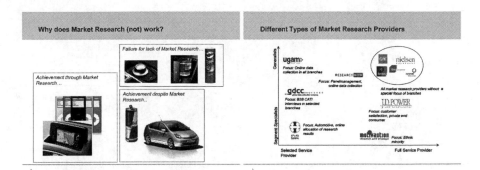

The book's web appendices are freely available on the accompanying website and provide supplementary information on analysis techniques, datasets, video files, and additional discussions of further methods not entirely covered in the book. Moreover, at the end of each chapter, there is a set of questions that can be used for in-class discussions.

If you have any remarks, suggestions, or ideas about this book, please drop us a line at emooi@feweb.vu.nl (Erik Mooi) or sarstedt@bwl.lmu.de (Marko Sarstedt). We appreciate any feedback on the book's concept and contents!

Final Note

We have many people to thank for making this book possible. First, we would like to thank Springer, and particularly Barbara Fess, for all of their help and for their willingness to publish this book. Second, Ilse Evertse, Ilze Hugo, Kobus Geldenhuys, and Daan Joubert have hugely contributed to this book by proofreading all the chapters. They are great proofreaders and we cannot recommend them enough! Drop them a line at stpubus@gmail.com (Ilse Evertse), ilzetjie@gmail.com (Ilze Hugo), gelden@iafrica.com (Kobus Geldenhuys), or chartsym@gmail.com (Daan Joubert) if you need proofreading help. Furthermore, without the constant support and enduring patience of our families, friends, and colleagues, this book would not have been possible – thank you so much! This book is dedicated to our wives Irma and Alexandra.

Finaly, a large number of people have contributed to this book by reading chapters, providing examples, or datasets. Thanks to all of you!

Amsterdam, The Netherlands   Erik Mooi
Munich, Germany   Marko Sarstedt

Contents

Contributors

Feray Adigüzel VU Universiteit Amsterdam, Amsterdam, The Netherlands

Saima Bantvawala VU Universiteit Amsterdam, Amsterdam, The Netherlands

Carolin Bock Technische Universität München, Munich, Germany

Cees J.P.M. de Bont TU Delft, Delft, The Netherlands

Eva M. Didden Ludwig-Maximilians-Universität München, Munich, Germany

Andrew M. Farrell Aston University, Birmingham, UK

David I. Gilliland Colorado State University, Fort Collins, CO, USA

Hester van Herk VU Universiteit Amsterdam, Amsterdam, The Netherlands

Emile F.J. Lancée VU Universiteit Amsterdam, Amsterdam, The Netherlands

Sabine Lengauer Azubiyo, Munich, Germany

Kobe Millet Katolieke Universiteit Leuven, Leuven, Belgium

Leonard J. Paas VU Universiteit Amsterdam, Amsterdam, The Netherlands

Johanna Pauge Procter & Gamble, Geneva, Switzerland

Marcelo Gattermann Perin Pontifícia Universidade Católica do Rio Grande do Sul, Porto Alegre, Brazil

Wybe T. Popma University of Brighton, Brighton, UK

Sascha Raithel Ludwig-Maximilians-Universität München, Munich, Germany

Irma Reçi VU Universiteit Amsterdam, Amsterdam, The Netherlands

Edward E. Rigdon Georgia State University, Atlanta, GA, USA

John Rudd Aston University, Birmingham, UK

Sebastian Scharf Biesalski & Company, Munich, Germany

Tobias Schütz Hochschule Reutlingen, Reutlingen, Germany

Charles R. Taylor Villanova University, Villanova, PA, USA

Eline de Vries and Van Ketel Intomart GFK, Hilversum, The Netherlands

Stefan Wagner Ludwig-Maximilians-Universität München, Munich, Germany

Eelke Wiersma VU Universiteit Amsterdam, Amsterdam, The Netherlands

Caroline Wiertz Cass Business School, City University London, London, UK

Chapter 1
Introduction to Market Research

Learning Objectives

After reading this chapter, you should understand:

- What market and marketing research are and how they differ.
- How practitioner and academic market(ing) research differ and where they are similar.
- When market research should be conducted.
- Who provides market research and the importance of the market research industry.

Keywords Full service and limited service providers · Market and marketing research · Syndicated data

Introduction

When Toyota developed the Prius – a highly fuel-efficient car using a hybrid petrol/electric engine – it took a gamble on a grand scale. Honda and General Motors' previous attempts to develop frugal (electric) cars had not worked well. Just like Honda and General Motors, Toyota had also been working on developing a frugal car but focused on a system integrating a petrol and electric engine. These development efforts led Toyota to start a development project called Global Twenty-first Century aimed at developing a car with a fuel economy that was at least 50% better than similar-sized cars. This project nearly came to a halt in 1995 when Toyota encountered substantial technological problems. The company solved these problems, using nearly a thousand engineers, and launched the car, called the Prius, in Japan in 1997. Internal Toyota predictions suggested that the car was either going to be an instant hit, or that the take-up of the product would be slow, as it takes time to teach dealers and consumers about the technology. In 1999, Toyota made the decision to start working on launching the Prius in the US. Initial market research showed that it was going to be a difficult task. Some consumers thought it was too small for the US, some thought the positioning of the controls was poor for US drivers, and there were other issues, such as the design, which many thought was too strongly geared toward Japanese drivers.

While preparing for the launch, Toyota conducted further market research, which could, however, not reveal who the potential buyers of the car would be. Initially, Toyota thought the car might be tempting for people concerned with the environment but market research dispelled this belief. Environmentalists dislike technology in general and money is a big issue for this group. A technologically complex and expensive car such as the Prius was therefore unlikely to appeal to them. Further market research did little to identify any other good market segment. Despite the lack of conclusive findings, Toyota decided to sell the car anyway and to await public reactions. Before the launch Toyota put a market research system in place to track the initial sales and identify where customers bought the car. After the formal launch in 2000, this system quickly found that the car was being bought by celebrities to demonstrate their concern for the environment. Somewhat later, Toyota noticed substantially increased sales figures when ordinary consumers became aware of the car's appeal to celebrities. It appeared that consumers were willing to purchase cars endorsed by celebrities.

CNW Market Research, a market research company specialized in the automotive industry, attributed part of the Prius's success to its unique design, which clearly demonstrated that Prius owners were driving a different car. After substantial increases in the petrol price, and changes to the car (based on extensive market research) to increase its appeal, Toyota reached total sales of over 2 million and is now the market leader in hybrid petrol/electric cars.

This example shows that while market research occasionally helps and greatly increases sales, sometimes it contributes little or even fails. There are many reasons for market research varying between being helpful and failing. These reasons include the budget available for research, support for market research in the organization, and the research skills of the market researchers. In this book, we will guide you through the practicalities of the basic market research process step by step. These discussions, explanations, facts, and methods will help you carry out market research successfully.

What is Market and Marketing Research?

Market research can mean several things. It can be the process by which we gain insight into how markets work, a function in an organization, or it can refer to the outcomes of research, such as a database of customer purchases or a report including recommendations. In this book, we focus on the market research process, starting by identifying and formulating the problem, continuing by determining the research design, determining the sample and method of data collection, collecting the data, analyzing the data, interpreting, discussing, and presenting the findings, and ending with the follow-up.

Some people consider *marketing research* and *market research* to be synonymous, whereas others regard these as different concepts. We understand marketing research as defined by the American Marketing Association, the largest marketing association in North America:

> The function that links the consumer, customer, and public to the marketer through information – information used to identify and define marketing opportunities and problems; generate, refine, and evaluate marketing actions; monitor marketing performance; and improve understanding of marketing as a process. Marketing research specifies the information required to address these issues, designs the method for collecting information, manages and implements the data collection process, analyzes the results, and communicates the findings and their implications (American Marketing Association 2004).

On the other hand, ESOMAR, the world organization for market, consumer and societal research, defines market research as:

> The systematic gathering and interpretation of information about individuals or organizations using the statistical and analytical methods and techniques of the applied social sciences to gain insight or support decision making. The identity of respondents will not be revealed to the user of the information without explicit consent and no sales approach will be made to them as a direct result of their having provided information (ICC/ESOMAR international code on market and social research 2007).

Both definitions overlap substantially but the definition of the AMA focuses on marketing research as a *function* (e.g., a department in an organization), whereas the ESOMAR definition focuses on the *process*. In this book, we focus on the process and, thus, on market research.

Whatever the case, practitioners and academics are involved in marketing and market research. These academic and practitioner views of market(ing) research differ in any ways but also have many communalities. For example, the tools and techniques developed and first applied by academics were subsequently adopted by practitioners. Examples of such tools include factor analysis and conjoint analysis. Although a small number of practitioner-developed tools were subsequently adopted by academics, in general, practitioners work with tools and techniques and concepts that academics developed. Although this is a similarity, in practice the rigor with which practitioners apply these tools is often less than when they are used by academics. This is partially due to the greater time pressures that practitioners face. Practitioners usually have a much shorter time span in which to carry out research than academics because, for example, research may need to be carried out in a hurry to study how the planned launch of a new product is impacted by competitors' moves. Thus, both the time available to carry out research, as well as the window of opportunity to do so, may differ between practitioners and academics. Another reason why practitioner and academic rigor differs is due to those who assess the research both parties undertake. Managers (who are mostly the "judges" of market research) may be predominantly concerned with the insights generated and market research's subsequent help with reaching targets and, consequently, less concerned with the rigor of the tools or techniques applied. In comparison, academic marketing research is judged mostly by editors and journal reviewers. These editors and reviewers are highly trained in research tools and techniques and focus on both rigor and relevance. Interestingly, practitioners often claim that their research is based on academic research but the reverse (academics claiming their research is based on practitioners' standards) never happens.

Besides these differences, there are also many similarities. For example, good measurement is paramount for academics as well as practitioners. Furthermore, academics and practitioners should be interested in each others' work; academics can learn much from the practical issues faced by practitioners while practitioners can gain much from understanding tools, techniques, and concepts that academics develop. The need to learn from each other was underlined by Reibstein et al. (2009), who issued an urgent call for the academic marketing community to focus on relevant business problems.[1] Finally, contributing to academic and practitioner research can be highly rewarding career paths!

When Should Market Research (Not) Be Conducted?

Market research serves a number of useful roles in organizations. Most importantly, market research can help organizations by providing answers to questions firms may have about their customers and competitors; answers that could help such firms increase their performance. Specific questions related to this include identifying market opportunities, measuring customer satisfaction, and assessing market shares. Some of these questions arise ad hoc, perhaps due to issues that the top management, or one of the departments or divisions have perceived. Much of the research is, however, programmatic; it arises because firms systematically evaluate elements of the market. An example of this type of research is conducted by Subway, the restaurant chain, that uses tools to systematically measure customer satisfaction. This type of research does not usually have a distinct beginning and end (contrary to much of ad hoc research) but continues over time and leads to daily, weekly, or monthly reports.

The decision to conduct market research may be taken when managers face an uncertain situation and when the costs of undertaking good research are (much) lower than the expected benefits of making good decisions. Therefore, researching trivial issues or issues that cannot be changed is likely to be bad decisions.

Other issues to consider are the politics within the organization; if the decision to go ahead has already been taken (as in the Prius example in the introduction), market research is unnecessary. If it is conducted and supports the decision, it is of little value (and those undertaking the research may be biased towards supporting the decision), while it is ignored if it rejects the decision.

Moreover, if organizations need to make very quick decisions (responding to competitive price changes, unexpected changes in regulation or the economic climate), research should mostly not be undertaken. Although market research may help, the need for timeliness is likely to mean that the research in support of

---

[1]See also Lee and Greenley (2010) on this discussion.

making decisions is likely to be concluded after the decisions have already been made.

Who Provides Market Research?

Many organizations have people, departments, or other companies working for them to provide market research. In Fig. 1.1, we show who these providers of market research are.

Most market research is provided internally through specialized market research departments or people tasked with this function. It appears that about 75% of organizations have at least one person tasked with carrying out market research. This percentage is similar across most industries, although it is much less in government sectors and, particularly, in health care (Churchill and Iacobucci 2005).

In larger organizations, internally provided market research is usually undertaken by a specific group within the marketing department. Sometimes this sub department is not connected to a marketing department but is connected to other organizational functions, such as corporate planning or sales. Certain large organizations even have a separate market research department. This system of having a separate marketing research department or attaching it to other departments seems to become more widespread with the marketing function increasingly devolving into other functions within organizations (Sheth and Sisodia 2006).

The external providers of market research are a powerful economic force. In 2008, external providers had a turnover of about 19.75 USD billion collectively (Honomichl 2009). The market research industry has also become a global field with companies such as the Nielsen Company (USA), Taylor Nelson (UK), GfK (Germany), Ipsos (France), and INTAGE (Japan) playing major roles outside their home markets. External providers of market research are either full or limited service providers.

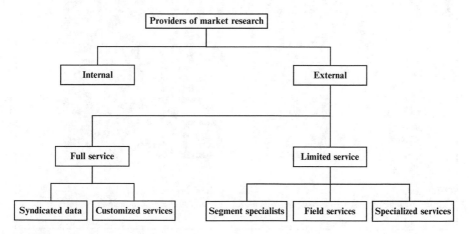

Fig. 1.1 The providers of market research

Full service providers are large market research companies such as the Nielsen Company, Taylor Nelson, and GfK. These large companies provide syndicated data as well as customized services. Syndicated data are data collected in a standard format and not specifically collected for a single client. These data, or analyses based on the data, are then sold to multiple clients. Syndicated data are mostly collected by large marketing research firms, as they have the resources to collect large amounts of data and can spread the costs of doing so over a number of clients. For example, the Nielsen company collects syndicated data in several forms: Nielsen's Netratings, containing information on digital media; Nielsen Ratings, which details the type of consumer who listens to the radio, watches TV, or reads print media; and Nielsen Homescan, which consists of panel information on the purchases consumers make. These large firms also conduct studies for a specific client, which is labeled a *customized service*. These customized services can be very specific, such as helping a client with a specific analysis technique.

Compared to full service providers, which undertake nearly all market research activities, *limited service providers* specialize in one or more services and tend to be smaller companies. In fact, many of the specialized market research companies are one-man businesses with the owner, after (or besides) a practitioner or academic career, offering his or her specialized services. Although there are many different types of limited service firms, we only discuss three of them: those focused on segmentation, field service, and specialized services.

Segment specialists focus on specific market segments. Examples of such specialists include RSA Ltd. (see Box 1.1), which focuses on market research in the airline and airport sector. Other segment specialists do not focus on a particular industry but on a type of customer. Ethnic Focus (see Box 1.1), a UK-based market research firm, for example, focuses on understanding ethnic minorities.

Box 1.1 Web links and mobile tags

RSA Ltd.
http://www.asm-global.com/page.php?id=918

Ethnic Focus
http://www.ethnicfocus.com/

(*continued*)

Survey Sampling International
http://www.surveysampling.com/

Field service firms, such as Survey Sampling International (see Box 1.1), focus on executing surveys, for example, determining samples, sample sizes, and collecting data. Some of these firms also deal with translating surveys, providing addresses and contact details.

Specialized Service firms are a catch-all term for firms that have specific technical skills, that only focusing on specific products, or aspects of products such as market research on taste and smell. Specialized firms may also focus on a few highly specific market research techniques, or may focus on one or more highly specialized analysis techniques, such as time series analysis, panel data analysis, or quantitative text analysis. These specialized firms are often subcontractors carrying out a part of a larger research project. Subcontractors are quite important and subcontractors undertake about 15% of all external market research activities regarding turnover in the Netherlands (MOA 2009).

The choice between these full service and limited service market research firms boils down to a tradeoff between what they can provide (if it is highly specialized, you may not have much choice) and the price of doing so. In addition, if you have to piece many studies together to gain further insight, full service firms may be better than multiple limited service firms. Obviously, the fit and feel *with* the provider are highly important too!

Questions

1. What is market research? Try to explain what market research is in your own words.
2. Imagine you are the head of a division of Procter & Gamble. You are just about ready to launch a new shampoo but are uncertain about who might buy it. Is it

useful to conduct a market research study? Should you delay the launch of the product?

3. Try to find the websites of a few market research firms. Look for example at the services provided by GfK and the Nielsen Company and compare the extent of their offerings to those of specialized firms such as those listed on, for example, http://www.greenbook.org

4. If you have a specialized research question, such as what market opportunities there are for selling music to ethnic minorities, would you use a full service or limited service firm (or both)? Please discuss the benefits and drawbacks.

Further Readings

American Marketing Association at http://www.marketingpower.com
Website of the American Marketing Association. Provides information on their activities and also links to two of the premier marketing journals, the Journal of Marketing and the Journal of Marketing Research.
Marketing Research Association at http://www.mra-net.org
The Marketing Research Association is based in the US and focuses on providing knowledge, advice, and standards to those working in the market research profession.
The British Market Research Society at http://www.mrs.org.uk
The website of the British Market Research society contains a searchable directory of market research providers and useful information on market research careers and jobs.
Associação Brasileira de Empresas de Pesquisa (Brazilian Association of Research Companies) at http://www.abep.org/novo/default.aspx
The website of the Brazilian Association of Research Companies. It provides some English documents as well as Brazilian documents on research ethics, standards, etc.
ESOMAR at http://www.esomar.org
The website of ESOMAR, the world organization for market, consumer and societal research. Amongst other activities, ESOMAR sets ethical and technical standards for market research and publishes books and reports on market research.
GreenBook: The guide for buyers of marketing research services at http://www.greenbook.org
This website provides an overview of many different types of limited service firms.

References

AMA definition of Marketing (2004) http://www.Marketingpower.com/AboutAMA/pages/definition ofmarketing.aspx
Churchill GA, Iaccobucci D (2005) Marketing research: methodological foundation, 9th edn. Mason, OH: Thomson

Honomichl J (2009) 2009 Honomichl Top 50. Mark News 43(11):12–72

ICC/ESOMAR international code on market and social research (2007) http://www.netcasearbitration. com/uploadedFiles/ICC/policy/marketing/Statements/ICCESOMAR_Code_English.pdf

Lee N, Greenley G (2010) The theory-practice divide: thoughts from the Editors and Senior Advisory Board of EJM. Eur J Mark 44(1/2):5–20

MOA-Center for Marketing Intelligence & Research (2009) http://moAwel.nL

Reibstein DJ, Day G, Wind J (2009) Guest editorial: is marketing academia losing its way?," J Mark 73(July):1–3

Sheth JN, Sisodia RS (eds) (2006) Does marketing need reform? In: Does marketing need reform? Fresh perspective on the future. Armonk, New York: M.E. Sharpe

Chapter 2
The Market Research Process

Learning Objectives

After reading this chapter, you should understand:
- How to determine a research design.
- The differences between, and examples of, exploratory research, descriptive research, and causal research.
- What causality is.
- The market research process.
- The difference between qualitative and quantitative research.

Keywords Descriptive research · Causal research · Ethnographies · Exploratory research · Focus groups · Hypotheses · Interviews · Lab and field experiments · Observational studies · Qualitative and quantitative research · Scanner data

---

Planning a successful market research process is complex as Best Western, a worldwide association of hotels headquartered in Phoenix Arizona, discovered. When they tried to expand the Best Western brand, they planned a substantial research process to find answers to seven major marketing questions. Answering these questions required involving several research firms, such as PriceWaterhouseCoopers. These firms then collected data to gain insights into customers, non-customers, and influencers in nine different countries.

How do organizations plan for market research processes? In this chapter, we explore the market research process and various types of research.

Introduction

Executing professional market research requires good planning. In this chapter, we introduce the planning of market research projects, starting with identifying and formulating the problem and ending with presenting the findings and the follow-up (see Fig. 2.1). This chapter is also an outline for the chapters to come.

E. Mooi and M. Sarstedt, *A Concise Guide to Market Research*,
DOI 10.1007/978-3-642-12541-6_2, © Springer-Verlag Berlin Heidelberg 2011

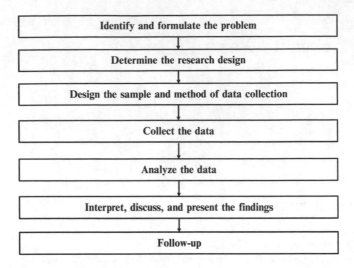

Fig. 2.1 The market research process

Identify and Formulate the Problem

The first step in setting up a market research process involves identifying and formulating the research problem. Identifying the research problem is valuable, but also difficult. To identify the "right" research problem, we have to first identify the marketing symptoms or marketing opportunities. The *marketing symptom* is the (usually tangible) problem that an organization faces. Examples of a marketing symptom include declining market shares, increasing numbers of complaints, or new products that consumers do not adopt. In some cases, there is no real existing problem but rather a *marketing opportunity*, such as potential benefits offered by new channels and products, or emerging market opportunities that need to be explored.

Organizations should identify the *marketing problem*, based on marketing symptoms or opportunities, if they want to undertake market research. The marketing problem explores what underlies the marketing symptom or opportunity by asking questions such as:

- *Why* is our market share declining?
- *Why* do the number of complaints increase?
- *Why* are our new products not successful?

Such marketing problems are divided into three categories: ambiguous problems, somewhat defined problems, and clearly defined problems.

Ambiguous problems occur when we know very little about the issues important to solve them. For example, the introduction of radically new technologies or products is often surrounded by ambiguity. When Amazon.com started selling products online, critical but little understood issues arose, such as how to deal with the logistics and encouraging customers to access the website.

When we face *somewhat defined problems*, we know the issues (and variables) that are important for solving the problem, but not how they are related. For example, when an organization wants to export products, it is relatively easy to obtain all sorts of information, for example, on market sizes, economic development, and the political and legal system. However, how these variables impact exporting success may be very uncertain.

When we face *clearly defined problems*, both the issues and variables that are important, and their relationships are clear. However, we do not know how to make the best possible choice. Thus, we face a problem of how to optimize the situation. A clearly defined problem may arise when organizations want to change their prices. While organizations know that increasing (or decreasing) prices generally results in decreased (increased) demand, the precise relationship (i.e., how many units do we sell less when the price is increased by 1 US Dollar (USD)?) is unknown.

Determine the Research Design

The research design is related to the identification and formulation of the problem. Research problems and research designs are highly related. If we start working on an issue that has never been researched before, we seem to enter a funnel where we initially ask exploratory questions because we as yet know little about the issues we face. These exploratory questions are best answered using an exploratory research design. Once we have a clearer picture of the research issue after exploratory research, we move further into the funnel. Typically, we want to learn more by describing the research problem in terms of descriptive research. Once we have a reasonably complete picture of all the issues, it may be time to determine exactly how key variables are linked. Thus, we move to the narrowest part of the funnel. We do this through causal (not *casual*!) research (Fig. 2.2).

Exploratory Research

As its name suggests, the objective of exploratory research is to explore a problem or situation. As such, exploratory research has several key uses in solving ambiguous problems. It can help organizations formulate their problems exactly. Through initial research, such as interviewing potential customers, opportunities and pitfalls may be identified that help to determine or refine the research problem. It is crucial to discuss this information with the client to ensure that your findings are helpful. Such initial research also helps establish priorities (what is *nice* to know and what is *important* to know?) and to eliminate impractical ideas. For example, market research helped Toyota dispel the belief that people concerned with the

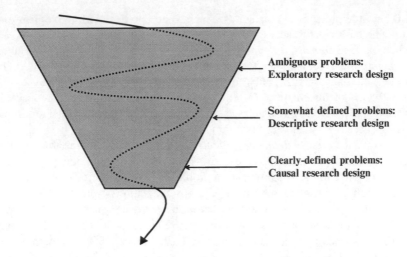

Ambiguous problems:
Exploratory research design

Somewhat defined problems:
Descriptive research design

Clearly-defined problems:
Causal research design

Fig. 2.2 The relationship between the marketing problem and the research design

environment would buy the Prius, as this target group has an aversion to high technology and lacks spending power.

Uses of Exploratory Research

Exploratory research may be used to formulate problems precisely. For example, interviews, focus groups, projective tests, observational studies, and ethnographies are often used to achieve this. When *personal interviews* are conducted, an interviewer asks the interviewee a number of questions. On the other hand, *focus groups* usually have between 4 and 6 participants who, led by a moderator, discuss a particular subject. The key difference between an interview and focus group is that focus group participants can react with one another (e.g., "What do you mean by...?", "How does this differ from...."), thereby providing insight into group dynamics. *Projective tests* present people with pictures, words, or other stimuli to which they respond. For example, a researcher could ask what people think of BMW owners ("A BMW owner is someone who....") or could show them a picture of a BMW and ask them what they associate the picture with. Moreover, when designing new products, market researchers can use different pictures and words to create analogies to existing products and product categories, thus making the adoption of new products more attractive (Feiereisen et al. 2008).

Observational studies are also frequently used to refine research questions and clarify issues. Observational studies require an observer to monitor and interpret participants' behavior. For example, someone could monitor how consumers spend their time in shops or how they walk through the aisles of a supermarket. These studies require the presence of a person, camera or other tracking devices, such as

RFID chips, to monitor behavior. Other observational studies may consist of click stream data that tracks information on the web pages people have visited. Observational studies can also be useful to understand how people consume and/or use products. Such studies found, for example, that baby wipes are frequently used to clean leather and cars!

Ethnographies (or ethnographic studies) originate from anthropology. In ethnographic research a researcher interacts with consumers over a period to observe and ask questions. Such studies can consist of, for example, a researcher living with a family to observe how people buy, consume, and dispose products. For example, the market research company BBDO used ethnographies to understand consumers' rituals. The company found that many consumer rituals are ingrained in consumers in certain countries, but not in others. For example, women in Colombia, Brazil, and Japan are more than twice as likely to apply make-up when in their cars than women in other countries. These findings can help marketers in many ways.

Exploratory research can help establish research priorities. What is important to know and what is less important? For example, a *literature search* may reveal that there are useful previous studies and that new market research is not necessary. Eliminating impractical ideas may also be achieved through exploratory research. Again, literature searches, just like interviews, may be useful to eliminate impractical ideas.

Another helpful aspect of exploratory research is the formulation of *hypotheses*. A hypothesis is a claim made about a population, which can be tested by using sample results. For example, one could hypothesize that at least 10% of people in France are aware of a certain product. Marketers frequently put forward such hypotheses because they help structure decision making processes. In Chap. 6, we discuss the nature of hypotheses and how they can be tested in further detail.

Another use of exploratory research is to develop *measurement scales*. For example, what questions can we use to measure customer satisfaction? What questions work best in our context? Do potential respondents understand the wording, or do we need to make changes? Exploratory research can help us answer such questions. For example, an exploratory literature search may contain measurement scales that tell us how to measure important variables such as corporate reputation and service quality. Many of these measurement scales are also included in the Marketing Handbook of Scales, such as the scale book published by Bruner et al. (2001).

Descriptive Research

As its name implies, descriptive research is all about describing certain phenomena, characteristics or functions. It can focus on one variable (e.g., profitability) or on two or more variables at the same time ("What is the relationship between market share and profitability?" and "How does temperature relate to sales of ice cream?"). Such descriptive research often builds upon previous exploratory research. After all, to describe something, we must have a good idea of what we need to measure and how we should measure it. Key ways in which descriptive research can help us include describing customers, competitors, market segments, and measuring performance.

Uses of Descriptive Research

Market researchers conduct descriptive research for many purposes. These include, for example, describing customers or competitors. For instance, how large is the UK market for pre-packed cookies? How large is the worldwide market for cruises priced 10,000 USD and more? How many new products did our competitors launch last year? Descriptive research helps us answer such questions. For example, the Nielsen Company has vast amounts of data available in the form of *scanner data*. Scanner data are mostly collected at the checkout of a supermarket where details about each product sold are entered into a vast database. By using scanner data, it is, for example, possible to describe the market for pre-packed cookies in the UK.

Descriptive research is frequently used to segment markets. As companies often cannot connect with all customers individually, they divide markets into groups of consumers, customers, or clients with similar needs and wants. These are called *segments*. Firms can then target each of these segments by positioning themselves in a unique segment (such as Ferrari in the high-end sports car market). There are many market research companies specializing in market segmentation, such as Claritas, which developed a segmentation scheme for the US market called PRIZM (Potential Ratings Index by Zip Markets). PRIZM segments consumers along a multitude of attitudinal, behavioral, and demographic characteristics and companies can use this to better target their customers. Segments have names, such as Up-and-Comers (young professionals with a college degree and a mid-level income) and Backcountry Folk (older, often retired people with a high school degree and low income).

Another important function of descriptive market research is to measure performance. Nearly all companies regularly track their sales across specific product categories to evaluate the firm, managers, or specific employees' performance. Such descriptive work overlaps the finance or accounting departments' responsibilities. However, market researchers also frequently measure performance using measures that are quite specific to marketing, such as *share of wallet* (i.e., how much do people spend on a certain brand or company in a product category?) and *brand awareness* (i.e., do you know brand/company X?).

Causal Research

Market researchers undertake causal research less frequently than exploratory or descriptive research. Nevertheless, it is important to understand the delicate relationships between variables that are important to marketing. Causal research is used to understand how changes in one variable (e.g., the wording in advertising) affect another variable (e.g., understanding as a result of advertising). The key usage of causal research is to uncover *causality*. Causality is the relationship between an event (the cause) and a second event (the effect), when the second event is a consequence of the first. To claim causality, we need to meet four requirements:

First, the variable that causes the other needs to be related to the other. Simply put, if we want to determine whether price changes cause sales to drop, there should be a relationship or correlation (see Chap. 5). Note that people often confuse correlation and causality. Just because there is some type of relationship between to variables does not mean that the one caused the other (see Box 2.1). Second, the cause needs to come before the effect. This is the requirement of time order. Third, we need to control for other factors. If we increase the price, sales may go up because competitors increase their prices even more. Controlling for other factors is difficult, but not impossible. In experiments, we design studies so that external factors' effect is nil, or as close to nil as possible. This is achieved by, for example, randomly giving participants a stimulus (such as information on a price increase) in an experiment, or by controlling environmental factors by conducting experiments in labs where, for example, light and noise conditions are constant (controlled). To control for other factors, we can also use statistical tools that account for external influences. These statistical tools include analysis of variance (see Chap. 6), regression analysis (see Chap. 7), and structural equation modeling (see end of Chap. 8). Finally, an important criterion is that there needs to be a good explanatory theory. Without theory our effects may be due to chance and no "real" effect may be present. For example, we may observe that when we advertise, sales decrease. Without any good explanation for this (such as that people dislike the advertisement), we cannot claim that there is a causal relationship.

Box 2.1 Correlation does not imply causation

Correlation between two variables does not automatically imply causality. For example, in Fig. 2.3 US fatal motor vehicle crashes (per 100,000 people) are plotted against the harvested area of melons (in 1,000 acres) between 1996 and 2005.

Clearly, the picture shows a trend. If the harvested area of melons increases, the number of US fatal motor vehicle crashes increases. This is a correlation and the first requirement to determine causality. Where the story falls short in determining causality is explanatory theory. What possible mechanism could explain the findings? Other examples include the following:

- As ice cream sales increase, the rate of drowning deaths increases sharply. Therefore, ice cream causes drowning.
- With a decrease in the number of pirates, there has been an increase in global warming over the same period. Therefore, global warming is caused by a lack of pirates.

If the above facts were to be presented, most people would be highly skeptical and would not interpret these facts as describing a causal mechanism.

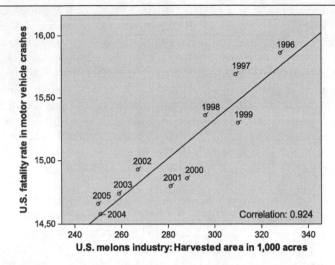

Fig. 2.3 Correlation and causation. The data were taken from the NHTSA Traffic Safety Facts, DOT HS 810 780, and the United States Department of Agriculture, National Agricultural Statistics Service

For other mechanisms, the situation is much less clear-cut. Think of claims that are part of everyday market research, such as "The new advertisement campaign caused a sharp increase in sales," "Our company's sponsorship activities helped improve our company's reputation," or "Declining sales figures are caused by competitors' aggressive price policies." Even if there is a correlation, the other requirements to determine causality may not be met. Causal research may help us to determine if causality really exists in these situations.

Some of the above and further examples can be found in Huff (1993) or on Wikipedia.

http://en.wikipedia.org/wiki/Correlation_does_not_imply_causation

Causal research is important, as it provides exact insights into how variables relate and may be useful as a test run for trying out changes in the marketing mix. Key examples of causal research include lab and field experiments and test markets.

Uses of Causal Research

Experiments are a key type of causal research and come in the form of either lab or field experiments. *Lab experiments* are performed in controlled environments (usually in a company or academic lab) to gain understanding of how changes in one variable (called *stimulus*) causes changes in another variable. For example, substantial experimental research is conducted to gain understanding of how changing websites helps people navigate better through online stores, thereby increasing sales. *Field experiments* are experiments conducted in real-life settings where a stimulus (often in the form of a new product or changes in advertising) is provided to gain understanding of how these changes impact sales. Field experiments are not set up in controlled environments (thus eliminating some of the causality claim's strength), but their realism makes them attractive for market research purposes. Field experiments are conducted regularly. For example, Procter & Gamble conducted a substantial number of field experiments to test the effects of different pricing strategies to help ease challenges and brand loyalty issues related to promotional pricing (see mobile tag and URL in Box 2.2 for more information). We discuss experimental set-ups in more detail in Chap. 4.

Box 2.2 Procter & Gamble's value pricing strategy

http://www.emorymi.com/neslin.shtml

Test markets are a particular form of field experiments in which organizations in a geographically defined area introduce new products and services, or change the marketing mix to gauge consumer reactions. For example, Acxiom and GFK's Behaviorscan provide test market services. Picking a controlled and geographically

Table 2.1 Types of research, uses, and examples

Type of research	Examples
Exploratory	Formulate problems precisely
	Establish priorities for research
	Eliminate impractical ideas
	Develop hypotheses
	Develop measurement scales
Descriptive	Describe customers/competitors
	Describe segments
	Measure performance
Causal	Explore causal relationships

defined test market is difficult. Test markets help marketers learn about consumer response, thus reducing the risks associated with a nationwide rollout of new products/services or changes in the marketing mix. In Chap. 4, we discuss test markets in more depth.

In Table 2.1 we provide several examples of the different types of research discussed.

Design the Sample and Method of Data Collection

After having determined the research design, we need to design a sampling plan and choose a data-collecting method. This involves deciding whether to use existing (secondary) data or to conduct primary research. We discuss this in further detail in Chap. 3.

Collect the Data

Collecting data is a practical but sometimes difficult part of the market research process. How do we design a survey? How do we measure attitudes toward a product, brand, or company if we cannot observe these attitudes directly? How do we get CEOs to respond? Dealing with such issues requires careful planning and knowledge of the marketing process. We discuss related key issues in Chap. 4.

Analyze the Data

Analyzing data requires technical skills. We discuss how to describe data in Chap. 5. After this, we introduce key techniques, such as hypothesis testing and analysis of variance (ANOVA), regression analysis, factor analysis, and cluster analysis in Chaps. 6–9. In each of these chapters, we discuss the key theoretical choices and issues market researchers face when using these techniques. We also illustrate how researchers can deal practically with these theoretical choices and issues, using the market-leading software package IBM SPSS Statistics.

Interpret, Discuss, and Present the Findings

When executing the market research process, one's immediate goals are interpreting, discussing, and presenting the findings. Consequently, researchers should provide detailed answers and actionable suggestions based on data (discussed in Chaps. 3 and 4) and analysis techniques (Chaps. 5–9). The last step is to clearly communicate the findings and recommendations to help decision making and implementation. This is further discussed in Chap. 10.

Follow-Up

Market researchers often stop when the results have been interpreted, discussed, and presented. However, following up on the research findings is important too. Implementing market research findings sometimes requires further research because suggestions or recommendations may not be feasible or practical and market conditions may have changed. From a market research firm's perspective, follow-up research on previously conducted research can be a good way of entering new deals to conduct further research.

Qualitative and Quantitative Research

In the discussion above on the market research process, we ignored the choice between qualitative and quantitative research. Nevertheless, market researchers often label themselves as either quantitative or qualitative researchers. The two types of researchers use different methodologies, different types of data, and focus on different research questions. Most people regard the difference between qualitative and quantitative as one between numbers and words, with quantitative researchers focusing on numbers and qualitative researchers on words. This distinction is not accurate, as many qualitative researchers use numbers in their analyses. Rather, the distinction should be made according to when the information is *quantified*. If we know that the possible values occur in the data before the research starts, we conduct quantitative research, while if we know only this after the data have been collected, we conduct qualitative research. Think of it in this way: if we ask survey questions and use a few closed questions such as "Is this product of good quality?" and the respondents can choose between "Completely disagree," "Somewhat disagree," "Neutral," "Somewhat agree," and "Completely agree," we know that the data we will obtain from this will – at most – contain five different values. Because we know all possible values beforehand, the data are also quantified beforehand. This is therefore quantitative research. If, on the other hand, we ask someone, "Is this product of good quality?," he or she could give many different answers, such as "Yes," "No," "Perhaps," "Last time yes, but lately...". This means we have no idea what the possible answer values are. Therefore, these data are qualitative. We can, however, recode these qualitative data and assign values to each response. Thus, we quantify the data, allowing further statistical analysis.

Qualitative and quantitative research are equally important in the market research industry in terms of money spent on services.[1]

Questions

1. What is market research? Try to explain what market research is in your own words.
2. Why do we follow a structured process when conducting market research? Are there any shortcuts you can take? Compare, for example, Polaris's market research process (http://www.polarismr.com/education/steps_index.html) with the process discussed above. What are the similarities and differences?
3. Describe what exploratory, descriptive, and causal research are and how these are related to one another. Provide an example of each type of research.
4. What are the four requirements for claiming causality? Do we meet these requirements in the following situations?

   – Good design caused the apple iPad to outsell its direct competitors.
   – Using Aspirin makes headaches disappear.
   – More advertising causes greater sales.

5. What is qualitative research and what is quantitative research? In which type of research (exploratory, descriptive, and causal) is qualitative or quantitative research most likely to be useful?

Further Readings

Levitt SD, Dubner SJ (2005) Freakonomics. A rogue economist explores the hidden side of everything. HarperCollins, New York, NY

An entertaining book that discusses statistical (mis)conceptions and introduces cases where people confuse correlation and causation.

Levitt SD, Dubner SJ (2009) Superfreakonomics. HarperCollins, New York, NY

---

[1]See http://www.e-focusgroups.com/press/online_article.html

The follow-up book on Freakonomics. Also worth a read.
Market Research Services, Inc. at http://www.mrsi.com/where.html
This website discusses how MRSI approaches the market research process.
Nielsen Retail Measurement at http://en-us.nielsen.com/tab/product_families/nielsen_retail_measurement
This website details some of the data the Nielsen company has available.
PRIZM by Claritas at http://www.claritas.com/MyBestSegments/Default.jsp?ID=20
This website allows looking up lifestyle segments at the zip level in the US.
Qualitative vs. Quantitative Research: Key Points in a Classic Debate at http://wilderdom.com/research/QualitativeVersusQuantitativeResearch.html
Explores differences between qualitative and quantitative research.

References

Bruner II, Gordon C, Karen J, Hensel PJ (2001) Marketing scales handbook: a compilation of multi-item measures, vol III. South-Western Educational Publishers, Cincinnati, OH
Feiereisen S, Wong V, Broderick AJ (2008) Analogies and mental simulations in learning for really new products: the role of visual attention. J Prod Innov Manage 25(6):593–607
Huff D (1993) How to lie with statistics. W. W. Norton & Company, New York, NY

Chapter 3
Data

Learning Objectives

After reading this chapter you should understand:
- How to explain what kind of data you use.
- The differences between qualitative and quantitative data.
- What the unit of analysis is.
- When observations are independent and when they are dependent.
- The difference between dependent and independent variables.
- Different measurement scales and equidistance.
- The differences between primary and secondary data.
- Reliability and validity from a conceptual viewpoint.
- How to set up several different sampling designs.
- How to determine acceptable sample sizes.

Keywords Case · Construct · Data · Equidistance · Item · Measurement scaling · Observation · Operationalization · Primary and secondary data · Qualitative and quantitative data · Reliability · Validity · Sample sizes · Sampling · Scale development · Variable

Introduction

Data lie at the heart of conducting market research. By *data* we mean a collection of facts that can be used as a basis for analysis, reasoning, or discussions. Think, for example, of the answers people give to surveys, existing company records, or observations of shoppers' behaviors.

In practice, "good" data are very important because they are the basis for good market research findings. In this chapter, we will discuss some of the different types of data. This will help you describe what data you use and why. Subsequently, we discuss strategies to collect data in Chap. 4.

E. Mooi and M. Sarstedt, *A Concise Guide to Market Research*,
DOI 10.1007/978-3-642-12541-6_3, © Springer-Verlag Berlin Heidelberg 2011

Types of Data

Before we start discussing data, it is a good idea to introduce some terminology. Data are present in the form of variables and cases for quantitative data and in the form of words and pictures for qualitative data (we will further discuss this distinction later in this chapter). A *variable* is an attribute whose value can change. For example, the price of a product is an attribute of that product and typically varies over time. If the price does not change, it is a *constant*. A *case* (or *observation*) consists of all the observed variables that belong to an object such as a customer, a company or a country. The relationship between variables and cases is that within one case we usually find multiple variables. In Table 3.1, you can see typical examples of data. In the columns, you find the variables. There are six variables; *type of car bought*, *age* and *gender*, as well as *brand_1*, *brand_2*, and *brand_3* which capture statements related to brand trust. In the lower rows, you can see the four observations we have.

Although marketers often talk about variables, they also use the word *item*, which usually refers to a survey question put to a respondent. Another important term that is frequently used in market research is *construct*, which refers to a variable that is not directly observable. For example, while *gender* and *age* are directly observable, this is not the case with concepts such as customer satisfaction, loyalty or brand trust. More precisely, a construct can be defined as a concept which cannot be directly observed, and for which there are multiple referents, but none all-inclusive. For example, *type of car bought* from Table 3.1 is not a hypothetical construct because, despite variation in brands and categories, there is an agreed upon definition for a car with specific characteristics that distinguish a car from, for example, a plane. Furthermore, the type of car can be directly observed (e.g., BMW 328i, Mercedes C180K). On the other hand, constructs consist of groups of functionally related behaviors, attitudes, and experiences and are psychological in nature. Researchers cannot directly measure satisfaction, loyalty, or brand trust. However, they can measure indicators or manifestations of what we have agreed to call satisfaction, loyalty, or trust, for example, in a brand, product or company. Consequently, we generally have to combine several items to form a so called multi-item scale which can be used to measure a construct.

This aspect of combining several items is called *scale development, operationalization*, or, in special cases, *index construction*. Essentially, it is a combination of theory and statistical analysis, such as factor analysis (discussed in Chap. 8) aiming at developing appropriate measures of a construct. For example, in Table 3.1, *brand_1*, *brand_2*, and *brand_3* are items that belong to a construct called brand trust (as defined by Erdem and Swait 2004). The construct is not an individual item that you see in the list, but it is captured by calculating the average of a number of related items. Thus, for brand trust, the score for customer 1 is $(6 + 5 + 7)/3 = 6$.

But how do we decide which and how many items to use when measuring specific constructs? To answer these questions, market researchers make use of scale development procedures which follow an iterative process with several steps

Table 3.1 Quantitative data

Variable name	type of car bought	age	gender	brand_1	brand_2	brand_3
Description	Name of car bought	Age in years	Gender (male = 0, female = 1)	This brand's product claims are believable (1 = fully disagree, 7 = fully agree)	This brand delivers what it promises (1 = fully disagree, 7 = fully agree)	This brand has a name that you can trust (1 = fully disagree, 7 = fully agree)
Customer 1	BMW 328i	29	1	6	5	7
Customer 2	Mercedes C180K	45	0	6	6	6
Customer 3	VW Passat 2.0 TFSI	35	0	7	5	5
Customer 4	BMW 525ix	61	1	5	4	5

and feedback loops. For example, DeVellis (2003) and Rossiter (2010) provide two different approaches to scale development. Unfortunately, these procedures require much (technical) expertise. Describing each step goes beyond the scope of this book. However, for many scales you do not need to use this procedure, as existing scales can be found in scale handbooks, such as the *Handbook of Marketing Scales* by Bearden and Netemeyer (1999). Furthermore, marketing and management journals frequently publish research articles that introduce new scales, such as for the reputation of non-profit organizations (Sarstedt and Schloderer 2010) or brand relevance (Fischer et al. 2010). Nevertheless, we introduce two distinctions that are often used to discuss constructs in Box 3.1.

Box 3.1 Type of constructs

Reflective vs. *formative constructs*: When considering reflective constructs, there is a causal relationship from the construct to the items. In other words, the items reflect the construct. This is also the case in our previous example, with three items reflecting the concept of brand trust. Thus, if a respondent changes his assessment of brand trust (e.g., because the respondent heard negative news concerning that brand), it is going to be reflected in the answers to the three items. Erdem and Swait (2004) use several (interrelated) items to capture different aspects of brand trust, which generally yields more exact and stable results. Moreover, if we have multiple items, we can use analysis techniques that inform us about the quality of measurement such as factor analysis or reliability analysis (discussed in Chap. 8). On the other hand, formative constructs consist of a number of items that define a construct. A typical example is socioeconomic status, which is formed by a combination of education, income, occupation, and residence. If any of these measures increases, socioeconomic status would increase (even if the other items did not change). Conversely, if a person's socioeconomic status increases, this would not go hand in hand with an increase in all four measures. This distinction is important when operationalizing constructs, as it requires different approaches to decide on the type and number of items. Moreover, reliability analyses (discussed in Chap. 8) cannot be used for formative measures. For an overview of this distinction, see Diamantopoulos and Winklhofer (2001) or Diamantopoulos et al. (2008).

Multi items vs. *single items*: Rather than using a large number of items to measure constructs, practitioners often opt for the use of single items to operationalize some of their constructs. For example, we may use only "This brand has a name that you can trust" to measure brand trust instead of all three items. While this is a good way to make measurement more efficient and the questionnaire shorter, it also reduces the quality of your measures. There is no general rule when the use of single items is appropriate but, in general, if a construct is concrete (which means that respondents across the board describe the construct's definition almost identically), the use of a single item to measure that construct is justifiable. For example, purchase intention is a rather concrete construct whereas corporate reputation is rather abstract. Thus, the former can be measured by means of a single item whereas multiple items should be used to measure the latter. See Bergkvist and Rossiter (2007) and Sarstedt and Wilczynski (2009) for a discussion. Fuchs and Diamantopoulos (2009) offer guidance on when to use multi items and single items.

Primary and Secondary Data

Generally, we can distinguish between two types of data: *primary* and *secondary data*. While *primary data* are data that a researcher has collected for a specific purpose, secondary data have already been collected by another researcher for another purpose. An example of secondary data is the US Consumer Expenditure Survey (http://www.bls.gov/cex/home.htm), which makes data available on what people in the US buy, such as insurances, personal care items, or food. It also includes the prices people pay for these products and services. Since these data have already been collected, they are secondary data. If a researcher sends out a survey with various questions to find an answer to a specific issue, the collected data are primary data. If these primary data are re-used to answer another research question, they become secondary data.

Secondary data can either be *internal* or *external* (or a mix of both). Internal secondary data are data that an organization or individual already has collected, but wants to use for (other) research purposes. For example, we can use sales data to investigate the success of new products, or we can use the warranty claims people make to investigate why certain products are defective. External secondary data are data that other companies, organizations, or individuals have available, sometimes at a cost.

Secondary and primary data have their own specific advantages and disadvantages. These are summed up in Table 3.2. Generally, the most important reasons for

Table 3.2 The advantages and disadvantages of secondary and primary data

	Secondary data	Primary data
Advantages	Tend to be cheaper	Are recent
	Sample sizes tend to be greater	Are specific for the purpose
	Tend to have more authority	Are proprietary
	Are usually quick to access	
	Are easier to compare to other research that uses the same data	
	Are sometimes more accurate	
Disadvantages	May be outdated	Are usually more expensive
	May not completely fit the problem	Take longer to collect
	There may be errors in the data	
	Difficult to assess data quality	
	Usually contains only factual data	
	May not be available	
	No control over data collection	
	May not be reported in the required form (e.g., different units of measurement, definitions, aggregation levels of the data)	

using secondary data are that they tend to be cheaper and quick to obtain access to (although there can be lengthy processes involved). For example, if you want to have access to the US Consumer Expenditure Survey, all you have to do is point your web browser to http://www.bls.gov/cex/csxmicro.htm and pay 145 USD. Furthermore, the authority and competence of some of these research organizations might be a factor. For example, the claim that Europeans spend 9% of their annual income on health may be more believable if it comes from Eurostat (the statistical office of the European Community) than if it came from a single survey conducted through primary research.

However, important drawbacks of secondary data are that they may not answer your research question. If you are, for example, interested in the sales of a specific product (and not in a product or service category), the US Expenditure Survey may not help much. In addition, if you are interested in reasons why people buy products, this type of data may not help answer your question. Lastly, as you did not control the data collection, there may be errors in the data. Box 3.2 shows an example of inconsistent results in two well-known surveys on Internet usage.

Box 3.2 Contradictory results in secondary data

The European Interactive Advertising Association (EIAA) (http://www.eiaa.net) is a trade organization for media companies such as CNN Interactive and Yahoo! Europe focused on interactive business. The Mediascope study issued yearly by EIAA provides insight into the European population's media consumption habits. For example, according to their 2008 study, 47% of all Germans are online every single day. However, this contradicts the results from the well-known German General Survey (ALLBUS) issued by the Leibniz Institute for Social Sciences (http://www.gesis.org), according to which merely 26% of Germans used the Internet on a daily basis in 2008.

In contrast, primary data tend to be highly specific because the researcher (you!) can influence what the research comprises. In addition, primary research can be carried out when and where it is required and cannot be accessed by competitors. However, gathering primary data often requires much time and effort and, there-fore, is usually expensive compared to secondary data.

As a rule, start looking for secondary data first. If they are available, and of acceptable quality, use them! We will discuss ways to gather primary and secondary data in Chap. 4.

Quantitative and Qualitative Data

Data can be *quantitative* or *qualitative*. Quantitative data are presented in values, whereas qualitative data are not. Qualitative data can therefore take many forms such as words, stories, observations, pictures, or audio. The distinction between qualitative and quantitative data is not as black-and-white as it seems, because quantitative data are based on qualitative judgments. For example, the questions on brand trust in Table 3.1 take the values of 1–7. There is no reason why we could not have used other values to code these answers, but it is common practice to code answers of a construct's items on a range of 1–5 or 1–7.

In addition, when the data are "raw," we often label them qualitative data, although researchers can code attributes of the data, thereby turning it into quantitative data. Think, for example, of how people respond to a new product in an interview. We can code this by setting neutral responses to 0, somewhat positive responses to 1, positives ones to 2, and very positive ones to 3. We have thus turned qualitative data contained in the interview into quantitative data. This is also qualitative data's strength and weakness; they are very rich but can be interpreted in many different ways. However, the process of how we interpret qualitative data is also subjective. To reduce some of these problems, qualitative data are often coded by highly trained researchers.

Most people think of quantitative data as being more factual and precise than qualitative data, but this is not necessarily true. Rather, what is important is how well qualitative data have been collected and/or coded into quantitative data.

Unit of Analysis

The unit of analysis is the level at which a variable is measured. Researchers often ignore this, but it is crucial because it determines what we can learn from the data. Typical measurement levels include individuals (respondents or customers), stores, companies, or countries. It is best to use data at the lowest possible level, because this provides more detail and if we need these data at another level, we can *aggregate the data*. Aggregating data means that we sum up a variable at a lower level to create a variable at a higher level. For example, if we know how many cars all car dealers in a country sell, we can take the sum of all dealer sales, to create a variable measuring countrywide car sales. This is not always possible, because, for example, we may have incomplete data.

Dependence of Observations

A key issue for any data is the degree to which observations are related. If we have exactly one observation from each individual, store, company, or country, we label the observations *independent*. That is, the observations are completely unrelated. If, however, we have multiple observations from each individual, store, company, or country, we label them *dependent*. The dependence of observations occurs if the number of observations is larger than the number of respondents (or objects) and if each individual respondent's (or object's) responses are related. For example, we could ask respondents to rate a type of Cola, then show them an advertisement, and again ask them to rate the same type of Cola. Although the advertisement may influence the respondents, it is likely that the first and second response will still be related. That is, if the respondents first rated the Cola negatively, the chance is higher that they will still rate the Cola negatively rather than positively after the advertisement. If the data are dependent, this often impacts what type of analysis we should use. For example, in Chap. 6 we discuss the difference between the independent samples t-test (for independent observations) and the paired samples t-test (for dependent observations).

Dependent and Independent Variables

An artificial distinction that market researchers make is the difference between dependent and independent variables. Independent variables are those that are used to explain another variable, the dependent variable. For example, if we use the amount of advertising to explain sales, then advertising is the independent variable and sales the dependent.

This distinction is artificial, as all variables depend on other variables. For example, the amount of advertising depends on how important the product is for a company, the company's strategy, and other factors. However, the distinction is frequently used and helpful, as it indicates what is being explained, and what variables are used to explain it.

Measurement Scaling

Not all data are equal! For example, we can calculate the average age of the respondents of Table 3.1 but it would not make much sense to calculate the average gender. Why is this? The values that we have assigned male (0) or female (1) respondents are arbitrary; we could just as well have given males the value of 1 and female the value of 0, or we could have used the values of 1 and 2. Therefore, choosing a different coding would result in different results.

The example above illustrates the problem of *measurement scaling*. Measurement scaling refer to two things: the measurements we use for measuring a certain construct (see discussion above) and the level at which a variable is measured which we discuss in this section. This can be highly confusing!

There are four levels of measurement: the *nominal scale*, the *ordinal scale*, the *interval scale*, and the *ratio scale*. These relate to how we quantify what we measure. It is vital to know the scale on which something is measured because, as the gender example above illustrates, the measurement scale determines what analysis techniques we can, or cannot, use. For example, it makes no sense to calculate the average of a variable indicating the gender of the respondent. We will come back to this issue in Chap. 5 and beyond.

The *nominal scale* is the most basic level at which we can measure something. Essentially, if we use a nominal scale, we substitute a word for a *label* (numerical value). For example, we could code what types of soft drinks are bought as follows: Coca-Cola = 1, Pepsi-Cola = 2, Seven-Up = 3. In this example, the numerical values represent nothing more than a label.

The *ordinal scale* provides more information. If we have a variable measured on an ordinal scale, we know that if the value of that variable increases, or decreases, this gives meaningful information. For example, if we code customers' usage of a product as non-user = 0, light user = 1, and heavy user = 2, we know that if the value of the usage variable increases the usage also increases. Therefore, something measured with an ordinal scale provides information about the *order* of our observations. However, we do not know if the differences in the order are equally spaced. That is, we do not know if the difference between "non-user" and "light user" is the same as between "light user" and "heavy user," even though the difference in the values (0–1 and 1–2) is equal.

If something is measured with an *interval scale*, we have precise information on the rank order at which something is measured and, in addition, we can interpret the magnitude of the differences in values directly. For example, if the temperature is 25°C, we know that if it drops to 20°C, the *difference* is exactly 5°C. This difference of 5°C is the same as the increase from 25°C to 30°C. This exact "spacing" is called *equidistance* and equidistant scales are necessary for certain analysis techniques, such as factor analysis (which we will discuss in Chap. 8). What the interval scale does not give us, is an absolute zero point. If the temperature is 0°C it may feel cold, but the temperature can drop further. The value of 0 therefore does not mean that there is no temperature at all.

The *ratio scale* provides the most information. If something is measured with a ratio scale, we know that a value of 0 means that that particular variable is not present. For example, if a customer buys no products (value = 0) then he or she really buys no products. Or, if we spend no money on advertising a new product (value = 0), we really spend no money. Therefore, the *zero point* or origin of the variable is equal to 0.

While it is relatively easy to distinguish the nominal and interval scales, it is quite hard to understand the difference between the interval and ratio scales. Fortunately, in practice, the difference between the interval and ratio scale is largely ignored and both categories are sometimes called the *quantitative scale* or *metric scale*. Table 3.3 could help you assess the difference between these four scales.

Table 3.3 Measurement Scaling

	Label	Order	Differences	Origin is 0
Nominal scale	✓			
Ordinal scale	✓	✓		
Interval scale	✓	✓	✓	
Ratio scale	✓	✓	✓	✓

Reliability and Validity

In any market research process, it is paramount to use "good" measures. Good measures are those that consistently measure what they are supposed to measure. For example, if we are interested in knowing if existing customers like a new TV commercial, we could show them the commercial and ask, for example, the following two questions afterwards (1) "Did you enjoy watching the commercial?," and (2) "Did the commercial provide the essential information necessary for a purchase decision?" How do we know if either of these questions really measures if the viewers like the commercial? We can think of this as a measurement problem through which we relate what we want to measure – whether existing customers like a new TV commercial – with what we actually measure in terms of the questions we ask. If these relate perfectly, our actual measurement is equal to what we intend to measure and we have no measurement error. If these do not relate perfectly, as is usual in practice, we have *measurement error*.

This measurement error can be divided into a *systematic* and a *random* error. We can express this as follows:

$$X_O = X_T + X_S + X_R$$

X_O stands for the observed score, X_T for the true score, X_S for the systematic error, and X_R for the random error. Systematic error is a measurement error through which we consistently measure higher, or lower, than we actually want to measure. If we were to ask, for example, customers to evaluate a TV commercial and offer them remuneration in return, they may provide more favorable information than they would otherwise have. This may cause us to think that the TV commercial is systematically more, or less, enjoyable than it is in reality. On the other hand, there may be random errors. Some customers may be having a good day and indicate that they like a commercial whereas others, who are having a bad day, may do the opposite.

Systematic errors cause the actual measurement to be consistently higher, or lower, than what it should be. On the other hand random error causes (random) variation between what we actually measure and what we should measure.

The systematic and random error concepts are important because they relate to a measure's validity and reliability. *Validity* refers to whether we are measuring what we want to measure and, therefore, to a situation where the systematic error X_S is zero. *Reliability* is the degree to which what we measure is free from random error and, therefore, relates to a situation where the X_R is zero. In Fig. 3.1, we explain the difference between reliability and validity by means of a target comparison. In this analogy, repeated measurements (e.g., of a customer's satisfaction with a specific service) are compared to arrows that are shot at a target. To measure each true score, we have five measurements (indicated by the

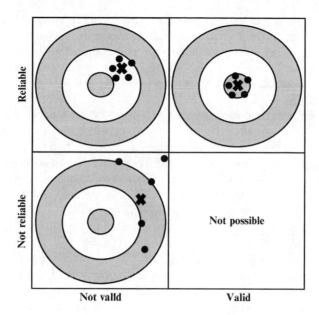

Fig. 3.1 Validity and reliability

black circles) whose average is indicated by a cross. Validity describes the cross's proximity to the bull's eye at the target center. The closer the average to the true score, the higher the validity. If several arrows are fired, reliability is the degree to which the arrows are apart. When all arrows are close together, the measure is reliable, even though it is not necessarily near the bull's eye. This corresponds to the upper left box where we have a scenario in which the measure is reliable but not valid. In the upper right box, both reliability and validity are given. In the lower left box, though, we have a situation in which the measure is neither reliable, nor valid. Obviously, this is because the repeated measurements are scattered quite heavily and the average does not match the true score. However, even if the latter were the case (i.e., if the cross were in the bull's eye), we would still not consider the measure valid. An unreliable measure can never be valid because there is no way we can distinguish the systematic error from the random error. If we repeated the measurement, say, five more times, the random error would likely shift the cross in a different position. Thus, reliability is a necessary condition for validity. This is also why the scenario not reliable/valid (lower right box) does not make sense.

For some variables, such as length or income, we can objectively verify what this true score should be, but for constructs that describe unobservable phenomena, such as satisfaction, loyalty or brand trust, this is virtually impossible (from a philosophical point of view, one could even argue that there is no "true" score for a construct). So how do we know if a measure is valid? Because there is no direct way to know what it is that we are measuring, there are several different aspects of validity, including face, content, construct, and predictive validity. These types of validity help us understand the association between what we should measure and what we actually measure.

Construct validity in a general term that includes the different types of validity discussed next.

Face validity is an absolute minimum requirement for a variable to be valid and refers to whether a variable reflects what you want to measure. Essentially, face validity exists if a measure seems to make sense. For example, if you want to measure trust, asking questions such as "this company is honest and truthful" makes quite a lot of sense whereas "this company is not well known" makes much less sense. Researchers should agree on face validity before starting the actual measurement (i.e., handing out the questions to respondents). Face validity is often determined by using a sample of experts who discuss and agree on the degree of face validity (this is also referred to as *expert validity*).

Content validity is strongly related to face validity but is more formalized. To assess content validity, researchers need to first define what they want to measure and discuss what is included in the definition and what not. For example, trust between businesses is often defined as the extent to which a firm believes that its exchange partner is honest and/or benevolent (Geyskens et al. 1998). This definition clearly indicates what should be mentioned in the questions used to measure trust (honesty and benevolence). After researchers have defined what they want to measure, questions have to be developed that relate closely to the definition. Consequently, content validity is mostly achieved before the actual measurement.

Predictive validity can be tested if we know that a measure should relate to an outcome. For example, loyalty should lead to people purchasing a product, or a measure of satisfaction should be predictive of people not complaining about a product or service. Assessing predictive validity requires collecting data at two points in time and therefore often takes a great deal of time.

Criterion validity is closely related to predictive validity, with the one difference that we examine the relationship between two constructs measured at the same time.[1]

Now that we know a bit more about validity, how do we know if a measure is reliable? Reliability can be assessed by three key factors: stability of the measurement, internal reliability, and inter-rater reliability.

Stability of the measurement means that if we measure something twice (also called *test–retest reliability*) we expect similar outcomes. Stability of measurement requires a market researcher to have collected two data samples and is therefore costly and could prolong the research process. Operationally, researchers administer the same test to the same sample on two different occasions and evaluate

---

[1]There are other types of validity, such as discriminant validity (see Chap. 8) and nomological validity. See Netemeyer et al. (2003) for an overview.

how strongly the measurements are related (more precisely, they compute correlations between the measurements; see Chap. 5 for an introduction to correlations). For a measure to be reliable, i.e., stable over time, we would expect the two measurements to correlate highly. This approach is not without problems. For example, it is often hard, if not impossible, to survey the same people twice. Furthermore, the respondents may learn from past surveys, leading to "practice effects." For example, it may be easier to recall events the second time a survey is administered. Moreover, test–retest approaches do not work when the survey is about specific time points. If we ask respondents to provide information on their last restaurant experience, the second test might relate to a different restaurant experience. Thus, test–retest reliability can only be assessed for variables that are relatively stable over time.

Internal consistency is by far the most common way of assessing reliability. Internal reliability requires researchers to simultaneously use multiple variables to measure the same thing (think of asking multiple questions in a survey). If these measures relate strongly and positively to one another there is a considerable degree of internal consistency. There are several ways to calculate indices of internal consistency, including split-half reliability and Cronbach's α (pronounced as alpha), which we discuss in Chap. 8.

Inter-rater reliability is a particular type of reliability that is often used to assess the reliability of secondary data or qualitative data (discussed later). If you want to measure, for example, which are the most ethical organizations in an industry, you could ask several experts to provide a rating and then check whether their answers relate closely. If they do, then the degree of inter-rater reliability is high.

Population and Sampling

A *population* is the group of units about which we want to make judgments. These units can be groups of individuals, customers, companies, products, or just about any subject in which you are interested. Populations can be defined very broadly, such as the people living in Canada, or very narrowly, such as the directors of large hospitals. What defines a population depends on the research conducted and the goal of the research.

Sampling is the process through which we select cases from a population. When we develop a sampling strategy, we have three key choices: the census, probability sampling, and non-probability sampling. The most important aspect of sampling is that the sample selected is *representative* of the population. With representative we mean that the characteristics of the sample closely match those of the population. How we can determine whether a sample is representative of the population is discussed in Box 3.3.

Box 3.3 Is my sample representative of the population?

Market researchers consider it important that their sample is representative of the population. How can we see if this is so?

- You can use (industry) experts to judge the quality of your sample. They may look at issues such as the type and proportion of organizations in your sample and population.
- To check whether the responses of people included in your research do not differ from non-respondents, you could use the *Armstrong and Overton procedure*. This procedure calls for comparing the first 50% of respondents to the last 50% with regard to key demographic variables. The idea behind this procedure is that later respondents more closely match the characteristics of non-respondents. If these differences are not significant (e.g., through hypothesis tests, discussed in Chap. 6), we find some support that there is little, or no, response bias (See Armstrong and Overton 1977).
- Perhaps the best way to test whether the sample relates to the population is to use a dataset with information on the population. For example, the Amadeus and Orbis databases provide information at the population level. We can (statistically) compare the information from these databases to the sample selected. The database is available at:

http://www.bvdinfo.com/Home.aspx

If we get lucky and somehow manage to include every unit of the population in our study, we have conducted a *census* study. Census studies are rare because they are very costly and because missing just a small part of the population can have dramatic consequences. For example, if we were to conduct a census study among directors of banks in Luxemburg, we may miss out on a few because they were too busy to participate. If these busy directors happen to be those of the very largest companies, any information we collect would underestimate the effects of variables that are more important in large banks. Census studies work best if the population is small, well-defined, and accessible. Sometimes census studies are also conducted for specific reasons. For example, the United States Census Bureau is required to hold a census of all persons resident in the US every 10 years. Check out the US Census Bureau's YouTube channel using the mobile tag or URL in Box 3.4 to find out more about the door-to-door census taking process of the US Census 2010.

Box 3.4 The US Census 2010

http://www.youtube.com/uscensusbureau#p/

If we select part of the population, we can distinguish two types of approaches: probability sampling and non-probability sampling.

Probability Sampling

Probability sampling approaches provide every individual in the population a chance (not equal to zero) of being included in the sample. This is often achieved by using an accurate *sampling frame*. A sampling frame is a list of individuals in the population. There are various sampling frames, such as Dun & Bradstreet's Selectory database (includes executives and companies), the Mint databases (includes companies in North and South Americas, Italy, Korea, The Netherlands, and the UK), or telephone directories. These sampling frames rarely completely cover the population of interest and often include some outdated information, but due to their ease of use and availability they are frequently used. If the sampling frame and population are very similar, we have little *sampling frame error*, which is the degree to which sample frames represent the population.

Starting from a good-quality sampling frame, we can use several methods to select units from the sampling frame. The easiest way is to use *simple random sampling*, which is achieved by randomly selecting the number of cases required. This can be achieved by using specialized software, or using Microsoft Excel. Specifically, Microsoft Excel can create random numbers between 0 and 1 (using the RAND() function to select cases). Next you choose those individuals from the sampling frame where the random value falls in a certain range. The range depends on the percentage of respondents needed. For example, if you wish to approach 5% of the sampling frame, you could set the range from 0.00 to 0.05. This method is easy to implement and works well for homogeneous sampling frames.

Systematic sampling uses a different procedure. We first number all the observations and subsequently select every n^{th} observation. For example, if our sampling frame consists of 1,000 firms and we wish to select just 100 firms, we could select the 1st observation, the 11th, the 21st, etc. until we reach the end of the sampling frame and have our 100 observations.

Stratified sampling and *cluster sampling* are more elaborate techniques of probability sampling, which require dividing the sampling frame into different groups. When we use stratified sampling, we divide the population into several different homogenous groups called *strata*. These strata are based on key sample characteristics, such as different departments in organizations or the area in which consumers live. Subsequently we draw a random number of observations from each strata. While stratified sampling is more complex and requires knowledge of the sampling frame and population, it also helps to assure that the sampling frame's characteristics are similar to those of the sample. Stratified sampling is very useful if the market research question requires comparing different groups (strata).

Cluster sampling requires dividing the population into different heterogeneous groups with each group's characteristics similar to those of the population. For example, we can divide the consumers of one particular country into different provinces, counties, or councils. Several of these groups can perhaps be created on the basis of key characteristics (e.g., income, political preference, household composition) that are very similar (representative) to those of the population. We can select one or more of these representative groups and use random sampling to select our observations. This technique requires knowledge of the sampling frame and population, but is convenient because gathering data from one group is cheaper and less time consuming.

Non-probability Sampling

Non-probability sampling procedures do not give every individual in the population an equal chance of being included in the sample. This is a drawback, because it can bias subsequent analyses. Nevertheless, non-probability sampling procedures are frequently used as they are easily executed, and are typically less costly than probability sampling methods.

Judgmental sampling is based on researchers taking an informed guess regarding which individuals should be included. For example, research companies often have panels of respondents who were previously used in research. Asking these people to participate in a new study may provide useful information if we know, from experience, that the panel has little sampling frame error.

Snowball sampling is predominantly used if access to individuals is difficult. People such as directors, doctors, or high-level managers often have little time and are, consequently, difficult to involve. If we can ask just a few of these people to provide names and details of others in a similar position, we can expand our sample quickly and access them. Similarly, if you send out a link to an online questionnaire and ask everyone to forward the link to at least five other persons, this is snowball sampling through referrals to people who would be difficult to access otherwise,

When we select a fixed number of observations from different groups, we use *quota sampling*. Quota sampling is similar to stratified random sampling, but we use a fixed number of observations for each group. For example, we can recruit 100 consumers of Pantene shampoo and 100 consumers of Nivea shampoo. Unlike in random stratified sampling, in which the number of observations for each group is determined by population characteristics, in the quota sampling process, the researcher determines the number for judgmental sampling. Once the required number of observations has been found, no observations are added.

Finally, *convenience sampling* is a catch-all term for methods (including the three non-probability sampling techniques just described) in which the researcher makes a subjective judgment. For example, we can use *mall intercepts* to ask people in a shopping mall if they want to fill out a survey. The researcher's control over who ends up in the sample is limited and influenced by situational factors.

Figure 3.2 provides an overview of the different sampling procedures.

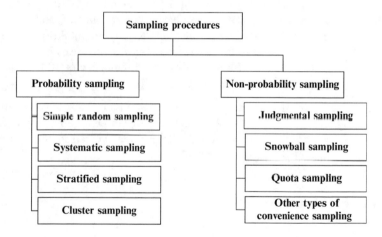

Fig. 3.2 Sampling procedures

Sample Sizes

After determining the sampling procedure, we have to determine the sample size. Larger sample sizes increase the precision of the research, but are also much more expensive to collect. Usually the gains in precision are very marginal if we increase the sample size far above 100–250 observations (in Box 6.3 we discuss the question whether a sample size can be too large in the context of significance testing). It may seem surprising that relatively small sample sizes are precise, but the strength of samples comes from accurately selecting samples, rather than through sample size. Furthermore, the required sample size has very little relation to the population size. That is, a sample of 100 employees from a company with 300 employees can be nearly as accurate as selecting 100 employees from a company with 100,000 employees. There are some problems in selecting sample sizes. The first is that market research companies often push their clients towards accepting large sample sizes. Since the fee for market research services is often directly dependent on the sample size, increasing the sample size increases the market research company's profit. Second, if we want to compare different groups (e.g., in a stratified sample design), we need to multiply the required sample by the number of groups included. That is, if 150 observations are sufficient to measure how much people spend on organic food, 2 times 150 observations are necessary to compare singles and couples' expenditure on organic food.

The figures mentioned above are net sample sizes; that is, these are the actual (usable) number of observations we should have. Owing to non-response (discussed in Chaps. 4 and 5), a multiple of the initial sample size (say, 400 or 800) is normally necessary to obtain the desired sample. Before collecting data, we should have an idea of the percentage of respondents we are likely to reach (often fairly high), a percentage estimate of the respondents willing to help (often low), as well as a percentage estimate of the respondents likely to fill out the survey correctly (often high). For example, if we expect to reach 80% of the identifiable respondents, and if 25% are likely to help, and 75% of those who help are likely to fully fill out the questionnaire, only 15% (0.80·0.25·0.75) of identifiable respondents are in this case likely to provide a usable response. Thus, if we wish to obtain a net sample size of 100, we need to send out $\left(\frac{\text{desired sample size}}{\text{likely usable responses}}\right) = 100/0.15 = 667$ surveys. That is a lot more than the sample size we are likely to use later on. These response issues have led many market researchers to believe that survey research may no longer be a good way to collect representative samples. In Chap. 4, we will discuss how we can increase response rates (the percentage of people willing to help).

Questions

1. Explain the difference between items and constructs.
2. What is the difference between reflective and formative constructs?
3. What are data? Give a few examples of quantitative and qualitative data.
4. What is the scale on which the following variables are measured?
   - The amount of money spent by a customer on shoes.
   - The country-of-origin of a product.
   - The number of times an individual makes a complaint.
   - The grades of a test.
   - The color of a mobile phone.

5. Try to find two websites that contain secondary data and also discuss what kind of data are described. Are these qualitative or quantitative data? What is the unit of analysis and how are the data measured?
6. What are "good data"?
7. Discuss the concepts of reliability and validity. How do they relate to each other?
8. Please comment on the following statement: "Face and content validity are essentially the same."
9. What is the difference between predictive and criterion validity?
10. Imagine you have just been asked to execute a market research study to estimate the market for notebooks prices 300 USD or less. What sampling approach would you propose to the client?
11. Imagine that a university decides to evaluate their students' satisfaction. To do so, employees issue a questionnaire to every tenth student coming to the student cafeteria on one weekday. Which type of sampling is conducted in this situation? Can the resulting sample be representative of the population?

Further Readings

Carmines EG, Zeller RA (1979) Reliability and validity assessment. Sage, Beverly Hills, CA.
Carmines and Zeller provide an in-depth discussion of different types of reliability and validity, including how to assess them.
Churchill GA (1979) A paradigm for developing better measures for marketing constructs. J Mark Res 16(1):64–73.
Probably the most widely cited marketing research article to this day. This paper marked the start of a rethinking process on how to adequately measure constructs.
Diamantopoulos A, Winklhofer HM (2001) Index construction with formative indicators: an alternative to scale development. J Mark Res 38(2):269–277.
In this seminal article the authors provide guidelines how to operationalize formative constructs.
Cochran WG (1977) Sampling techniques. Wiley series in probability and mathematical statistics, 3rd edn, Wiley, New York, NY.
This is a seminal text on sampling techniques which provides a thorough introduction into this topic. However, please note that most descriptions are rather technical and require a sound understanding of statistics.
DeVellis RF (2003) Scale development: theory and applications, 2nd edn. Sage, Thousand Oaks, CA.
This is a very accessible book which guides the reader through the classic way of developing multi-item scales. The text does not discuss how to operationalize formative constructs, though.
Marketing Scales Database at http://www.marketingscales.com/search/search.php

This website offers an easy-to-search database of marketing-related scales. For every scale a description is given, the scale origin and reliability and validity are discussed and the items are given.
Netemeyer RG, Bearden WO, Sharma S (2003) Scaling procedures: issues and applications, Sage, Thousand Oaks, CA.
Like DeVellis (2003), this book presents an excellent introduction into the principles of scale development of measurement in general.

References

Armstrong JS, Overton TS (1977) Estimating nonresponse bias in mail surveys. J Mark Res 14 (August):396–403
Bearden WO, Netemeyer RG (1999) Handbook of marketing scales. Multi-item measures for marketing and consumer behavior research, 2nd edn. Sage, Thousand Oaks, CA
Bergkvist L Rossiter JR (2007) The predictive validity of single-item versus multi-item measures of the same construct. J Mark Res 44(2):175–184.
DeVellis RF (2003) Scale development: theory and applications, 2nd edn. Sage, Thousand Oaks, CA
Diamantopoulos A, Riefler P, Roth KP (2008) Advancing formative measurement models. J Bus Res 61(12):1203–1218
Diamantopoulos, A, Winklhofer HM (2001) Index construction with formative indicators: an alternative to scale development. J Mark Res 38(2):269–277
Erdem T, Swait J (2004) Brand credibility, brand consideration, and choice. J Consum Res 31 (June):191–198
Fischer M, Völckner F, Sattler H (2010) How important are brands? A cross-category, cross-country study. J Mark Res 47(5):823–839
Fuchs C, Diamantopoulos A (2009) Using single-item measures for construct measurement in management research. Conceptual issues and application guidelines. Die Betriebswirtschaft 69 (2):195–210
Geyskens I, Steenkamp J-BEM, Kumar N (1998) Generalizations about trust in marketing channel relationships using meta-analysis. Int J Res Mark 15(July):223–248
Netemeyer RG, Bearden WO, Sharma S (2003) Scaling procedures: issues and applications. Sage, Thousand Oaks, CA
Rossiter JR (2010) Measurement for the social sciences. Springer, New York
Sarstedt M, Schloderer MP (2010) Developing a measurement approach for reputation of non-profit organizations. Int J Nonprofit Volunt Sect Mark 15(3):276–299
Sarstedt M, Wilczynski P (2009) More for less. A comparison of single-item and multi-item measures. Die Betriebswirtschaft 69(2):211–227

Chapter 4
Getting Data

Learning Objectives

After reading this chapter, you should understand:
- How to gather secondary data.
- How to collect primary data.
- How to design a basic questionnaire.
- How to set up basic experiments.
- How to set up basic qualitative research.

Keywords CRM · Constant sum scale · Directly and indirectly observed qualitative data · Ethnographies · Experiments · Face-to-face interviewing · Focus groups · Internal and external secondary data · Interviews · Likert scale · Mail surveys · Mixed mode · Observational studies · Projective techniques · Semantic differential scale · Surveys · Telephone interviews · Test markets · Web surveys

Introduction

In the previous chapter, we discussed some of the key theoretical concepts and choices prior to collecting data such as validity, reliability, sampling, and sample sizes. We also discussed different types of data. Building on Chap. 3, this chapter discusses the practicalities of collecting data. First, we discuss how to collect quantitative and qualitative secondary data. Subsequently, we discuss how to collect primary data through surveys. We also introduce experimental research and some basics of primary qualitative research.

We discuss the practicalities of secondary data prior to those of primary data. Market researchers should always consider secondary before collecting primary data as secondary data tends to be cheaper, usually takes less time to collect, and does not depend on the respondents' willingness to participate. However, if secondary data are unavailable or outdated, primary data may have to be collected. All secondary and primary data can be divided into quantitative and qualitative data. In Table 4.1, we provide an overview of some types of secondary and primary, quantitative, and qualitative data. These and some other types will be discussed in this chapter.

E. Mooi and M. Sarstedt, *A Concise Guide to Market Research*,
DOI 10.1007/978-3-642-12541-6_4, © Springer-Verlag Berlin Heidelberg 2011

Table 4.1 Types of data: secondary vs. primary and quantitative vs. qualitative data

	Secondary data	Primary data
Quantitative data	Examples: – CIA-The World Factbook – Existing customer satisfaction databases, e.g., J.D. Power's Initial Quality Study – Existing sales figures, e.g., Nielsen's Retail Management Services	Examples: – Survey undertaken by management to measure customer satisfaction – Experiment used to design a new product
Qualitative data	Examples: – Written reports, e.g., the McKinsey Quarterly, industry reports by OliverWyman	Examples: – Interviews – Focus groups – Mystery shopping – Ethnographies – Projective techniques – Test markets

Secondary Data

Secondary data are data that have already been gathered, often for a different research purpose. Secondary data comprise internal secondary data, external secondary data, or a mix of both. In Fig. 4.1, we show an overview of different types of secondary data.

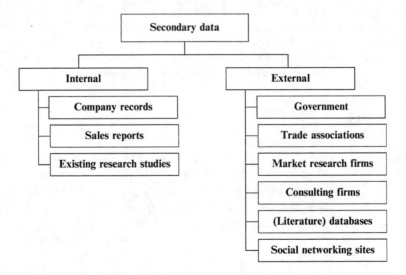

Fig. 4.1 Sources of secondary data

Internal Secondary Data

Internal secondary data are contained within the company and are mostly tailored towards specific needs. Large companies specifically have systems in place, such as accounting and enterprise resource planning (ERP) systems, in which vast amounts of data on customers, transactions, and performances are stored. In general terms, internal secondary data comprise internal company records, sales reports, and existing research studies.

Company records are a firm's repository of information. Internal company records may contain data from different business functions, such as controlling or CRM (*Customer Relationship Management*). Controllers provide internal reviews of organizations' financial well-being and may provide strategic advice. Controllers may therefore have access to much of the firm's financial and operational data. CRM is a term that refers to a system of databases and analysis software to track and predict customer behavior. The database systems, on which the analysis software runs, are marketed by firms such as IBM, Microsoft, and Oracle. These database management systems often include information on, for example, purchasing behavior, (geo-)demographic customer data, and after-sales service provided. This information is often compiled and coordinated so that marketers can track individual customers over different sales channels and types of products to tailor offerings to customers. The analysis software that runs on top of these databases is sold by a number of information technology companies such as SAP, Oracle, and Salesforce.com. Companies often use CRM systems to, for example, identify customer trends, calculate profitability per customer, or identify opportunities for selling new, or different products. The CRM market is substantial, generating over USD 9 billion in sales during 2008.[1]

Sales reports are created when products and services are sold to clients. Many of these reports contain details of the discussions held with clients and the products/ services sold. Consequently, they can provide insights into customers' needs. Sales reports also provide a means to retain customers' suggestions regarding products and services. These reports can be a highly productive source of market research information. For example, DeMonaco et al. (2005) discovered that 59% of existing drugs have uses other than described by the producing company. Evidently, it is important to be aware of a drug's uses. Discussions with doctors, hospitals, and research institutes can help reveal the different uses of these drugs. When sales reports are available, they are often part of a CRM system.

Existing research studies are a good source of secondary data, even if they were conducted for a (slightly) different purpose. Carefully consider whether existing research studies are still useful and what you can learn from them. Even if you deem the findings of such studies as outdated, the measures that they contain may be very useful. In order to use existing research studies, it is important that enough of their details are available. Clients ask market research agencies with which they do business to make the data and a detailed description of the analysis available. If only the final report is received, you need to go back to the market research agency to re-analyze the findings.

---

[1]See http://www.gartner.com/it/page.jsp?id=1074615.

External Secondary Data

Governments often provide general data that can be used for market research purposes. For example, The CIA-The World Factbook (see Box 4.1) provides information on the economy, politics, and other issues of nearly every country in the world. Eurostat (the statistics office of the European Union) provides detailed information on the economy and different market sectors (see Box 4.1). Much of this information is free of charge and provides an easy starting point for market research studies.

Box 4.1 Web links and mobile tags

CIA World Fact Book
https://www.cia.gov/library/publications/the-
  world-factbook/

Eurostat
http://epp.eurostat.ec.europa.eu/

Nielsel's Retail Management Services
http://en-us.nielsen.com/tab/product_
  families/nielsen_retail_direct

IRI's Etilize
http://www.etilize.com/index.en.html

Trade associations are organizations representing different companies and are aimed at promoting their common interests. For example, the Auto Alliance, consisting of US automakers, provides information on the sector and lists the key issues it faces. The European Federation of Pharmaceutical Industries and Associations represents 2,200 pharmaceutical companies operating in Europe. The federation provides a detailed list of key figures and facts and regularly offers statistics on the industry. Most other trade associations also provide lists that include the members' names and addresses. These can be used, for example, as a sampling frame (see Chap. 3). Most trade associations consider identifying their members' opinions a key task and consequently collect data on a regular basis. These data are then typically included in reports that may be downloadable from the organization's website. Such reports can be a short-cut to identifying key issues and challenges in specific industries. Sometimes, these reports are free of charge but non-members usually need to pay a (mostly substantial) fee.

Market research firms are another source of secondary information. Particularly large market research firms provide syndicated data (see Chap. 1) used for many different clients. Some examples of syndicated data include Nielsen's Retail Management Services, IRI's Etilize, and J.D. Power's Initial Quality Study. Nielsen's Retail Management Services (see Box 4.1) provides detailed information on the sales of individual products across different retailers. IRI's Etilize (see Box 4.1) offers aggregated data on more than 7 million products from 20,000 manufacturers in 30 countries, and in 20 languages. J.D. Power's Initial Quality Study provides insights into the initial quality of cars in the US, while J.D. Power's Vehicle Ownership Satisfaction Study contains similar data for other markets, such as New Zealand or Germany.

Consulting firms are a rich source of secondary data. Most firms publish full reports or summaries of reports on their website. For example, McKinsey & Company provides the McKinsey Quarterly, a business journal that includes articles on current business trends, issues, problems, and solutions. Oliver Wyman publishes regular reports on trends and issues across many different industries. Other consulting firms, such as Gartner and Forrester, also provide panel data on various topics. These data can be purchased and used for secondary analysis. For example, Forrester maintains databases on market segmentation, the allocation of budgets across firms, and the degree to which consumers adopt various innovations. Consulting firms provide general advice, information, and knowledge as opposed to market research firms, which only focus on marketing-related applications. In practice, there is however some overlap in the activities undertaken by consulting and market research firms.

(Literature) databases contain professional and academic journals, newspapers, and books. Some of the prominent literature databases are ProQuest (http://www.proquest.co.uk) and JSTOR (http://www.jstor.org). ProQuest is unique in that it contains over 9,000 trade journals, business publications, and leading academic journals, including highly regarded publications in the market research area, such as the Journal of Marketing and the Journal of Marketing Research. However, one needs a subscription to gain access to this literature. Students, and sometimes

alumni, can often access this site via their academic institution. Certain companies also provide access. JSTOR is similar to ProQuest but is mostly aimed at academics. Consequently, it provides access to nearly all leading academic journals. A helpful feature of JSTOR is that the first page of academic articles (which usually contains the abstract) can be read free of charge. In addition, nearly all of JSTOR's information is searchable via Google Scholar (discussed in Box 4.2). Certain database firms make firm-level data, such as names and addresses, available. For example, Bureau van Dijk (http://www.bvdep.com) as well as Dun and Bradstreet (http://www.dnb.com) publish extensive lists that contain the names of firms, the industry in which they operate, their profitability, key activities, and address information. This information is often used as a sampling frame for survey studies.

Social networking sites, such as LinkedIn, Twitter, Facebook, or MySpace, can provide market researchers with valuable information since social networking profiles often reflect how people would like to be perceived by others and, thus, display consumers' intentions. Product or company-related user groups are of specific interest to market researchers. Take, for example, comments posted on a Facebook group site such as: "I bet I can find 1,000,000 people who dislike Heineken." An analysis of these postings could help one understand how people perceive this brand. Interpretations of such postings usually include analyzing five elements: the agent (who is posting?), the act (what happened, i.e., what aspect is the posting referring to?), the agency (what vehicle is used to perform the action), the scene (what is the background situation?), and the purpose (why do the agents act?). By analyzing this information, market researchers can gain insight into consumers' motives and actions. For example, Casteleyn et al. (2009) show that the Facebook posts regarding Heineken reveal a negative image of the brand in Belgium. Another example of a website that provides social networking facilities is tripadvisor.com, which provides customer ratings of holidays, trips, and excursions and includes detailed customer feedback. Even some online stores, such as Amazon.com and eBay.com provide social networking facilities. Amazon.com, for example, provides customer ratings and feedback on the products it sells. Several companies, such as Attensity (http://www.attensity.com) have software tools to analyze text information and to provide all sorts of statistics. An analysis of Twitter feeds on the iPad just after the launch revealed that 87% of all posts on the iPad leaned towards purchasing while 13% leaned towards not purchasing. Further, 26% of all posts complained that the iPad did not replace iPhone functionality.

Accessing Secondary Data

Many of the sources of secondary data we have just discussed can be very easily accessed by means of *search engines*. Search engines provide access to many sources of secondary information. Both generalist search engines (such as Google, Bing, or Yahoo) and specialist databases (see the ⌐ Web Appendix → Chap. 4) have links to vast amounts of secondary data. Generalist search engines are regularly updated, their search results depend on what other people are searching for, and how websites are interlinked. Furthermore, they integrate data from different sources, including universities, news websites, and governments. However, undertaking correct searches in generalist search engines requires careful thought. For example, the word order is important (put key words first) and operators may need to be added (such as +, −, and ∼) to restrict searches. In Box 4.2, we discuss some basics of searching the Web using the search engine Google.

Box 4.2   Searching for secondary data using Google

Google has an easy to use interface but if you use the standard search box you may not find the secondary data you are looking for. So, how does one find secondary data?

- You could use Google Scholar (http://scholar.google.com) if you are looking for scholarly information such as that found in academic journals. While you can *search* for information from anywhere, it can usually only be accessed if you have an organizational, university, or library password.
- By using Google Books (http://books.google.com/books), you can enter several keywords to easily search within a very large catalogue of digital books. Google clearly indicates in which books the search results are found and also on which pages the keywords occur.
- Under *advanced search* on the Google homepage, you can command Google to only return searches from Excel documents by selecting *Microsoft Excel* under *file type*. Since data are often stored in spreadsheets, this is a good way to search for data. Under advanced search, you can also command Google to return searches from universities only by typing in.*edu* in *Search Within Site or Domain*.
- If you want to see news from some time ago to, for example, see how the press received a new product launch, you can use Google News Archive Search (http://news.google.com/archivesearch).
- Try using operators. Operators are signs that you use to restrict your research. For example, putting a minus symbol (–) (without a space) before a search word *excludes* this word from your findings. Putting a sequence of words or an entire sentence in quotation marks (e.g., "a concise guide to market research") indicates that Google should search for exactly these elements.
- You can use a dedicated search tool to find secondary data such as the *Internet Crossroads in Social Science Data* (http://www.disc.wisc.edu/newcrossroads/index.asp). These dedicated search tools and lists often work well if you are looking for specialized datasets.

Primary Data

Primary data are gathered for a specific research project or task. This distinguishes primary data from secondary data gathered previously for another purpose. Primary data can be quantitative or qualitative data. Quantitative primary data are mostly gathered through surveys and experiments. Most qualitative primary data are collected in the form of interviews, focus groups, observational studies, projective techniques, and test markets. We provide an overview of various types of quantitative and qualitative primary data in Fig. 4.2. Next, we discuss how to set up surveys in detail. Since surveys are the main means of collecting quantitative primary data, we discuss the process of undertaking survey research in enough detail to allow you to set up your own survey-based research project (Table 4.2). We also discuss some aspects of experimental research. Subsequently, we provide an overview of different types of qualitative research.

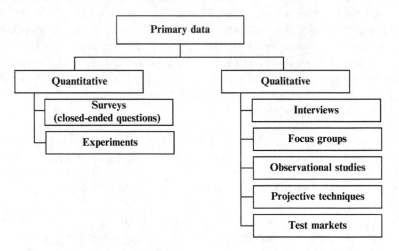

Fig. 4.2 Quantitative and qualitative primary data

Collecting Quantitative Data: Designing Questionnaires

There is little doubt that questionnaires are higly important in market research. While it may seem easy to create a questionnaire (just ask what you want to know, right?), there are many issues that could turn good intentions into bad results. In this section, we will discuss the key design choices to produce good surveys. A good survey requires at least six steps. First, set the goal of the survey. Next, determine the type of questionnaire and method of administration. Thereafter, decide on the questions and their formulation, and conclude by pre-testing and administering the questionnaire. We show these steps in Fig. 4.3.

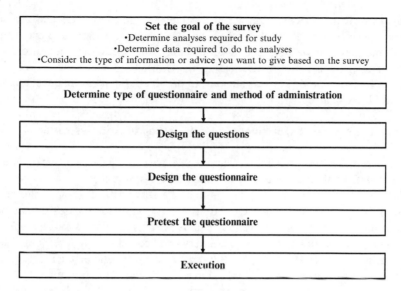

Fig. 4.3 Steps in designing questionnaires

Set the Goal of the Survey

Before you start designing the questionnaire, it is vital to consider the goal of the survey. Is it to collect quantitative data on the background of customers, to assess customer satisfaction, or do you want to understand why and how customers complain? These different goals influence the type of questions asked (such as open-ended or closed-ended questions), the method of administration (e.g., mail or the Web), and other design issues discussed below. We discuss three sub-aspects that are important to consider when designing surveys.

First, it is important to consider the analyses required for the study. For example, if a study's goal is to determine market segments, cluster analysis is the technique most likely to be used (cluster analysis is discussed in Chap. 9). Similarly, if the study's goal is to develop a way of systematically measuring customer satisfaction, factor analysis will most likely be used (see Chap. 8).

A second step is to consider what types of data these analyses require. Cluster analysis, for example, often requires equidistant data, meaning that we need to use a type of questionnaire that can produce these data. Conducting factor analysis, on the other hand, usually requires data that include different, but related, questions. If we use factor analysis to distinguish between the different aspects of consumer satisfaction, we need to design a survey that allows us to conduct factor analysis.

A third point to consider is the information or advice you want to give based on the study. Imagine you are asked to provide help to reach an understanding of waiting times for check-in at an airport. If the specific question is to understand how many minutes travelers are willing to wait before becoming dissatisfied, you should be able to provide answers to how much travelers' satisfaction decreases as the waiting time increases. If, on the other hand, the specific question is to understand how people perceive waiting time (short or long), your questions should focus on how travelers perceive waiting time and, perhaps, what influences their perception. Thus, the information or advice you want to provide influences the questions that you should ask in a survey.

Determine the Type of Questionnaire and Method of Administration

After determining the goal of the survey, we need to decide on what type of questionnaire we should use and how it should be administered.

There are four different ways to administer a survey: face-to-face interviews, telephone interviews, Web surveys, and mail surveys. In some cases, researchers combine different ways of administering surveys. This is called a *mixed mode*.

Face-to-face interviews (or personal interviews) can obtain high response rates, since engagement with the respondents are maximized, thereby collecting rich information (visual expressions, etc.). Moreover, since people find it hard to walk away from interviews, it is possible to collect answers to a reasonably lengthy set of questions. For this reason, face-to-face interviews can support long surveys. It is also the best type of data collection for open-ended responses. In situations where the respondent is initially unknown, this may be the only feasible data collection type. Consequently, face-to-face interviews seem highly preferable but they are also the most costly per respondent. This is less of a concern for small samples (where face-to-face interviewing could be the most efficient). Other issues with face-to-face interviewing include the possibility of interviewer bias, respondent bias to sensitive items, as well as slow data collection time. Typically, researchers use face-to-face interviewing when we require the in-depth exploration of opinions. Such interviewing may also help if systematic drop out is a key concern. For example, if we collect data from executives around the globe, using methods other than face-to-face interviewing may lead to excessive non-response in countries such as Russia or China. A term that is frequently used in the context of face-to-face interviewing is CAPI, which is an abbreviation of Computer-Assisted Personal Interviews. CAPI involves using computers during the interviewing process to, for example, route the interviewer through a series of questions or to enter responses directly.

Telephone interviewing allows one to collect data quickly. It also supports open-ended responses, though not as well as face-to-face interviewing. Moreover, there is only moderate control of interviewer bias, since interviewers follow predetermined protocols, and there is strong control of the respondent's interactions with others during the interview. Telephone interviewing can be a good compromise between the low cost of mail and the richness of face-to-face survey research. Similar to CAPI, CATI refers to Computer-Assisted Telephone Interviews. Telephone surveys were dominant in the 1990s but since the 2000s, people have increasingly dropped their landlines, making access to respondents harder. The use of mobile phones has, however, increased rapidly and many countries have mobile phone adoption rates that are higher than landline adoption has ever been (especially in African countries and India). This has caused market researchers to be increasingly interested in using mobile phones for survey purposes. The cost of calling mobile phones is still higher than calling landlines, but the cost involved in calling mobile phones is decreasing. Can market researchers switch to calling mobile phones without problems? Research suggests not. In many countries, users of mobile phones differ from the general population of a country in that they are younger, more educated, and represent a smaller household size. Moreover, the process of surveying through mobile phones is different from using landlines. For example, the likelihood of full completion of surveys is higher for mobile calling, and completion takes around 10% longer (Vincente et al. 2008). Researchers should be aware that calling to mobile phones differs from calling to landlines and that those who use mobile phones are unlikely to represent the general population of a country.

Web surveys (sometimes referred to as CAWI, or Computer-Assisted Web Interviews) are often the least expensive to administer and can be fast in terms of data collection, particularly since they can be set up very quickly. We can administer Web surveys to very large populations, even internationally, as the marginal cost of administering additional Web surveys is relatively low beyond the fixed cost of setting up the survey. Many firms specializing in carrying out Web surveys will ask USD 0.30 (or more) for processing an additional respondent, which is substantially lower than the cost of telephone interviews, face-to-face interviews or mail surveys. Web surveys also support complex survey designs with elaborate branching and skip patterns that depend on the response. For example, through Web surveys we can create different surveys for different types of products and route respondents. In addition, Web surveys can be created to automatically skip questions if they do not apply. For example, if a respondent has no experience using Apple's iPad, we can create surveys that do not ask questions about this product. The central drawback of Web surveys is the difficulty of drawing random samples, since Web access is known to be biased by income, race, gender, and age. Some firms, like Toluna (http://www.toluna.com) and Research Now (http://www.researchnow.co.uk), provide representative panels that can be accessed through Web surveys. An issue with Web surveys is that they impose almost as high a burden on the respondents as mail surveys do. This makes administering long Web surveys difficult. Moreover, open-ended questions tend to be problematic in that few respondents are likely to provide answers, thereby leading to low item response. There is evidence that properly conducted Web surveys lead to data as good as those obtained by mail surveys and that they can provide better results than personal interviews due to the absence of an interviewer and subsequent interviewer bias (Bronner and Kuijlen 2007; Deutskens et al. 2006). In addition, in Web surveys, the respondents are less exposed to evaluation apprehension and are less inclined to respond with socially desirable behavior.[2] Web surveys are also used when a quick "straw poll" is needed on a subject.

---

[2]For a comparison between CASI, CAPI and CATI with respect to differences in response behavior, see Bronner and Kuijlen (2007).

It is important to distinguish between true Web-based surveys used for collecting information on which marketing decisions will be based and polls or very short surveys on websites that are used to increase interactivity. These polls/short surveys are used to attract and keep people interested in websites and are thus not part of market research. For example, the USA Today (http://www.usatoday.com), an American newspaper, regularly publishes short polls on their main website.

Mail surveys are paper-based surveys sent out to respondents. They are a more expensive type of survey research and are best used for sensitive items. As no interviewer is present, there is no interviewer bias. However, mail surveys are a poor choice for complex survey designs, such as when respondents need to skip a large number of questions depending on previously asked questions, as this means that the respondent bears the burden of having to correctly interpret the survey. Open-ended items are also problematic in that few people are likely to provide answers to open-ended questions if the survey is administered on paper. Other problems include a lack of control over the environment in which the respondent fills out the survey and that mail surveys take longer than telephone or Web surveys. However, in some situations, mail surveys are the only way to gather data. For example, while executives rarely respond to Web-based surveys, they are more likely to respond to paper-based surveys. Moreover, if the participants cannot easily access the Web (such as employees working in supermarkets, cashiers, etc.), handing out paper surveys is likely to be more successful.

Mixed-mode approaches are increasingly used by market researchers. An example of a mixed-mode survey is when potential respondents are first approached by phone and then asked to participate and confirm their email addresses, after which they are given access to a Web survey. Mixed-mode approaches could also be used in cases where people are first sent a paper survey and are then called if they fail to respond to the survey.

Mixed-mode approaches may help because they signal that the survey is important. They may also help response rates as people who are more visually oriented prefer mail and Web surveys, whereas those who are aurally oriented prefer telephone surveys. By providing different modes, people can use the mode they most prefer. A downside of mixed-mode surveys is that they are expensive and require a detailed address list (including a telephone number and matching email address). The key issue with mixed-mode surveys is the possibility of systematic response issues. For example, when filling out mail surveys, respondents have more time than when providing answers by telephone. If respondents need more time to think about their answers, the responses obtained through mail surveys may differ systematically from those obtained through telephone surveying.

Design the Questions

Designing questions (items) for a survey, whether it is for an interview, the Web, or mail, requires a great deal of thought. Take, for example, the following survey item (Fig. 4.4):

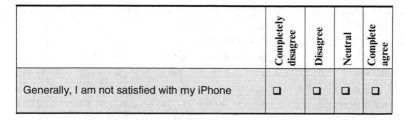

	Completely disagree	Disagree	Neutral	Complete agree
Generally, I am not satisfied with my iPhone	❑	❑	❑	❑

Fig. 4.4 Example of a survey item

It is unlikely that people are able to give meaningful answers to such a question. First, using a negation ("not") in sentences makes questions hard to understand. Second, the reader may not have an iPhone or perhaps not even know what it is. Third, the answer categories are unequally spaced. These issues are likely to create difficulties in understanding and answering questions and may cause validity and reliability issues.

Rules for Question Design

When designing survey questions, as a first rule, ask yourself whether everyone will be able to answer each question asked. If the question is, for example, about the quality of train transport and the respondent always travels by car, his or her answers will be meaningless. However, the framing of questions is important since, for example, questions about why that particular respondent does not use the train can lead to meaningful answers.

In addition, you should check whether respondents are able to construct or recall an answer. If you require details that possibly occurred a long time ago (e.g., what information did the real estate agent provide when you bought/rented your current house?), respondents may "make up" an answer, which could lead to validity and reliability issues.

As a third rule, assess if respondents will be willing to fill out questions. If questions are considered sensitive (e.g., sexuality, money, etc.), respondents may consciously adjust their own answers (e.g., by reporting higher or lower incomes than are actually true) or not be willing to answer at all. You have to determine whether these questions are necessary to attain the research objective. If they are not, omit them from the survey. What comprises a sensitive question is subjective and differs across cultures, age categories, and other variables. Use your common sense and, if necessary, expert judgment to decide whether the questions are appropriate. In addition, make sure you pre-test the survey and ask those participants whether they were reluctant to provide certain answers. In some cases, the reformulation of the question can circumnavigate this issue. For example, instead of directly asking about a respondent's disposable income, you can provide various answering categories, which usually increase willingness to answer this question. Another issue that may make respondents reluctant to answer questions is a survey's length. Many people are willing to provide answers to a short question but are reluctant to even start with a lengthy survey. As the length of the survey increases, the respondent's willingness and ability to complete it decrease.

In addition to these three general rules, there are also a few specific rules that deal with how to write particular questions. One of those is the choice between open-ended and closed-ended questions. Open-ended questions provide little or no structure for respondents' answers. Generally, the researcher asks a question and the respondent writes down his or her answer in a box. Open-ended questions (also called verbatim items in the market research world) are flexible and allow explanation but a drawback is that respondents may feel reluctant to provide such detailed information. In addition, their interpretation requires substantial coding. This coding issue arises when respondents provide many different answers (such as "sometimes," "maybe," "occasionally," or "once in a while") and the researcher has to divide these into categories (such as very infrequently, infrequently, frequently, and very frequently) for further statistical analysis. This coding is very time-consuming, subjective, and difficult. Closed-ended questions, on the other hand, provide a few categories from which the respondent can choose by ticking an appropriate answer. When comparing open-ended and closed-ended questions, open-ended questions usually have much lower response rates.

Types of Scales

When using closed-ended questions, an answer scale has to be determined. In its simplest form, a survey could use just two answer categories (yes/no). Multiple categories (such as, "completely disagree," "disagree," "neutral," "agree," "completely agree") are used more frequently to allow for more nuances. The type of scaling where all categories are named and respondents indicate the degree to which they agree is called a *Likert scale*. Likert scales used by academics commonly have 5-point and 7-point answer categories. A study analyzing 259 academic marketing studies suggests that 5-point (24.2%) and 7-point (43.9%) scales are the most common (Peterson 1997). For practical market research, 10-point scales are frequently used.

In determining how many scale categories to use, one has to balance having more variation in responses vs. asking too much of the respondents. There is some evidence that 7-point scales are better than 5-point scales in terms of obtaining more variation in responses. However, scales with a large number of answer categories often confuse respondents because the wording differences between the scale points become trivial. For example, differences between "tend to agree" and "somewhat agree" are subtle and may not be picked up by respondents. Moreover, scales with many answer categories increase a survey's length, and are therefore more difficult to answer.

You could of course also use 4- or 6-point scales (by deleting the neutral choice). If you force the respondent to be positive or negative, you use a forced-choice (Likert) scale since you "force" the respondent to be either positive or negative. This could bias the answers, thereby leading to reliability issues. By providing a "neutral" category choice the respondents are not forced to give a positive or negative answer. Many respondents feel more comfortable about participating in a survey when offered free-choice scales. In any case, provide descriptions to all answer categories (such as agree or neutral) to facilitate answering by the respondents. When designing answer categories, also use scale categories that are exclusive, so that answers of questions do not overlap (e.g., age categories 0–4, 5–10 etc.).

A related choice is to include an "undecided" category in the scaling. This choice also plays a role for other scale types and we discuss this in Box 4.3.

Box 4.3 Should we use an undecided category?

Using an undecided category allows the researcher to distinguish between those respondents who have a clear opinion and those who do not. Moreover, it may make answering the survey slightly easier for the respondent. While these are good reasons for including this category, the drawback is that we then have missing observations. If a large number of respondents choose not to answer, this will substantially reduce the number of surveys that can be used for analysis. Generally, when designing surveys, you should include an "undecided" or "don't know" category as answers to questions that the respondent might genuinely not know, for example, when factual questions are asked. For other types of questions (such as on attitudes or preferences) the "undecided" or "don't know" category should not be included, as we are interested in the respondents' perceptions regardless of their knowledge of the subject matter.

Moreover, when designing surveys, you need to ensure that the scaling is balanced. A *balanced scale* has an equal number of positive and negative scale categories. For example, in a 5-point Likert scale, we have two negative categories (completely disagree and disagree); a neutral option, and two positive categories (agree and completely agree). Besides this, the wording in a balanced scale should reflect equal distances between the scale items. A caveat is that some constructs cannot take on negative values. For example, one can have some trust in a company or very little trust, but negative trust is highly unlikely. If a scale item cannot be negative, you will have to resort to an unbalanced scale in which the endpoints of the scales are unlikely to be exact opposites.

The *semantic differential scale* uses an opposing pair of words (young-old, masculine-feminine) and the respondent can indicate to what extent he or she agrees with that word. These scales are widely used by market researchers. Like with Likert scales, five or seven answer categories are commonly used. We provide an example of the semantic differential scale in Fig. 4.5 in which a respondent marked his or her perception of two mobile phone brands across four semantic pairs.[3] The answers provided by the respondent are subsequently linked, using lines

---

[3]The categories stem from Aaker's (1997) brand personality scale which describes brands in terms of human characteristics and which is commonly applied in marketing research and practice.

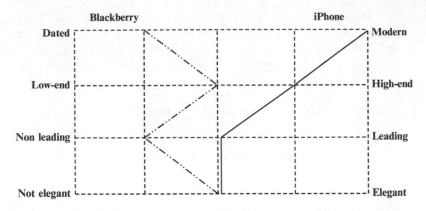

Fig. 4.5 Example of a four-point semantic differential scale

as shown in Fig. 4.3. Sometimes a scaling with an infinite number of answer categories is used (without providing answer categories). This seems very precise because the respondent can tick any answer on the scale. However, in practice these are imprecise because respondents do not, for example, know where along the line "untrustworthy" falls. Another drawback of an infinite number of answer categories is that entering and analyzing the responses are time-consuming because it involves measuring the distance from one side of the scale to the answer ticked by the respondent. We provide two examples of such a semantic differential scale in the Web Appendix (⌁ Web Appendix→Chap. 4). The advantages of semantic differential scales include their ability to profile respondents or objects (such as products or companies) in a simple way.

Rank order scales are a unique type of scale, as they force respondents to compare alternatives. In its basic form, a rank order scale (see Fig. 4.6 for an example) asks the respondent to indicate which alternative is the most important, which one second most important, etc. As a consequence, respondents need to balance their answers instead of merely stating that everything is important. In a more complicated form, rank order scales ask the respondent to allocate a certain total number of points (often 100) over a number of alternatives. This is called the *constant sum scale*. Constant sum scales work well when a small number of answer categories is used, such as four or five. Generally, respondents find constant scales that have six or seven answer categories somewhat challenging while constant

---

Rank the reasons for buying an Apple iPhone from most to least applicable:

___ To listen to music

___ To browse the Web

___ To take photos

___ To make/receive phone calls

___ To send/receive emails

Fig. 4.6 Example of a rank order scale

Table 4.2 A summary of some of the key choices when designing questions

Choice	Actions
Can all the respondents answer the question asked?	Ensure that all items are answerable by all potential respondents. If this is not the case, ask screener questions to direct the respondents. If the respondents cannot answer questions, they should be able to skip those questions.
Can the respondents construct/recall answers?	If the answer is no, you should use other methods to obtain information (e.g., secondary data or observations). Moreover, you may want to ask the respondents about major aspects that occurred before zooming in on details to help them recall answers.
Do the respondents want to fill out each question?	If the questions concern "sensitive" subjects, check whether they can be omitted. If not, stress the confidentiality of the answers and mention why these answers are useful for the researcher, the respondent, or society before introducing the questions.
Should you use open-ended or closed-ended questions?	Keep the subsequent coding in mind. If easy coding is possible beforehand, design a set of exhaustive answer categories. Also, remember that open-ended scale items have a much lower response rate than closed-ended items.
What scaling categories should you use (closed-ended questions only)	Use Likert scales, the semantic differential scale, or rank order scales.
Should you use a balanced scale?	Check the wording and number of items There should be an exact number of positive and negative scale items. The words at the ends of the scale should be exact opposites.
Should you want to use a forced-choice or open-choice scale?	Respondents feel most comfortable with the open-choice scale. However, when an even number of scale categories is used, the forced-choice scale is most common since the scaling can become uneven if it isn't.
Should you include an "undecided"/"don't know" category?	Only for questions that the respondent might genuinely not know, should a "don't know" category be included. If included, place this at the end of the scale.

scales that have eight or more categories are very difficult to answer. The latter are thus best avoided.

In addition to these types of scaling, there are other types, such as graphic rating scales, which use pictures to indicate categories, and the MaxDiff scale in which respondents indicate the most and least applicable items. We introduce the MaxDiff scale as a ⊕ Web Appendix (→ Chap. 4). Table 4.2 provides a summary of some key changes when designing questions.

Do's and Don'ts in Designing Survey Questions

When designing survey questions, there are a number of do's and don'ts. Always use simple words and avoid using jargon or slang if not all the respondents are likely to understand it. There is good evidence that short sentences work better than longer sentences because they are easier to understand (Holbrook et al. 2006).

Thus, try to keep survey questions short and simple. Moreover, avoid using the word *not* or *no* where possible. This is particularly important when other words in the same sentence are negative, such as "unable," or "unhelpful" because generally sentences with two negatives (called a double negative) are hard to understand. For example, a question such as "I do not use the email function in my iPhone because it is unintuitive" is quite hard to understand.

Also avoid the use of "vague" quantifiers such as "frequent" or "occasionally" (Dillman 2007). Vague quantifiers make it difficult for respondents to answer questions (what exactly is meant by "occasionally"?). They also make comparing responses difficult. After all, what one person considers "occasionally," may be "frequent" for another. Instead, it is better to use frames that are precise ("once a week").

Never suggest an answer, for example, by asking "Company X has done very well, how do you rate company X?" In addition, avoid double-barreled questions at all costs, in which a respondent can agree with one part of the question but not the other, or cannot answer without accepting a particular assumption. Examples of double-barreled questions include: "Is the sales personnel polite and responsive?" and "In general, are you satisfied with the products and services of company X?"

Lastly, when you run simultaneous surveys in different countries, make use of professional translators as translation is a complex process. Functionally translating one language into another is quite easy and many websites, such as Google translate (http://translate.google.com) can do this. However, translating surveys requires preserving conceptual equivalence of whole sentences and paragraphs; current software applications and websites cannot ensure this. In addition, cultural differences may require changes to the entire instrument format or procedure. A technique to establish conceptual equivalence across languages is back-translation. Back-translation requires translating a survey instrument into another language after which the translated survey instrument is translated into the original language by another translator. After the back-translation, the original and back-translated instruments are compared and points of divergence are noted. The translation is then corrected to more accurately reflect the intent of the wording in the original language.

In Fig. 4.7, we provide a few examples of poorly designed survey questions followed by better-worded equivalents. These questions relate to how satisfied iPhone users are with performance, reliability, and after-service.

Design the Questionnaire

After determining the individual questions, the market researcher has to integrate these, together with other elements, to create the questionnaire. This involves including an explanation, choosing the order of the questions, and designing the layout and format.

At the beginning of each questionnaire, the importance and goal are usually described to stress that the results will be treated confidentially, and to mention what they will be used for. This is usually followed by an example question (and answer), to demonstrate how the survey should be filled out.

Poor: The question is double-barreled: it asks about performance and reliability

	Strongly disagree	Somewhat disagree	Neutral	Somewhat agree	Completely agree
I am satisfied with the performance and reliability of my Apple iPhone	❑	❑	❑	❑	❑

Better: The question is separated into two questions

	Strongly disagree	Somewhat disagree	Neutral	Somewhat agree	Completely agree
I am satisfied with the performance of my Apple iPhone	❑	❑	❑	❑	❑
I am satisfied with the reliability of my Apple iPhone	❑	❑	❑	❑	❑

Poor: The question cannot be answered by those who have not experienced after-sales service.

	Strongly disagree	Somewhat disagree	Neutral	Somewhat agree	Completely agree
I am satisfied with the after-sales service of my Apple iPhone	❑	❑	❑	❑	❑

Better: Question uses branching

	No	Yes
1.1: Did you use Apple's after-sales service for your iPhone?	❑	❑
If you answered yes, please proceed to question 1.2, otherwise, skip question 1.2 and proceed to question 1.3		

	Strongly disagree	Somewhat disagree	Neutral	Somewhat agree	Completely agree
1.2: I am satisfied with the after-sales service provided by Apple for my iPhone	❑	❑	❑	❑	❑

Fig. 4.7 Examples of good and bad practice in designing survey questions

If questions relate to a specific issue, moment, or transaction, you should indicate this clearly. For example, "Please provide answers to the following questions, keeping the purchase of product X in mind". If applicable, you should also point out that your survey is conducted in collaboration with a university, a recognized research institute, or a known charity as this generally increases respondents' willingness to participate. Moreover, do not forget to provide a name and contact details for those participants who have questions or in case technical problems

Poor: Question design will likely cause inflated expectations ("everything is very important")

	Not at all important	Not important	Neutral	Important	Very important
Which of the following iPhone features are most important to you?					
Camera	☐	☐	☐	☐	☐
Music player (iPod)	☐	☐	☐	☐	☐
App store	☐	☐	☐	☐	☐
Web browser (Safari)	☐	☐	☐	☐	☐
Mail client	☐	☐	☐	☐	☐

Better: Use rank order scale

	Rank
Rank the following iPhone features from most to least important. Begin by picking out the feature you think is most important and assign it a number 1. Then find the second most important and assign it a number 2 etc.	
Camera	—
Music player (iPod)	—
App store	—
Web browser (Safari)	—
Mail client	—

Fig. 4.7 (continued)

should arise. Lastly, you should thank the respondents for their time and describe how the questionnaire should be returned (for mail surveys).

The order of questions is usually as follows:

1. Screeners or classification questions come first. These questions determine what parts of the survey a respondent should fill out.
2. Next, insert the key variables of the study. This includes the dependent variables, followed by the independent variables.
3. Use the funnel approach. That is, ask questions that are more general first and then move on to details. This makes answering the questions easier as the order aids recall. Make sure that sensitive questions are put at the very end of this section.
4. Demographics are placed last if they are not part of the screening questions. If you ask demographic questions, always check whether they are relevant with regard to the research goal. In addition, check if these demographics are likely to lead to non-response. Asking about demographics, like income, may result in a substantial number of respondents refusing to answer. If such sensitive demographics are not necessary, omit them from the survey. When asking

about demographics, providing a few response categories instead of open-ended questions can increase the respondent's willingness to answer. For example, you could provide income categories when requesting information on the annual household income. In certain countries, asking about a respondent's demographic characteristics means you have to abide by specific laws, such as the Data Protection Act 1998 in the UK.

If your questionnaire contains several sections (e.g., in the first section you ask about the respondents' buying attitudes and in the following section about their satisfaction with the company's services), you should make the changing context clear to the respondents.

Moreover, the layout and format of the survey need to be considered. For both mail and Web-based surveys, the layout should be concise and should conserve space where possible.

A few final recommendations: Avoid using small and colored fonts, which reduce readability. For mail-based surveys, booklets work well, since they are less costly to send as they can be made to fit into standard envelopes. If this is not possible, single-sided stapled paper can also work. For Web-based surveys, it is good to have a counter to let the respondents know what percentage of the questions they have already filled out. This gives them some indication of how much time they still have to spend on completing the survey. Make sure the layout is simple and follows older and accepted Web standards. This allows respondents with older and/or non-standard browsers or computers to fill out the survey. In addition, take into consideration that many people access Web surveys through mobile phones and tablet computers. Using older and accepted Web standards is likely to cause a minimum number of technical problems for these respondents.

Pretest the Questionnaire

We have already mentioned the importance of pretesting the survey several times. Before any survey is sent out, you should pre-test the questionnaire to enhance its clarity and to ensure the client's acceptance of the survey. Once the questionnaire is in the field, there is no way back! You can pretest questionnaires in two ways. In its simplest form, you can use a few experts (say 3–6) to read the survey, fill it out, and comment on it. Many Web-based survey tools allow researchers to create a pretest version of their survey in which there is a text box for comments behind every question. Experienced market researchers are able to spot most issues right away and should be employed to pretest surveys. If you aim for a very high quality survey, you should also send out a set of preliminary (but proofread) questionnaires to a small sample consisting of 50–100 respondents. The responses (or lack thereof) usually indicate possible problems and preliminary data may be analyzed to determine potential results. Never skip pretesting because of time issues, since you are likely to run into problems later!

An increasingly important aspect of survey research is to induce potential respondents to participate. In addition to Dillman's (2007) recommendations (see Box 4.4), incentives are increasingly used. A simple example of such an incentive is to provide potential respondents with a cash reward. In the US, one-Dollar bills are often used for this purpose. Respondents who participate in (online) research panels often receive points that can be exchanged for products and services. For example, Research Now, a market research company, provides its Canadian panel members with AirMiles that can be exchanged for free flights, amongst others. A special type of incentive is to indicate that, for every returned survey, money will be donated to a charity. The ESOMAR, the world organization for market and social research (see Chap. 10), suggests that incentives for interviews or surveys should "be kept to a minimum level proportionate to the amount of their time involved, and should not be more than the normal hourly fee charged by that person for their professional consultancy or advice".

Another incentive is to give the participants a chance to win a product or service. For example, you could randomly give away iPods or holidays to a number of participants. By providing them with a chance to win, the participants need to disclose their name and address so that they can be reached. While this is not part of the research, some respondents may feel uncomfortable doing so, which could potentially reduce response rates.

Finally, a type of incentive that may help participation (particularly in professional settings) is to report the findings back to the participants. This can be done by providing a general report of the study and its findings, or by providing a customized report detailing the participant's responses and comparing them with all the

Box 4.4 Dillman's (2007) recommendations

It is becoming increasingly difficult to get people to fill out surveys. This may be due to over surveying, dishonest firms that disguise sales as research, and a lack of time. In his book, Mail and Internet Surveys, Dillman (2007) discusses four steps to increase response rates:

1. Send out a pre-notice letter indicating the importance of the study and announcing that a survey will be sent out shortly.
2. Send out the survey with a sponsor letter again indicating the importance of the study.
3. Follow up after 3–4 weeks with both a thank you note (for those who responded) and a new survey plus a reminder (for those who did not respond).
4. Call or email those who have not responded still and send out a thank you note to those who replied in the second round.

Further, Dillman (2007) points out that names and addresses should be error free. Furthermore, he recommends, using a respondent-friendly questionnaire in the form of a booklet, providing return envelopes, and personalizing correspondence.

---

other responses. Obviously, anonymity needs to be assured so that the participants cannot compare their answers with those of other individual responses.

Collecting Quantitative Data: Basic Experimental Research

In Chap. 2, we discussed causal research and briefly introduced experiments as a means of conducting research. The goal of designing experiments is to control for as much as possible and to avoid other variables' unintended influences. Experiments are typically conducted by manipulating one or a few variables at a time. For example, we can change the price of a product, the type of product, or the package size to determine whether these changes affect important outcomes such as attitudes, satisfaction, or intentions. Often, simple field observations cannot establish these relationships.

Imagine a company were to introduce a new type of soft drink aimed at health-conscious consumers. If the product were to fail, the managers would probably conclude that consumers did not like the product. However, many (often unobserved) variables, such as price cuts by competitors, changing health concerns, or a lack of availability, can also influence new products' success.

Experiments attempt to isolate how one particular change affects an outcome. The outcome is called the dependent variable (we may have several) and the several independent variable(s) explain the outcome(s). The independent variables are often *stimuli* or *treatments* manipulated in the experiment by providing the participants with different situations. A simple form of a treatment could take the shape of a yes/no manipulation in which, for example, respondents are shown an advertisement with or without humor. The number of treatments are the different *factors* or *levels* of a variable. If we manipulate price between low, medium, and high, we have three factors. If we manipulate using or not using humor we have two factors. When selecting independent variables, we typically include changeable variables marketers care about related to marketing and design of products and services. Care should be taken not to include too many of these variables in order to keep the experiment manageable. An experiment that includes four manipulations, each of which have three levels, and that includes every possible combination (called a *full factorial design*) would already require conducting $4^3 = 64$ experiments. Large numbers of levels (five or more) will increase the complexity and cost of the research dramatically. *Extraneous variables*, such as the age or income of the participant in the experiment, are not changed as part of the experiment but may be important.

Experimental design refers to the conducted experiment's structure. There are various types of experimental designs. To clearly separate the different experimental designs, researchers have developed the following notation:

O: A formal observation or measurement of the dependent variable. Subscripts such as O_1, O_2, etc, are used to indicate measurements in different points in time.

X: Test participants' exposure to an experimental manipulation or treatment.

R: Random assignment of participants. Randomization ensures control over extraneous variables and increases the reliability of the experiment.

If one symbol follows after another it means that the first symbol precedes the next one in time.

The simplest form of experiment is the *one-shot case study*. This type of experiment is structured as follows:

$$X \quad O_1$$

This means we have only one manipulation (e.g., increasing advertising). After the manipulation, we await reactions and then measure the outcome of the manipulation, such as attitude towards a brand. This type of experiment is common but does not tell us if the effect is causal. One reason for this is that we did not measure anything before the manipulation and therefore cannot assess what the relationship between the manipulation and outcome is. Moreover, other explanations, such as a competing brand's negative publicity, are not controlled for. Thus, causality cannot be established with this design.

The simplest type of experiment that allows us to make causal inferences – within certain limits – is the *before-after design* for one group. The notation for this is:

$$O_1 \quad X \quad O_2$$

Thus, we have one measurement before and one after a manipulation. This type of design can be used to determine whether customers find a product's health claim credible before and after seeing an advertisement.

However, the initial measurement O_1 may alert participants that they are being studied, which may bias the post measurement O_2. Likewise, participants may drop out of the experiment, which may threaten the experiment's validity. The key issue with drop out is that the reason for the participant dropping out may be confused with the effect studied. For example, if we study attitudes towards the iPhone as a product, people with a job may have little time and, consequently, refuse to participate. However, since they have a job, they will have a higher income, making their attitudes underrepresented in the study.

A more common approach to understanding causal effects is to use two different groups in an experiment. An important feature that helps come to causal conclusions is if the participants are randomly assigned to two groups. This means that, for any given treatment, every participant has an equal probability of being chosen for one of the two groups. This ensures that participants with different characteristics are spread equally among the treatment(s), which will neutralize extraneous variables' effects. A simple form of this is the *posttest-only control group experiment*. In this type of experiment, we have a single manipulation and two measurements.

Experimental group   (R) X O_1
Control group   (R) O_2

We can use this type of experiment to determine whether a higher service level increases satisfaction. For example, the Omni hotel chain has introduced a new service for selected guests: they can have two pieces of clothing pressed for free. Using a posttest-only experiment, we can determine if such a service change influences guests' satisfaction.

If we want to identify how strong the effect of a manipulation is, we need a more complex (but also more rigorous) setup, called the *before-after experiment with a control group*. The notation of this type of experiment is:

Experimental group   (R) O_1 X O_2
Control group   (R) O_3 O_4

The effect attributed to the experiment is the difference between O_1 and O_2 minus that of O_3 and O_4. That is, the difference between O_1 and O_2 is probably mostly due to the experiment. However, to control for effects that may cause a repeat measurement to differ (the respondents become experienced, bored, etc.), we subtract the difference between O_3 and O_4 from the difference between O_1 and O_2.[4]

In Chap. 6, we discuss how the data resulting from experiments can be analyzed using various tests and ANOVA.

Collecting Qualitative Data: Basic Qualitative Research

Qualitative research is mostly used to gain an understanding of *why* certain things happen or to work on developing measures. Qualitative research leads to the collection of qualitative data as discussed in Chap. 3. One can collect qualitative data by explicitly informing the participants that you are doing research (*directly observed qualitative data*), or you can simple observe the participants' behavior without the participants being explicitly aware of the research goals (*indirectly observed qualitative data*). There are ethical issues associated with conducting research in which the participants are not aware of the research purpose. Always check regulations regarding what is allowed in your context and what not. It is always advisable to brief the participants on their role and the goal of the research after data have been collected. Figure 4.8 shows the most important types of qualitative research and we will discuss these in turn.

The two key forms of directly observed qualitative data are interviews and focus groups. Together, focus groups and interviews comprise most of the conducted qualitative market research. As the terms suggests, interviews are conducted with one participant at a time while focus groups include multiple participants.

---

[4]To learn more about experimental research and different designs, take a look at Campbell and Stanley (1966) or Cook and Campbell (1979).

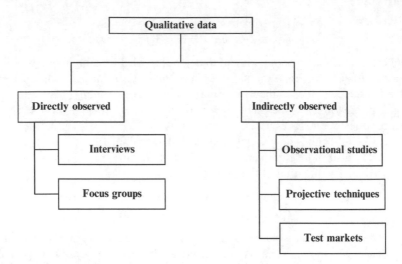

Fig. 4.8 Types of qualitative research

Interviews are qualitative conversations with participants about a specific issue. Often, these participants are consumers but they might also be the decision-makers in a market research study who are interviewed to gain an understanding of their clients' needs. They could also be government or other company representatives. Interviews vary in their level of structure. In their simplest form, interviews are unstructured and the participants talk about a topic in general. This works well if you want to obtain insight into an issue or as an initial step in a research process. Interviews can also be fully structured, meaning all questions and possible answer categories are decided in advance. This leads to the collecting of quantitative data. However, most interviews are semi-structured and contain a series of questions that need to be addressed but that have no specific format as to what the answers should look like. The person interviewed can make additional remarks or discuss somewhat related issues, but is not allowed to wander off too far. In these types of interviews, the interviewer often asks questions like "that's interesting, could you explain?", or "how come. . .?" to probe further into the issue. In highly structured interviews, the interviewer has a fixed set of questions and often a fixed amount of time allocated to each person's response. The goal of structured interviews is to maximize the comparability of the answers. Consequently, the set-up of the questions and the structure of the answers need to be similar.

Interviews are unique in that they allow for interaction and probing on a one-to-one basis. Interviews also work well when the person interviewed has very little time available and when he or she does not want the information to be shared with the other participants in the study. This is, for example, likely to be the case when you discuss marketing strategy decisions with CEOs. The drawbacks of interviews include the amount of time the researcher needs to spend on the interview itself and traveling (if the interview is conducted face-to-face and not via the telephone), as well as transcribing the interview. When conducting interviews, a set format is usually followed. First, the interview details are discussed, such as confidentiality issues, the topic of the interview, the structure, and the duration. Moreover, the interviewer should disclose whether the interview is being recorded and inform the interviewee that there is no right or wrong answer, just opinions on the subject. The interviewer should also try to be open and keep eye contact with the interviewee. The interview can be ended by informing the respondent that you have reached the last question and thanking him or her for being helpful.

Interviews are often used (together with other qualitative techniques, such as focus groups) to investigate *means-end* issues in which researchers try to understand what ends consumers try to satisfy through which means (consumption). A means-end approach involves first determining the *attributes* of a product. These are the functional product features, such as the speed a car can reach or its acceleration. Subsequently, we look at the *functional consequences* that follow from the product benefits. This could be driving fast. The *psychosocial consequences*, or personal benefits, are derived from the functional benefits and, in our example, could include an enhanced status or being regarded as successful. Finally, the psychosocial benefits are linked to people's personal *values* or life goals, such as a desire for success or acceptance. Analyzing and identifying the relationships between these steps is called *laddering*.

Focus groups are interviews conducted among a number of respondents at the same time and led by a *moderator*. This moderator leads the interview, structures it, and often plays a central role in later transcribing the interview. Focus groups are usually semi- or highly structured. The group usually comprises between 4 and 6 people to allow for interaction between the participants and to ensure that all the participants can have a say. The duration of a focus group interview varies, but is often between 30 and 90 minutes for focus groups of company employees and between 60 and 120 minutes for consumers. When focus groups are held with company employees, the moderator usually travels to the company and conducts his or her focus group in a reserved room. When consumers are involved, moderators often travel to a market research company or hotel where a conference room is used for the focus group. Market research companies often have special conference rooms with equipment like one-way mirrors, built-in microphones, and video recording devices.

Focus groups usually start with the moderator introducing the topic and discussing the background. Everyone is introduced to establish rapport. Subsequently, the moderator tries to get the members of the focus group to speak to one another, instead of asking the moderator for confirmation. Once the focus group members start discussing topics with one another, the moderator tries to stay in the background while ensuring that the discussions stay on-topic. Afterwards, the participants are briefed and the discussions are transcribed for further analysis. Focus groups have distinct advantages: they are relatively cheap compared to face-to-face interviews, they work well with issues that have important social aspects or require spontaneity, and are also useful for developing new ideas. On the downside, focus groups do not offer the same ability as interviews to probe and run a greater risk of going off-course. Moreover, a few focus group members may dominate the discussion and, in larger focus groups, "voting" behavior may occur, hindering real discussions and the development of new ideas.

Observational studies are relatively rare but can provide important insights that are unavailable through other market research techniques. Observational techniques shed light on consumers' and employees' behavior and can help answer questions, such as how consumers walk through supermarkets, how they consume and dispose of products, and how employees spend their working day. Observational techniques are not used to understand why people behave in a certain way but rather aim to understand what they are doing. Observational studies work well when people find it difficult to put what they are doing in words, such as when people from different ethnic backgrounds shop for food. Most observational studies use video recording equipment or trained researchers who observe what people do unobtrusively (e.g., through one-way mirrors or by using recording equipment). Recently, researchers have also used computer chips (called RFIDs) to trace consumers' shopping paths within a supermarket. Other types of observational studies include *mystery shopping*, in which a trained researcher is asked to visit a store or restaurant and consume their products/services. For example, McDonalds and Selfridges, a UK retail chain, use mystery shoppers (see Box 4.5 for an MSNBC video on mystery shopping).

Box 4.5   Using mystery shopping to improve customer service

http://tiny.cc/myst_msnbc

Sometimes observational studies are conducted in households with researchers participating in a household to see how people buy, consume, and dispose of products/services. The type of studies in which the researcher is a participant is called an *ethnography*. An example of an ethnography is Volkswagen's Moonraker project in which a number of Volkswagen's employees follow American drivers to gain an understanding of how their usage of and preferences for automobiles different from those of drivers in Europe.[5]

---

[5]See http://www.businessweek.com/autos/autobeat/archives/2006/01/there_have_been.html

Projective techniques work by providing a participant with a stimulus and gauging his or her response. Although participants in projective techniques know that they are participating in a market research study, they may not be aware of the specific purpose of the research. The stimuli provided in projective techniques are ambiguous and require a response from the participants. A key form of projective techniques is *sentence completion*, for example:

An iPhone user is someone who: ....
The Apple brand makes me think of: ....
iPhones are most liked by: ....

In this example, the respondents are asked to express their feelings, ideas, and opinions in a free format.

Projective techniques' advantage is that they allow for responses when people are unlikely to respond if they were to know the exact purpose of the study. Thus, projective techniques can overcome self-censoring and allow expression and fantasy. In addition, they can change a participant's perspective. Think of the previous example. If the participant is a user of the Apple iPhone, the sentence completion example asks how he or she thinks other people see him or her, not what he or she thinks of the Apple iPhone. A drawback is that projective techniques require interpretation and coding of responses, which can be difficult.

Test markets are a costly type of market research in which a company introduces a new product or service in a specific geographic market. Sometimes, test markets are also used to see how consumers react to different marketing mix instruments, such as changes in pricing, distribution, or advertising and communication. Thus, test marketing is about changing the product or service offering in a real market and gauging consumers' reactions. Test markets are expensive and difficult to conduct. Some common test markets include Hassloch in Germany as well as Indianapolis and Nashville in the USA.

Questions

1. What is the difference between primary and secondary data? Can primary data become secondary data?
2. Please provide a few examples of secondary data sources that you found through the Internet.
3. Imagine you are asked to understand what consumer characteristics make them likely to buy a Honda Insight hybrid car (see http://automobiles.honda.com/insight-hybrid). How would you collect the data? Would you start with secondary data or do you directly start collecting primary data? Do you think it is appropriate to collect qualitative data? If so, at what stage of the process?
4. If you were to set up an experiment to ascertain what type of package (new or existing) current customers prefer, what type of experiment would you choose? Please discuss.

5. What are the different reasons for choosing interviews over focus groups? What choice would you make if you want to understand CEOs' perceptions of the economy and what would seem appropriate when you want to understand how consumers feel about a newly introduced TV program?

Further Readings

http://www.focusgrouptips.com

This website provides a thorough explanation of how to set-up focus groups from planning to reporting the results.

http://www.mysteryshop.org

This website discusses the mystery shopping industry in Asia, Europe, North America, and South America.

Dillman DA, Smyth JD, Christian LM (2009) Internet, mail, and mixed-mode surveys: the tailored design method. Wiley, Hoboken, NJ

This book gives an excellent overview on how to set-up questionnaires and how to execute them. Specifically mixed-mode surveys and web surveys are paid significant attention.

Lietz P (2010) Current state of the art in questionnaire design: a review of the literature. Int J Mark Res 52(2):249–272

This article reviews survey design choices from an academic perspective.

Veludo-de-Oliveira TM, Ikeda AA, Campomar MC (2006) Laddering in the practice of marketing research: barriers and solutions. Qual Mark Res: An Int J 9(3):297–306

This article provides an overview of laddering, the various forms of laddering, and biases that may result and how these should be overcome.

References

Aaker JL (1997) Dimensions of brand personality. J Mark Res 34(3):347–357

Bronner F, Kuijlen T (2007) The live or digital interviewer. A comparison between CASI, CAPI and CATI with respect to differences in response behaviour. Int J Mark Res 49(2):167–190

Campbell DT, Stanley JC (1966) Experimental and quasi-experimental designs for research. Wadsworth Publishing, Chicago, IL

Casteleyn J, Mottart A, Rutten K (2009) How to use Facebook in your market research. Int J Mark Res 51(4):439–447

Cook TD, Campbell DT (1979) Quasi-experimentation: design and analysis issues for field settings. Wadsworth Publishing, Chicago, IL

Deutskens E, de Jong A, de Ruyter K, Wetzels M (2006) Comparing the generalizability of online and mail surveys in cross-national service quality research. Mark Lett 17(2):119–136

DeMonaco HJ, Ali A, Hippel EV (2005) The major role of clinicians in the discovery of off-label drug therapies. Pharmacotherapy 26(3):323–332

Dillman DA (2007) Mail and internet surveys. Wiley, Hoboken, NJ

Holbrook A, Cho YIK, Johnson T (2006) The impact of question and respondent characteristics on comprehension and mapping difficulties. Public Opin Q 70(4):565–595

Peterson R (1997) A quantitative analysis of rating-scale response variability. Mark Lett 8(1):9–21

Vincente P, Reis E, Santos M (2008) Using mobile phones for survey research. Int J Mark Res 51(5):613–633

Chapter 5
Descriptive Statistics

Learning Objectives

After reading this chapter, you should understand:
- The workflow involved in a market research study.
- Univariate and bivariate descriptive graphs and statistics.
- How to deal with missing values.
- How to transform data (z-transformation, log transformation, creating dummies, aggregating variables).
- How to identify and deal with outliers.
- What a codebook is.
- The basics of using IBM SPSS Statistics.

Keywords Bar chart · Codebook · Correlation · Covariance · Cross tabs · Dummies · Frequency table · Histogram · Line chart · Log transformation · Mean · Median · Mode · Outliers · Pie chart · Scatter plots · SPSS · Standard deviation · Variance · Workflow · z-transformation

This chapter has two purposes: first, we discuss how to keep track of, enter, clean, describe, and transform data. We call these steps the *workflow* of data. Second, we discuss how we can describe data using a software package called IBM SPSS Statistics (abbreviated as SPSS).

The Workflow of Data

Market research projects involving data become more efficient and effective if a proper *workflow* is in place. A workflow is a strategy to keep track of, enter, clean, describe, and transform data. These data may have been collected through surveys or may be secondary data. Haphazardly entering, cleaning, and analyzing bits of data is not a good strategy, since it increases one's likelihood of making mistakes and makes it hard to replicate results. Moreover, without a good workflow of data, it becomes hard to document the research process and cooperate on projects. For example, how can you outsource the data analysis, if you cannot indicate what the data are about or what specific values mean? Finally, a lack of good workflow

E. Mooi and M. Sarstedt, *A Concise Guide to Market Research*,
DOI 10.1007/978-3-642-12541-6_5, © Springer-Verlag Berlin Heidelberg 2011

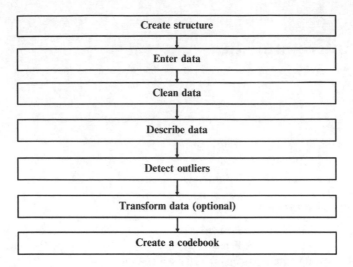

Fig. 5.1 The workflow of data

increases one's risk of having to duplicate work or even of losing all of your data due to accidents. In Fig. 5.1, we show the steps necessary to create and describe a dataset after the data have been collected.

Create Structure

The basic idea of setting up a good workflow is that good planning allows the researcher to save time and allows other researchers to do their share of the analysis and/or replicate the research. After the data collection phase, the first step is to save the available data. We recommend keeping track of the dataset by providing data and data-related files in separate directories. We can do this with Windows Explorer or the Apple Mac's Finder. This directory should have subdirectories for at least the data files, the output, syntax, a temporary directory, and a directory with files that are directly related, such as the survey used to collect the data. In Table 5.1, we show an example of a directory structure. Within the main directory, there are five subdirectories, each with distinct files. Notice that in the *Data files* directory, we have the original dataset, two modified datasets (one without missing data and one which includes several transformations of the data) as well as a *.zip* file that contains the original dataset. If the data file is contained in a *.zip* file, it is unlikely to be modified and can be easily opened if the working file is accidentally overwritten or deleted. In the *Output*, *Syntax*, and *Temporary* directories, we provided each file with the suffix *rev1* or *rev2*. We use *rev* (abbreviation of revision), however, you could choose to use another file name, as long as it clearly indicates the revision on which you are working. Finally, in the *Related Files* directory, we have a codebook (more on this later), the survey, two presentations, and two documents containing recommendations.

Table 5.1 Example of a directory structure for saving market research related files

Directory name	Subdirectory name	Example file names
2010_retailing project	Data files	Retailer.sav
		Retailer.zip
		Retailer rev1.sav
		Retailer rev2.sav
	Output files	Missing data analysis rev2.spv
		Descriptives rev2.spv
		Factor analysis rev2.spv
		Regression analysis rev2.spv
	Syntax files	Missing data analysis.sps
		Descriptives.sps
		Factor analysis.sps
		Regression analysis.sps
	Temporary	Missing data analysis rev1.spv
		Descriptives rev1.spv
		Factor analysis rev1.spv
		Regression analysis rev1.spv
	Related files	Codebook.doc
		Survey.pdf
		Initial findings – presentation to client.ppt
		Final findings – presentation to client.ppt
		Recommendations rev1.doc
		Recommendations rev2.doc

Another aspect to creating structure is to properly set up the variables for your study. Provide clear names for each variable. In SPSS, and most other statistical software programs, you can indicate a name for each variable and a description (in SPSS, this is called a *variable label* and is discussed later). The name of the variable should be short so that it can be read in the dialog boxes. For example, if you have three questions on web browsing enjoyment, three on time pressure during browsing, and several descriptors (age and gender), you could code these as *enjoy1-enjoy3*, *time1-time3*, and *age* and *gender*. The description of the variables should be more informative than the variable name. The description typically includes the original question if the data were collected using surveys. It is also a good idea to indicate what types of data have been collected. For example, you can collect data based on values (*Numeric* in SPSS) or on text (*String* in SPSS). In SPSS, you can indicate the measurement level; nominal data, ordinal data, or scale data (for ratio and interval scaled data). Another point to consider is *coding*. Coding means assigning values to specific questions. When quantitative data are collected, the task is relatively easy; for Likert and semantic differential scales, we use values that correspond with the answers. For example, for a five-point Likert scale, responses can be coded as 1–5 or as 0–4 (with 0 being the most negative and 4 being the most positive response).

Open-ended questions (qualitative data) require more effort; typically, a three-step process is involved. First, we collect all responses. In the second step, we group all responses. Determining the number of groups and to which group a response belongs is the major challenge in this step. To prevent the process from becoming too subjective, usually two or three market researchers code the responses and discuss any arising differences. The third step is providing a value for each group.

Once a system is set up to keep track of your progress, you need to consider safeguarding your files. Large companies usually have systems for creating *backups* (extra copies of files as a safeguard). If you are working alone or for a small company, you will most probably have to take care of this yourself. You could save your most recent and second most recent version of your file on a separate drive. Always keep two copies and never keep both backups in the same place as theft, fire, or an accident could still mean you'll lose all of your work!

Enter Data

Capturing the data is the next step for primary data. How do we enter survey or experimental data into a dataset? For large datasets, or datasets created by professional firms, specialized software is often used. For example Epidata (http://www.epidata.dk) is frequently used to enter data from paper-based surveys, Entryware's mobile survey (http://www.techneos.com) is commonly deployed to enter data from personal intercepts or face-to-face interviewing, while, for example, Voxco's Interviewer CATI is often used for telephone interviewing. The SPSS Data Collection Family (http://www.spss.com/software/data-collection) is a suite of different software packages specifically designed to collect and (automatically) enter data collected from online, telephone, and paper-based surveys.

Small firms or individual firms may not have access to such software and may need to enter data manually. You can enter data directly into SPSS. However, a drawback of directly entering data is the risk of making typing errors. Professional software such as Epidata can directly check if values are admissible. For example, if a survey question has only two answer categories such as gender (coded 0/1), Epidata and other packages can directly check if the value entered is 0 or 1, and not any other value. Moreover, if you are collecting very large amounts of data that require multiple typists, specialized software needs to be used. When entering data, check whether a substantial number of surveys or survey questions were left blank and note this.

Clean Data

Cleaning data is the next step in the workflow. It requires checking for data entry errors, interviewer fraud, and missing data. Datasets often contain wrongly entered data, missing data, blank observations, and other issues that require some decision making by the researcher.

First, one should check if there are any data entry errors. Data entry errors are easy to spot if they occur outside the variable's range. That is, if an item is measured using a 5-point scale, then the lowest value should be 1 (or 0) and the highest 5 (or 4).

Using descriptive statistics (minimum, maximum, and range), we can check if this is indeed true. Data entry errors should always be corrected by going back to the original survey. If we cannot go back (e.g., because the data were collected using face-to-face interviews), we need to delete that particular observation for that particular variable. More subtle errors, for example, incorrectly entering a score of 4 as, say, 3 are difficult to detect using statistics. One way to check for these data entry errors is to randomly select observations and compare the entered responses with the original surveys. You would expect a small number of errors (below 1%). If many typing errors occurred, the dataset should be entered again.

Interviewer fraud is a difficult issue to deal with. It ranges from interviewers "helping" actual respondents provide answers to the falsification of entire surveys. Interviewer fraud is a serious issue and often leads to incorrect results. Fortunately, we can avoid and detect interviewer fraud in several ways. First, never base interviewers' compensation on the number of completed responses. Once data have been collected, interviewer fraud may be detected in several ways. If multiple interviewers are used, the way in which they select respondents should be similar, if a reasonably large number of responses (> 100) is collected per interviewer. We would therefore expect the responses obtained to also be similar. Using the testing techniques discussed in Chap. 6, we can test if this is indeed likely. Furthermore, the persons interviewed can be contacted afterwards to obtain their feedback on survey. If a substantial number of people do not claim to have been interviewed, interviewer fraud is likely. Furthermore, if people have been previously interviewed on a similar subject, we would expect factual variables (education, address, etc.) to change little. Using descriptive statistics, we can check if this is indeed true. If substantial interviewer fraud is suspected, the data should be discarded. Of course, the costs of discarding data are substantial. Therefore, firms should check for interviewer fraud during the data collection process as well.

Missing data are a frequently occurring issue that market researchers have to deal with. There are two levels at which missing data occur, namely at the survey level (entire surveys are missing) and at the item level (respondents have not answered some item). The first issue is called *survey non-response* and the second *item non-response*.

Survey non-response is very common. In fact, routinely, only 5–25% of all surveys are filled out by respondents. Although higher percentages are possible, they are not the norm for one-shot surveys. Issues such as inaccurate address lists, a lack of interest and time, people confusing market research with selling, and privacy issues, have led response rates to drop over the last decade. Moreover, the amount of market research has increased, leading to respondent fatigue and a further decline in response rates. However, the issue of survey response is best dealt with by properly designing surveys and the survey procedure (see Box 4.4 in Chap. 4 for suggestions). Moreover, survey response issues are only detected once there is a tabulation of all responses. The response percentage of a survey is calculated by dividing the number of usable responses by the total number of surveys sent out (called the *net response*) or by dividing the number of surveys received, including blank returned surveys or those partially completed, by the total number of surveys sent out (called the *gross response*). Occasionally, researchers send out multiple surveys to the same respondent. If so, it is common to calculate how many respondents have provided at least one response and to divide this by the number of unique respondents to which a survey was sent out. This calculation is also followed for mixed-mode surveys.

Item non-response occurs when respondents do not provide answers to certain questions. This is common and typically 2–10% of questions remain unanswered. However, this number strongly depends on several factors such as the subject matter, the length of the questionnaire and the method of administration. For questions considered sensitive by many people (such as income), non-response can be much higher. The key issue with non-response is if the items are missing completely at random or if they are systematically missing. Items missing completely at random means that the observations answered are a random draw from the population. If data are systematically missing, the observations are not a random draw. For example, if we ask respondents what their incomes are, those with higher incomes are less likely to answer. We might therefore underestimate the overall income. Item non-response with a systematic component to it, nearly always leads to validity issues. How can we check if systematic item non-response issues are present? If we believe that the pattern of missing values is systematic, we could tabulate the occurrence of non-responses against responses for different groups. If we put the variable about which we have concerns on one side of the table, and the number of (non-)response on the other, a table similar to Table 5.2 is produced.

Using a χ^2-test (pronounced as *chi-square*; which we discuss under nonparametric tests in the ⌨ Web Appendix $\rightarrow$ Chap. 6), we can test if there is a significant relationship between the respondents' (non-)response and their income.

You can deal with these missing values in several ways. If the percentage of item non-response is low and the sample large, most researchers choose to completely delete all observations with missing data. However, with a moderate level of item non-response and a large number of items per survey, this leads to high percentages of surveys needing to be deleted (10% or more). In that case, most researchers choose to *impute* observations. Imputation means substituting a missing observation for a likely value. Several imputation procedures exist. However, before deciding on one, always check if imputation makes sense. The key issue is to check if an observation could have been answered. If so, imputation may make sense. If not, imputation should not be carried out. An example is to ask how satisfied someone is with his or her car(s). Even if no answer is provided, a car-owning respondent could have provided an answer and therefore imputation may make sense. However, if the respondent does not own a car, the question could not be answered, and imputation makes no sense.

Table 5.2 Example of response issues

	Low income	High income
Response	95	80
Non-response	5	20

N = 200

Table 5.3 Data cleaning issues and how to deal with them

Problem	Action
Data entry errors	Use descriptive statistics (minimum, maximum, range) to check for obvious typing errors and/or compare a subset of surveys to the dataset to check for inconsistencies.
Typing errors	Check descriptive statistics (minimum, maximum, range); use a sample of the surveys and check consistency between the surveys and data.
Interviewer fraud	Check respondents; correlate with previous data if available.
Survey non-response	Before sending out survey use Dillman's (2008) design principles (see Box 4.4 in Chap. 4).
Item non-response	Check type of non-response: is non-response systematic or random? If small percentage of items is missing: delete cases. Otherwise, use an imputation method such as regression imputation.

A simple imputation procedure is *mean substitution*, which is nothing more than a substitution of a missing value by the average of all observed values of that variable. Mean substitution is simple and easily carried out in most analysis software. However, a drawback of mean substitution is that it reduces correlations (discussed later). We can also apply more complex methods (e.g., EM or regression substitution), which are also included in SPSS (these methods are not discussed here). Hair et al. (2010) provide a basic introduction to imputation. Table 5.3 summarizes the data issues discussed in this section.

Describe Data

Once we have performed the previous steps, we can turn to the task of describing the data. Data can be described one variable at a time (*univariate descriptives*) or the relationship between two variables can be described (*bivariate descriptives*). We further divide univariate and bivariate descriptives into graphs/charts/tables and statistics.

The choice between graphs/charts/tables and statistics depends on what information you want to convey. Often graphs/charts/tables can tell a reader with a limited background in statistics a great deal. However, graphs/charts/tables can also mislead readers, as we will discuss later in Chap. 10 (Box 10.1). On the other hand, statistics require some background knowledge but have the advantage that they take up little space and are exact. We summarize the different types of descriptive statistics in Fig. 5.2.

Univariate Graphs/Charts/Tables

In the next section, we discuss the most prominent types of univariate graphs/charts/tables: the histogram, pie chart, frequency table, bar chart, and line chart. In Fig. 5.3, these different types of charts are used to show the different sales tax rates in the US. Notice how the charts display the same information in different ways.

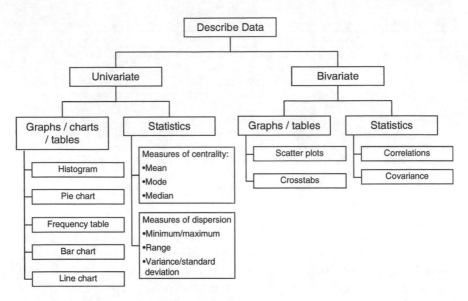

Fig. 5.2 The different types of descriptive statistics

The *histogram* is a graph that shows how frequently a particular variable's values occur. The values a variable can take on are plotted on the *x*-axis, where the values are divided into (non-overlapping) classes that are directly adjacent to one another. These classes usually have an equal width. For example, if you create a histogram for the variable *age*, you can use classes of 0–10, 11–20, etc. where the width is equal. However, you could also choose classes such as 0–20, 21–25, 26–30. If you think important information will be left out if too many variables are included in the same class, it is best to use classes with an unequal width or to increase the number of classes. Because histograms use classes, they are helpful for describing interval or ratio scaled data. A histogram can also be used if you want to show the distribution of a variable. If you have a variable with a very large number of categories (more than ten), a histogram becomes difficult to understand. Similarly, if the difference between the least frequently and most frequently occurring values is very high, histograms become difficult to read.

The *pie chart* visualizes how a variable's different values are distributed. Pie charts are easy to understand and work well if the number of values a variable takes on is small (less than 10). Pie charts are particularly useful for displaying percentages of variables, because people interpret the entire pie as being 100%, and can easily see how often a variable's value occurs.

A *frequency table* is a table that includes all possible values of a variable and how often they occur. It is similar to both the histogram and pie chart in that it shows the distribution of a variable's possible values. However, in a frequency table, all values are indicated exactly.

A *bar chart* plots the number of times a particular value occurs in a data set, with the height of the bar representing the number of times a value is observed. Bar

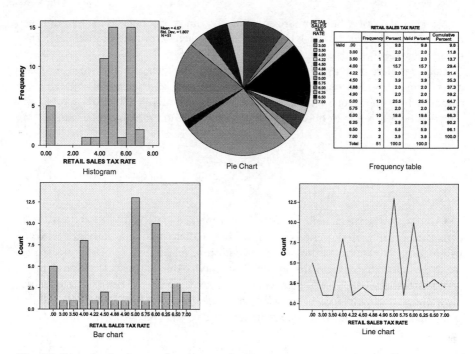

Fig. 5.3 Several univariate graphs, charts, and tables

charts are useful for describing nominal or ordinal data. The bars of bar charts are not directly adjacent, as some blank space is included between each bar. A bar chart is somewhat similar to a histogram, but bar charts can indicate how often the different values of a variable occur (e.g., 20 females, 30 males), can describe different variables next to each other (e.g., average income is 30,000 USD, average age is 39) or show the values of each observation (e.g., observation 1, age = 31, observation 2, age = 25, etc.)

A *line chart* also describes the different values occurring in a variable but connects each value, thereby giving the impression that that particular variable is continuous. Line charts work well if you want to visualize how a variable changes over time.

Univariate Statistics

Univariate statistics fall into two groups: those describing centrality and those describing the dispersion of variables. Centrality-based measures include the mean, the mode, and the median. The *mean* (or average) is the sum of each individual observation of a variable divided by the number of observations. The *median* is the value that separates the lowest 50% of cases from the highest 50% of cases. The *mode* is the most frequently occurring value in the dataset.

Nominal data may be summarized using the mode, but not the median nor the mean. The median and also the mode are useful when describing ordinal data. The mean is useful if our data are interval or ratio-scaled.

Each measure of centrality has its own uses. The mean (abbreviated as $\bar{x}$) is most frequently used but is sensitive to unexpected large or small values. It is calculated by the sum of each observation's value divided by the number of observations. x_i refers to observation i of variable x and n to the total number of observations.

$$\bar{x} = \frac{1}{n} \sum_{i=1}^{n} x_i$$

Contrary to the mean, neither the mode nor median are sensitive to outliers. As a consequence, the relationship between mean, median and mode provides us with valuable information regarding the distribution of a variable. For example, if the mean is much higher than the median and mode, this suggests that the dataset contains outliers which shift the mean upwards. This is the case when we observe the values 4, 5, 5, and 50, where both median and mode are 5 while the mean is 16. If the mean, median, and mode are more or less the same, the variable is likely to be symmetrically distributed.

For the measures of dispersion, the *minimum* and *maximum* indicate a particular variable's highest and lowest value. The *range* is the difference between the highest value and the lowest value. The *variance* (abbreviated as s^2) measures the sum of the squared differences between all of a variable's values and its mean divided by the number of observations minus 1.

$$s^2 = \frac{\sum_{i=1}^{n} (x_i - \bar{x})^2}{n - 1}$$

Variance is one of the most frequently used measures of dispersion. It tells us how strongly observations vary around the mean. By using squared differences between observations and the mean, positive and negative differences cannot cancel each other out. Likewise, values that lie far from the mean increase the variance more strongly than those that are close to the mean.

The *standard deviation* (abbreviated as s) is the square root of – and, therefore, a special case of – the variance. Whereas the mean is usually easy to interpret, the variance and standard deviation are less intuitive. A rule of thumb is that in large (normally distributed – this will be discussed in later chapters) datasets, about two-thirds of all observations are between plus and minus one standard deviation away from the mean. Thus, if the standard deviation is 0.70 and the mean 3, 64% of all observations will likely fall between 2.30 and 3.70. Approximately 2 standard deviations plus, or minus the mean, usually indicates that 95% of all observations fall between 1.60 and 4.40.

Bivariate Graphs/Tables

There is only a small number of bivariate graphs and tables of which the *scatter plot* and the *crosstab* are the most prominent. The scatter plot uses both the y and x-axis (and sometimes a third z-axis) to show how two or three variables relate to one another. Scatter plots are useful to identify outliers and to show the relationship between two variables. Relationships are much harder to visualize when there are three variables. Scatter plots work well if the sample size is not too large (about 100 observations or less). We give an example of a scatter plot later on.

Bivariate Statistics

While univariate statistics provide insights regarding one variable, bivariate statistics allow for measuring how two variables are associated. Next we will discuss two bivariate measures, the covariance and the correlation.

Covariance

Two key measures to discuss associations between two variables are the *covariance* and the *correlation*. The covariance is the degree to which variables vary together. It is the sum of the multiplications of the differences between every value of the x and y variable and their means.

$$Cov(x_i, y_i) = \frac{1}{n-1} \sum_{i=1}^{n} (x_i - \bar{x}) \cdot (y_i - \bar{y})$$

Correlations

A *correlation* (abbreviated as r^2) is a measure of how strongly two variables relate to each other. Correlation coefficients are frequently used to describe data because they are relatively easy to use and provide a great deal of information in just a single value. A (Pearson) correlation coefficient is calculated as follows:

$$r^2 = \frac{Cov(x_i, y_i)}{s_x \cdot s_y} = \frac{\sum_{i=1}^{n} (x_i - \bar{x}) \cdot (y_i - \bar{y})}{\sqrt{\sum_{i=1}^{n} (x_i - \bar{x})^2} \cdot \sqrt{\sum_{i=1}^{n} (y_i - \bar{y})^2}}$$

The numerator contains the covariance of x and y ($Cov(x_i, y_i)$) and the denominator contains the product of the standard deviations of x and y.[1] Thus, the

---

[1] Note that the terms *n-1* in the numerator and denominator cancel each other out and, thus, are not displayed here.

Table 5.4 Types of descriptive statistics for differently scaled variables

	Nominal	Ordinal	Interval & ratio (*Scale* in SPSS)
Display distribution	Frequency table	Frequency table	Frequency table
Measure of centrality	Mode	Mode and median	Mode, median, and mean
Measures of dispersion	–	Range	Standard deviation, variance
Measures of association	–	Spearman's correlation coefficient	Pearson correlation coefficient, covariance

correlation is the covariance divided by the product of the standard deviation. Therefore, the correlation is no longer dependent on the variables' original measurement as it is the case with the covariance. As such, the calculated value of the correlation coefficient ranges from -1 to 1, where -1 indicates a perfect negative relation (the relationship is perfectly linear) and 1 indicates a perfectly positive relationship. A correlation coefficient of 0 indicates that there is no correlation.

Cohen (1988) defined standards to describe how "strong" a correlation is. He argued that absolute correlation coefficients below 0.30 indicate a weak effect, coefficients between 0.30 and 0.49 indicate a moderate effect, and values of 0.50 and higher indicate a strong effect.

There are several types of correlations that can be calculated but two are most prominent. A Pearson correlation coefficient is the most commonly used and is often simply referred to as correlation. It is appropriate for calculating correlations between two interval or ratio scaled variables. When at least one variable is ordinally scaled, we use Spearman's correlation coefficient.

In Table 5.4, we indicate which descriptive statistics are useful for differently scaled variables.

Detect Outliers

Data often contain *outliers*. Outliers are values that are uniquely different from all the other observations and influence results substantially. For example, if we compare the average amounts different households spend on transport, we may find that some spend as little as 200 USD per year, whereas a few households may spend millions (e.g., because they own very expensive cars). If we were to calculate the mean, including those people who spend millions, this would substantially increase the average.

Outliers come in different forms. The first type of outlier is produced by data collection or entry errors. For example, if we ask people to indicate their household income in thousands of USD, some respondents may just indicate theirs in USD (not thousands). Obviously, there is a substantial difference between 30 and 30,000! Moreover, clear data entry errors (55 instead of 5) often occur. Outliers produced by data collection or entry errors either need to be deleted or we need to find the correct values, for example, by going back to the respondents.

A second type of outlier occurs because exceptionally high or low values are a part of reality. While such observations can significantly influence results, they are sometimes specifically important for researchers as characteristics of outliers can be insightful. Think for example of companies that are extremely successful or users that face needs long before the bulk of that marketplace encounters them (so called lead users). Malcolm Gladwell's (2008) book "Outliers: The Story of Success" provides entertaining study of what really explains exceptionally successful people (outliers).

A third type of outlier occurs when combinations of variables are exceptionally rare. For example, if we look at income and expenditure on holidays, we may find someone who earns 500,000 USD but spends 300,000 USD of his/her income on holidays. Such combinations are unique and have a very strong impact on particularly correlations.

Finding outliers means finding very low or very high variable values. This can be achieved by calculating the minimum, maximum and range of each variable and through scatter plots (if outliers are a rare combination of variables). The next step is to determine whether we have an explanation for those high or low values. If there is an explanation (e.g., because some exceptionally wealthy people were included in the sample), outliers are typically retained. If the explanation is that it is most probably a typing or data entry error, we always delete these outliers. If there is no clear explanation, the decision to delete or retain outliers is not clear-cut and outliers are generally retained.

Transform Data

Transforming data is an optional step in the workflow. Researchers transform data for several reasons. The key reasons are that transforming data may be necessary for some analysis techniques, because it may help interpretation or because it is necessary to meet assumptions of techniques discussed in the subsequent chapters. Transforming data means that the original values of a variable are changed consistently by means of a mathematical formula. An example of a simple transformation is coding a variable into two categories. For example, if we have a variable measuring a respondent's income, we may code incomes below 20,000 USD as *low* and those above as *high*. Thus, we use a simple rule to recode our original variable as a new variable.

If we choose to use cluster analysis (see Chap. 9), we often need to *standardize* our variables. Standardizing variables means that we rescale the data so that the mean of the variable is 0 and the standard deviation is 1. This type of standardization is called the *z-transformation* and is applied by subtracting the mean $\bar{x}$ of every observation x_i and dividing it by the standard deviation s. That is:

$$z_i = \frac{(x_i - \bar{x})}{s}$$

The *log transformation* is another type of transformation, which is commonly used if we have *skewed data*. Skewed data arises if we have a variable that is asymmetrically distributed. For example, family income is often a highly skewed variable. The majority of people will have incomes around the median, but a few people will have very high incomes. However, no one will have a negative income leading to a "tail" at the right of the distribution. A histogram will quickly show if data are skewed. Skewed data can be problematic in analyses and it has therefore become common practice to use a log transformation. A log transformation applies a base 10 logarithm to every observation.[2] We should only use the log transformations for skewed variables that have positive numbers. The log cannot be calculated for negative numbers. Another complication is that we cannot calculate the log for the value of 0. A way around this is to add 1 to every observation and then apply a logarithmic transformation. This of course leads to a different interpretation.

Dummy coding is a special way of recoding data. *Dummies* are binary variables that indicate if a variable is present or not. For example, we can use dummies to indicate that advertising was used during a particular period (value of the dummy is 1) but not in other periods (value of the dummy is 0). We can use multiple dummies at the same time, for example to indicate if advertising or a special product promotion was used. We can also use multiple dummies to capture categorical variables' effects. For example, if we want to understand the effects of no, some, and intensive advertising, we can create two dummies, one where the dummy takes the value of 1 if intensive advertising was used (else 0) and one where the value of 1 is used for some advertising (else 0). In this way, we always construct one dummy less than the amount of categories used (in this example, if both dummies take the value zero, this indicates no advertising). We explain dummies in further detail in the Web Appendix (🖰 Web Appendix → Chap. 5)

A frequently used type of recoding is to create *constructs*. As described in Chap. 3, a construct can be defined as a concept which cannot be directly observed, and for which there are multiple referents, but none all-inclusive. The construct is not an individual item that you see in the list, but it is captured by calculating the average of a number of related items. For example, if we want to measure the construct brand trust using three items ("This brand's product claims are believable," "This brand delivers what it promises," and "this brand has a name you can trust"), and one respondent indicated 4, 3, and 6 for these three items, then the construct score for this respondent would be $(4 + 3 + 6)/3 = 4.33$.

---

[2]The logarithm is calculated as follows: If $x=y^b$, then $y=log_b(x)$ where x is the original variable, b the logarithm's base, and y the exponent. For example, log 10 of 100 is 2 because 10^2 is 100. Logarithms cannot be calculated for negative values (such as household debt) and the value of zero.

A special type of data transformation is *aggregation*. Aggregation means that we bring variables measured at a lower level to a higher level. For example, if we know the average of customers' satisfaction and from which stores they buy, we can calculate average satisfaction at the store level. Aggregation only works one way (from lower to higher levels) and is useful if we want to compare groups.

There are also drawbacks to transforming data, such as that we lose information through most transformations. For example, recoding income in USD (measured at the ratio scale) into a "low" and "high" income category will result in an ordinal variable. Thus, in the transformation process, we have lost information. A simple rule of thumb is that information will be lost if we cannot move back from the transformed to the original variable. Another drawback is that transformed data are often more difficult to interpret. For example, log USD or log EUR are much more difficult to interpret and less intuitive.

Create a Codebook

After all the variables have been organized and cleaned and some initial descriptives have been calculated, a *codebook* is often created. A codebook contains essential details of the data file to allow the data to be shared. In large projects, multiple people usually work on data analysis and entry. Therefore, we need to keep track of the data to minimize errors. Even if just a single researcher is involved, it is still a good idea to create a codebook, as this helps the client use the data and helps if the same data are used later on. On the website accompanying this book (⌘ Web Appendix → Chap. 5), we briefly discuss how a codebook can be created using SPSS. Codebooks usually have the following structure:

Introduction: In the introduction, we discuss the goal of the data collection, why the data are useful, who participated, and how the data collection effort was conducted (mail, Internet, etc.).

Questionnaire(s): It is common practice to include copies of all types of questionnaires used. Thus, if different questionnaires were used for different respondents (e.g., for French and Italian respondents), a copy of each original questionnaire should be included. Differences in wording may explain the results of the study afterwards, particularly in cross-national studies, even if a back-translation was used (see Chap. 4). These are not the questionnaires received from the respondents themselves but blank copies of each type of questionnaire used. Most codebooks include details of the name of each variable behind the items used. If a dataset was compiled using secondary measures (or a combination of primary and secondary data), the secondary datasets are often briefly discussed (what version was used, when it was accessed, etc.).

Description of the variables: This section includes a verbal description of each variable used. It is useful to provide the variable name as used in the data file, a description of what the variable is supposed to measure, and whether the measure has been used previously. You should also describe the measurement level (see Chap. 3).

Summary statistics: We include descriptive statistics of each variable in the summary statistics section. The average (only for interval and ratio-scaled data), minimum, and maximum are often calculated. In addition, the number of observations and usable observations (excluding observations with missing values) are included, just like a histogram.

Datasets: This last section includes the names of the datasets and sometimes the names of all the revisions of the used datasets. Sometimes, codebooks include the file date to assure that the right files are used.

Introduction to SPSS

SPSS is a computer package specializing in quantitative data analysis. It is widely used by market researchers. It is powerful, able to deal with large datasets, and relatively easy to use.

In this book, we use version 18 of SPSS, officially called IBM SPSS Statistics. The SPSS screens somewhat confusingly display the name PASW. For simplicity, we refer to version 18 as SPSS. Versions 16 and 17 are similar and can also be used for all examples throughout this book. Versions 16, 17, and 18 are available for Microsoft Windows (XP or higher), the Mac (OS X version 10.5 or higher), and Linux. The differences between these versions are small enough so that all examples in the book should work with all versions.

The regular SPSS package is available at a substantial fee for commercial use. However, large discounts are available for educational use. To obtain these discounts, it is best to go to your university's IT department and enquire if (and where) you can purchase a special student license. You can also download a trial version from www.spss.com.

> In the next sections, we will use the ▶ sign to indicate that you have to click on something with your mouse. Options, menu items or drop-down lists that you have to look up in dialog boxes are printed in **bold**, just like elements of SPSS output. Variable names, data files or data formats are printed in *italics* to differentiate those from the rest of the text.

Finding Your Way in SPSS

If you start up SPSS for the first time, it presents a screen similar to Fig. 5.4, unless a previous user has ticked the **Don't show this dialog in the future** box. In that case, you will see a screen similar to Fig. 5.5, but without an active dataset.

In the startup screen, SPSS indicates several options to create or open datasets. The options that you should use are either **Open an existing data source**, under which you can find a list with recently opened data files, or **Type in data**. To open

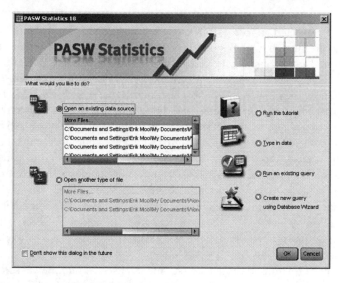

Fig. 5.4 The start up screen of SPSS

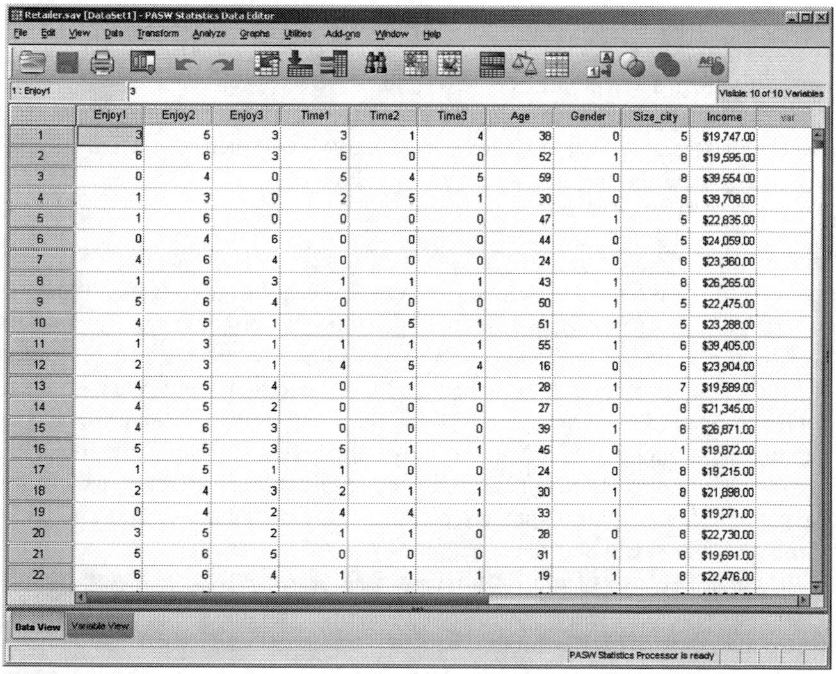

Fig. 5.5 The SPSS data editor

an unlisted file, simply choose **More Files**... and click **OK** (alternatively, you can click **Cancel**, and then go to ▶ File ▶ Open ▶ Data). Then search for the directory in which the files are kept, click on the file and then on ▶ Open. For the subsequent examples and illustrations, we use a dataset called *retailer.sav* (⌂ Web Appendix → Chap. 5). This dataset contains information on how participants feel about the Internet and how they experienced their last Internet session. Moreover, it contains the participant's age, gender, income and the size of city he/she lives in.

SPSS uses two windows, the **SPSS Statistics Data Editor** and the **SPSS Statistics Viewer**. The data editor has two tab fields in the lower left corner. The first is the **Data View** and the second the **Variable View**. Both provide details on the same dataset. The data view shows you the data itself with the variable names in the columns and the observations in the rows. Under the variable view tab, you will see many details of the variables, such as the variable name and type. The **SPSS Statistics Viewer** is a separate window, which opens after you carry out an action in SPSS. The viewer contains the output that you may have produced. If you are used to working with software such as Microsoft Excel, where the data and output are included in a single screen, this may be a little confusing at first. Another aspect of the viewer screen is that it does not change your output once made. Unlike, for example, Microsoft Excel, changing the data after an analysis does not dynamically update the results.

Tip: the notation you will see in this book follows the US style. That is, commas are used to separate thousands (1,000) while decimal points are used to separate whole values from fractions. If you want to change the notation to US style, go to SPSS, then ▶ File ▶ New ▶ Syntax and type in *"SET LOCALE = 'English'"*. You also need to type in the last point. Now press enter and type in *"EXECUTE."* (again, including the point) in the next line. Now run the syntax by choosing Run ▶ All in the syntax window. SPSS will then permanently apply the US style notation the next time you use SPSS.

SPSS uses multiple file formats. The *.sav* file format contains data only. SPSS also allows you to open other file formats such as Excel (*.xls* and *.xlsx*) and text files (such as *.txt* and *.dat*). Once these files are open, they can be conveniently saved into SPSS's own *.sav* file format. If you are on SPSS's main screen (see Fig. 5.4) simply go to File ▶ Open ▶ Files of type (select the file format) and double click on the file you wish to open. The output produced in SPSS can be saved using the *.spv* file format that is particular to SPSS. To partially remedy this, SPSS provides the option to export the output to Microsoft Word, Excel, or PowerPoint, PDF, HTML, or text. It is also possible to export output as a picture. You can find these export options in the **Statistics Viewer** under File ▶ Export.

In the **SPSS Statistics Data Editor** (Fig. 5.5), you will find the dataset *retailer. sav*. This dataset's variables are included in the columns and their names are indicated at the top of each column. The cases are in the rows, which are numbered from 1 onwards. If you click on the **Variable View** tab, SPSS will show you a

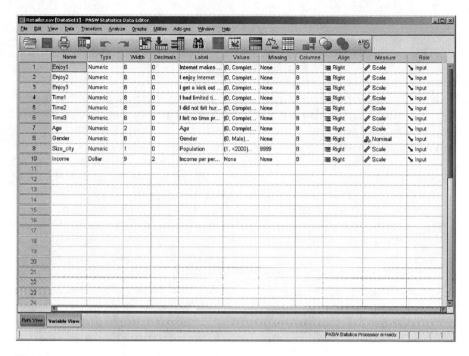

Fig. 5.6 The variable view

screen similar to Fig. 5.6. In the **Variable View**, SPSS provides information on the variables included in your dataset:

- **Name**: here you can indicate the name of the variable. It is best to provide very short names here. Variable names must begin with letters (A to Z) or one of the following special characters (@, # or $). Subsequent characters can include letters (A to Z), numbers (0–9), a dot (.), and _, @, #, or $. Note that neither spaces nor other special characters (e.g., %, &,/) are allowed.
- **Type**: here you can specify what your variable represents. **Numeric** refers to values and **String** refers to words. String is useful if you want to type over open-ended answers provided by respondents. With **Dollar** or **Custom Currency**, you can indicate that your variable represents money. **Width** and **Decimals** indicate the amount of space available for your variables.
- **Labels**: here you can provide a longer description of your variables (called variable labels). This can either be the definition of the variables or the original survey question.
- **Values**: here you can indicate what a certain value represents (called value labels). For example, for gender, which is measured on a nominal scale, 0 could represent "female" and 1 "male."
- **Missing**: here you can indicate one or more missing value(s). Generally, SPSS deals with missing values in two ways. If you have blanks in your variables (i.e.,

you haven't entered any data for a specific observation), SPSS treats these as system-missing values. These are indicated in SPSS by means of a dot (·). Alternatively, the user (you!) can define user-missing values that are meant to signify a missing observation. By defining user-missing values, we can indicate why specific scores are missing (e.g., the question didn't apply to the respondent or the respondent refused to answer). In SPSS, you should preferably define user-missing values as this at least allows the true missing values to be separated from data that were not recorded (no value was entered). The options under **Missing** provide three options to indicate user-defined missing values. The first option is **No missing values**, which is the default setting and indicates that no values are user-defined missing values. The other two options, **Discrete missing values** and **Range plus one optional discrete missing value**, provide a means to express user-defined missing values. To do so, simply enter values that record that an observation is missing. Each separate value should indicate separate reasons for missing values. For example -999 may record that a respondent could not answer, and -998 that the respondent was unwilling to answer, and -997 might record "other" reasons. Thus, missing values can provide us with valuable information on the respondents' behavior. More importantly, observations with user-missing values (just like with system-missing values) are excluded from data manipulation and analyses. This is of course essential as, for example, including a user-missing value of -999 in descriptive analyses would greatly distort the results. One tip: When picking missing values, take values that would not otherwise occur in the data. For example, for a variable *age*, 1,000 might be an acceptable value, as that response cannot occur. However, the same missing value for a variable *income* might lead to problems, as a respondent might have an income of 1,000. If 1,000 is indicated as (user-defined) missing value, this observation would be excluded from analysis.

– **Columns** and **Align**: these are rarely necessary, so we will skip these.
– **Measure**: here you can specify the measurement level of your variable. SPSS provides you with the option to indicate whether your variable is nominal, ordinal, or whether it is interval or ratio-scaled. The combination of the last two categories is called **Scale** in SPSS.
– The last **Role** option is not necessary for basic analysis.

In SPSS, you also find a number of commands in the menu bar. These include ▶ File, ▶ Edit, ▶ View, ▶ Data, and ▶ Transform. Next, we will describe these commands. Thereafter, we will describe ▶ Analyze ▶ Graphs to discuss how descriptive statistics and graphs/charts can be produced. The last four commands are ▶Utilities, ▶ Add-ons, ▶ Windows, and ▶ Help. You are unlikely to need the first three functions but the help function may come in handy if you need further guidance. Under help, you also find a set of tutorials that can show you how to use most of the commands included in SPSS.

In addition to the menu functionalities, we can run SPSS by using its command language, called SPSS syntax. You can think of it as a programming language that SPSS uses to "translate" those elements on which you have clicked in the menus into commands that SPSS can understand. Discussing the syntax in great detail is beyond the scope of this book but, as the syntax offers a convenient way to execute analysis, we offer an introduction in the Web appendix ($^{\circlearrowleft}$ Web Appendix → Chap. 5). Also, Collier (2010) provides a thorough introduction into this subject. Syntax can be saved (as a *.sps* file) for later use. This is particularly useful if you conduct the same analyses over different datasets. Think, for example, of standardized marketing reports on daily, weekly, or monthly sales.

Under ▶ File, you find all the commands that deal with the opening and closing of files. Under this command, you will find subcommands that you can use to open different types of files, save files, and create files. If you open a dataset, you will notice that SPSS also opens a new screen. Note that SPSS can open several datasets simultaneously. You can easily switch from dataset to dataset by just clicking on the one which you would like to activate. Active datasets are marked with a green plus sign at the top left of the **Data View** and **Variable View** screen.

Under ▶ Edit, you will find subcommands to copy and paste data. Moreover, you will find two options to insert cases or variables. If you have constructed a dataset but need to enter additional data, you can use this to add an additional variable and subsequently add data. **Edit** also contains the **Find** subcommand with which you can look for specific cases or observations. This is particularly useful if you want to determine, for example, what the income of 60-year old respondents is (select the *Age* column, then ▶ Edit ▶ Find and type in 60). Finally, under ▶ Edit ▶ Options, you find a large number of options, including how SPSS formats tables, and where the default file directories are located.

Under ▶ View, you find several options, of which the **Value Labels** option is the most useful. Value labels are words or short sentences used to indicate what each value represents. For example, *Male* could be the value label used to indicate that responses coded with a 1 correspond to males. SPSS shows value labels in the SPSS Data Editor window if you click on ▶ View, and then on **Value Labels**.

Under the ▶ Data command, you will find many subcommands to change or restructure your dataset. The most prominent option is the ▶ Sort Cases subcommand with which you can sort your data based on the values of a variable. You could, for example, sort your data based on the income of the respondent. The ▶ Split File subcommand is useful if you want to compare output across different groups, for example, if you want to compare males and females' yearly income. Moreover, we can carry out separate analyses over different groups using the **Split File** command. After clicking on split file, SPSS shows a dialog box similar to Fig. 5.7. All you need to do is to enter the variable that indicates the grouping (select **Compare groups**) and move the grouping variable into **Groups Based on**: SPSS will automatically carry out all subsequent analyses for each subgroup separately. If you want to revert to analyzing the whole dataset, you need to go to ▶ Data ▶ Split File, then click on **Analyze all cases, do not create groups**. Attention! It is a common mistake to forget to turn off the split file command. Failing to turn off the command results in all subsequent analyses being carried out over part of the dataset, and not the whole dataset.

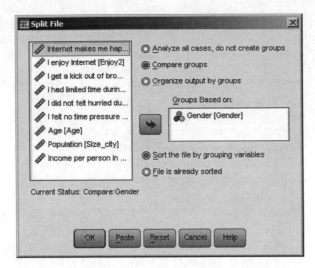

Fig. 5.7 Split file command

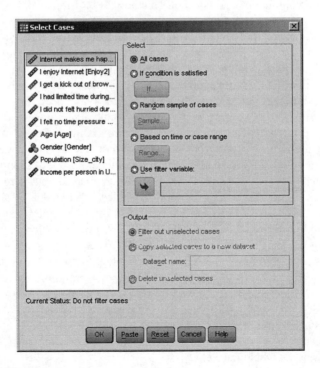

Fig. 5.8 Select cases

Another very useful command is ▶ Data ▶ Select cases (SPSS). After clicking on this, SPSS shows a dialog box similar to Fig. 5.8. Here, you can select the cases that you want to analyze. If you go to **If condition is satisfied** and click on **If**, you will see a new screen that you can use to select a subset of the data. For example, you can tell SPSS to analyze females only by entering *gender = 0* (assuming gender is 0 for females). Back in the data view, SPSS will cross out the observations that will not be included in any subsequent analyses. Remember to turn the selection off if you do not need it by going back to ▶ Data ▶ Select Cases and then click on **All cases**.

Under ▶ Transform, we find several options to create new variables from existing variables. The first subcommand is **Compute variable (SPSS)**. This command allows you to create a new variable from one (or more) existing variables. For example, if you want to create a construct (see Chap. 3), you need to calculate the average of several variables. After you click on ▶ Transform ▶ Compute Variable, SPSS shows a dialog box similar to Fig. 5.9.

In this dialog box, you can enter the name of the variable you want to create under **Target Variable** and under **Numeric Expression** you need to indicate how the new variable will be created. In the example, we create a new construct called *Enjoy* which is the average of variables *Enjoy1*, *Enjoy2*, and *Enjoy3*. You can use the buttons in the dialog box to build the formulas that create the new variable (such as the + and − button), or you can use any of the built-in functions that are found under **Function group**. SPSS provides a short explanation of each function. The compute variable command is very useful to transform variables, as we discussed

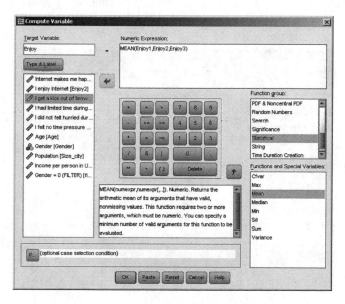

Fig. 5.9 Compute new variables

earlier in this chapter. For example, log transformations can be performed with the *Ln* function.

Also included under the ▶ Transform command are two subcommands to recode variables; ▶ Recode into Same Variables and ▶ Recode into Different Variables. We always recommend using the recode into different variables option. If you were to use recode into the same variables, any changes you make to the variable will result in the deletion of the original variable. Thus, if you ever want to go back to the

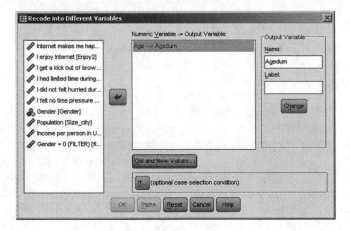

Fig. 5.10 Recode into different variables

original data, you either need to have saved a previous version, or enter all data again as SPSS cannot undo these actions! The recode subcommands allow you to change the scaling of a variable. This is useful if you want to create dummies or create

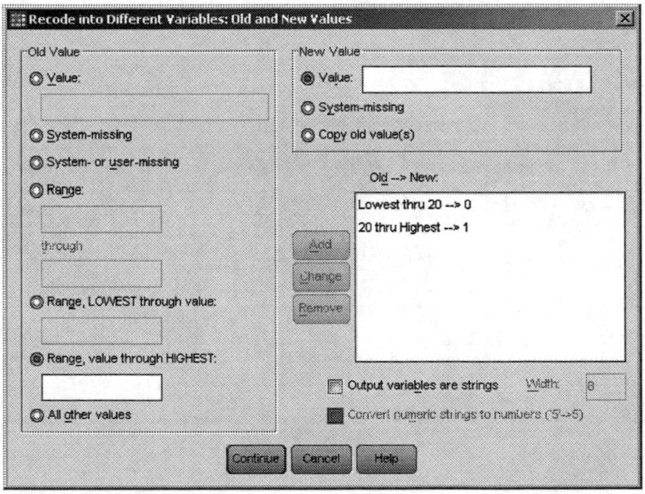

Fig. 5.11 Recode options

categories of existing variables. For example, if you want to create a dummy variable to compare the younger and older respondents, you could divide the variable age into young (say, younger than 20) and old (say, 20 and older). Figure 5.10 illustrates dialog box for recode into different variables.

In Fig. 5.10, we see several boxes. The first box at the far left shows all variables included in the dataset. This is the input for the recode process. To recode a variable, move it to the middle box by using the arrow located between the left and middle boxes. On the far right, you see an **Output Variable** box in which you should enter the name of the variable and an explanatory label you want to create. Next, click on **Change**. You will then see that in the middle box an arrow is drawn between the original and new variables. The next step is to tell SPSS what values need to be recoded. Do this by clicking on **Old and New Values**. After this, SPSS will present a dialog box similar to Fig. 5.11.

Table 5.5 Shortcuts symbols

Symbol	Action
	Open dataset
	Save the active dataset
	Recall recently used dialogs
	Undo a user action
	Find
	Split file
	Select cases
	Show value labels

On the left of this dialog box, you should indicate the values of the original variable that you want to recode. On the right, you can indicate the new values for the new variable.

Some of the previous commands are also accessible by means shortcut symbols in **Data View** screen's menu bar. As these are very convenient, we describe the most frequently used shortcuts in Table 5.5.

Creating Univariate Graphs, Charts, and Tables in SPSS

In SPSS, all descriptives are included in ▶ Analyze, and ▶ Graphs. The ▶ Graphs command is divided into two subcommands, the **Chart Builder** and **Legacy Dialogs**. The chart builder provides more functionality than the legacy dialogs but is slightly more difficult to use. The legacy dialog provides simple and quick access to the most commonly used graph types, such as the bar chart, pie chart, and scatter plot. Descriptive statistics are included under ▶ Analyze ▶ Descriptive Statistics. In Fig. 5.12, we show how to calculate each previously discussed descriptive statistic in SPSS.

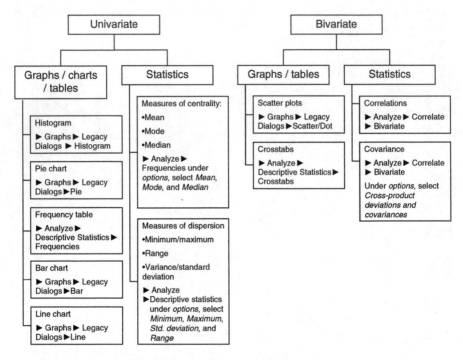

Fig. 5.12 How to calculate descriptive statistics and graphs in SPSS

Histograms

Histograms are created by clicking on ▶ Graphs ▶ Legacy Dialogs and then on ▶ Histogram. SPSS will then produce a dialog box in which you should enter the variable for which you want to produce a histogram under **Variable**. If you want to create multiple histograms on top of, or next to each other, you can add a variable for which multiple histograms need to be made under **Rows** or **Columns**. If you just move *Internet makes me happy* into the **Variable** box, SPSS will produce a histogram as in Fig. 5.13.

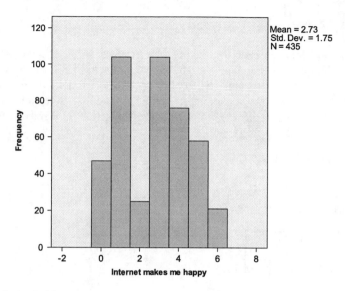

Fig. 5.13 A simple histogram

Pie Charts

Pie charts can be made by clicking on ▶ Graphs ▶ Legacy Dialogs ▶ Pie. SPSS will then ask you to make one of three choices. For a standard pie chart, the first option (**Summaries for groups of cases**) is best. In the subsequent dialog box, all you need to do is enter the variable from which you want to make a pie chart in the box, titled **Define Slices by**. If we move *Gender* into the **Define Slices by** box, and click on **OK**, SPSS will show a pie chart similar to Fig. 5.14.

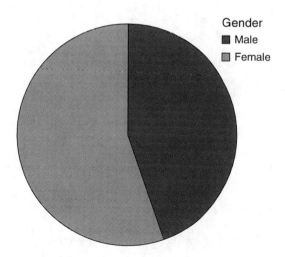

Fig. 5.14 A pie chart

Frequency Tables

A frequency table can be made by clicking on ▶ Analyze ▶ Descriptive Statistics ▶ Frequencies. You can enter as many variables as you want, as SPSS will make separate frequency tables for each variable. Then click on **OK**. If we use *Internet makes me happy*, SPSS will produce tables similar to Table 5.6. The first table includes just the number of observations, while the second includes the actual frequency table.

Table 5.6 A frequency table

Statistics

Internet makes me happy

N	Valid	435
	Missing	0

Internet makes me happy

		Frequency	Percent	Valid Percent	Cumulative Percent
Valid	Completely disagree	47	10.8	10.8	10.8
	Disagree	104	23.9	23.9	34.7
	Somewhat disagree	25	5.7	5.7	40.5
	Neutral	104	23.9	23.9	64.4
	Somewhat agree	76	17.5	17.5	81.8
	Agree	58	13.3	13.3	95.2
	Completely agree	21	4.8	4.8	100.0
	Total	435	100.0	100.0	

Bar Charts

Bar charts are made by clicking on ▶ Graphs ▶ Legacy Dialogs ▶ Bar. Next, SPSS will ask you to choose a type of bar chart (**Simple**, **Clustered**, or **Stacked**) and what the data in the bar chart represent (**Summaries for groups of cases**, **Summaries of separate variables**, or **Values of individual cases**). For a simple bar chart, click on **Define** and then move the variable for which you want to create a bar chart in the **Category Axis** box. Under **Bars Represent**, you can indicate what the bars are. Choosing for **N of cases** or **% of Cases** results in a graph similar to a histogram, while choosing **Other statistic (e.g., mean)** can be helpful to summarize a variable's average values across different groups. The groups then need to be identified in the **Category Axis** and that which is summarized in the **Variable** box. For example, go to ▶ Graphs ▶ Legacy Dialogs ▶ Bar, then click on **Simple** and **Define**. Subsequently, enter *Internet makes me happy* under **Category axis**. SPSS will then show a graph similar to Fig. 5.15.

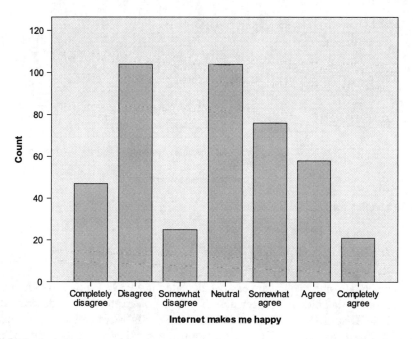

Fig. 5.15 A bar chart

Line Charts

Line charts are made by clicking on ▶ Graphs ▶ Legacy Dialogs ▶ Line. SPSS will then ask you what type of line chart you want: a **Simple** line chart, a **Multiple** line chart or a line indicating a variable's values for different groups called **Drop-line**. You also need to indicate what the data need to represent: **Summaries for groups of cases** (used in most cases), **Summaries of separate variables**, or **Values of individual cases**. As an example, go to ▶ Graphs ▶ Legacy Dialogs ▶ Line, then click on **Simple** and **Define**. Enter *Internet makes me happy* into the **Category Axis** box and click on **OK**. The resulting graph will be similar to Fig. 5.16.

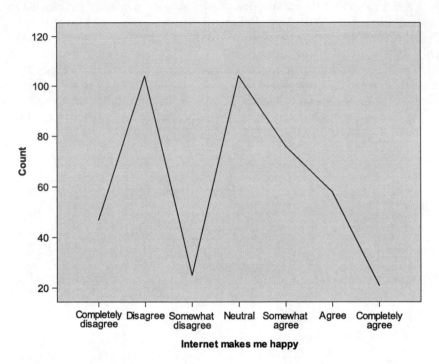

Fig. 5.16 A line chart

Calculating Univariate Descriptive Statistics in SPSS

The mean, mode, and median are easily calculated in SPSS by going to ▶ Analyze ▶ Descriptive Statistics ▶ Frequencies. If you just need these three descriptives, uncheck the **Display Frequency tables** box. Under **Statistics**, you can then check **Mean**, **Median**, and **Mode**. Clicking on **Continue** and then **OK** will show you the requested statistics in the output window. Notice that if you ask SPSS to calculate descriptives, it will also display **Valid N (listwise)**. The value indicated behind this, are the number of observations for which we have full information available (i.e., no missing values).

You can also create a z-transformation under descriptive statistics. Go to ▶ Analyze ▶ Descriptive statistics ▶ Descriptives. Then click on **Save standardized values as variables**. For every variable you enter in the **Variable(s)** box, SPSS will create a new variable (including the prefix *z*), standardize the variable, and save it. In the **Label** column under **Variable View** it will even show the original value label preceded by *Zscore:* to indicate that you have transformed that particular variable.

Measures of dispersion are most easily created by going to Analyze ▶ Descriptive Statistics ▶ Descriptives. Enter the variables for which you want to calculate descriptives into the **Variable(s)** box. Under **Options**, you can check **Std. deviation**, **Minimum**, **Maximum**, and **Range**. You can also check **Mean** but no options are included to calculate the mode or median (for this, you have to go back to ▶ Analyze ▶ Descriptive Statistics ▶ Frequencies).

Creating Bivariate Graphs and Tables in SPSS

Scatter Plots

Scatter plots are made easily by going to ▶ Graphs ▶ Legacy Dialogs ▶ Scatter/Dot. Subsequently, SPSS shows five different options: a **Simple Scatter** plot, a **Matrix Scatter** plot (showing different scatter plots for different groups), a **Simple Dot** graph, an **Overlay Scatter** plot (showing different groups within one scatter plot, and the **3-D Scatter** plot (for relationships between three variables). As an example, go to ▶ Graphs ▶ Legacy Dialogs ▶Scatter/Dot. Then click on **Simple Scatter** and **Define**. Enter *Internet makes me happy* under **Y Axis** and *Income per person in USD* under **X Axis**. The resulting graph will look like Fig. 5.17.

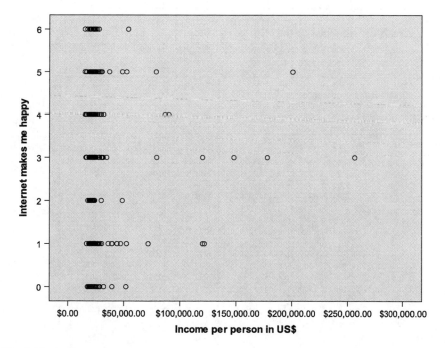

Fig. 5.17 A simple scatter plot

Crosstabs

Crosstabs are useful to describe data, particularly if your variables are nominally or ordinally scaled. Crosstabs are made by going to ▶ Analyze ▶ Descriptive Statistics ▶ Crosstabs. You can enter multiple variables under **Row(s)** and **Column(s)**, but crosstabs are easiest to interpret if you enter just one variable under **Row(s)** and one under **Column(s)**. Try making a crosstab by going to ▶ Analyze ▶ Descriptive Statistics ▶ Crosstabs. Under **Row(s)** you can enter *Internet makes me happy* and *Gender* under **Column(s)**. If you then click on **OK**, SPSS produces a table (see Table 5.7).

Table 5.7 Example of a crosstab

Case Processing Summary

	Cases					
	Valid		Missing		Total	
	N	Percent	N	Percent	N	Percent
Internet makes me happy * Gender	435	100.0%	0	.0%	435	100.0%

Internet makes me happy * Gender Crosstabulation

Count

		Gender		
		Male	Female	Total
Internet makes me happy	Completely disagree	24	23	47
	Disagree	46	58	104
	Somewhat disagree	11	14	25
	Neutral	54	50	104
	Somewhat agree	33	43	76
	Agree	19	39	58
	Completely agree	7	14	21
Total		194	241	435

Calculating Bivariate Descriptive Statistics in SPSS

Correlations

In SPSS, we can calculate correlations by going to ▶ Analyze ▶ Correlate ▶ Bivariate. In the dialog box that pops up, we can select whether we want SPSS to calculate Pearson's or Spearman's correlation coefficient. Table 5.8 is an example of a correlation matrix produced in SPSS.

Table 5.8 Correlation matrix produced in SPSS

Correlations

		Internet makes me happy	I enjoy Internet
Internet makes me happy	Pearson Correlation	1	.466 **
	Sig. (2-tailed)		.000
	N	435	435
I enjoy Internet	Pearson Correlation	.466 **	1
	Sig. (2-tailed)	.000	
	N	435	435

**. Correlation is significant at the 0.01 level (2-tailed).

The correlation matrix in Table 5.8 shows the correlation between two variables labeled as *Internet makes me happy* and *I enjoy Internet*. The correlation is 0.466. SPSS also indicates the number of observations used to calculate each correlation (435 observations) and indicates the significance, indicated by *Sig. (2-tailed)*. We discuss what this means in Chap. 6.

Case Study

The UK chocolate market achieved annual sales of 6.40 billion GBP in 2008. Six sub-categories of chocolates are used to identify the different chocolate segments: boxed chocolate, molded bars, seasonal chocolate, countlines, straightlines, and "other".

To understand the UK chocolate market for molded chocolate bars, we have a dataset (*chocolate.sav*) that includes a large supermarket's weekly sales of 100 g

Chocolate Confectionery Industry Insights

http://www.globalbusinessinsights.com/content/rbcg0125m.pdf

molded chocolate bars from January 2009 onwards. This data file can be downloaded on the book's website (⚲ Web Appendix → Chap. 5). This file contains a set of variables. Once you have opened the dataset and clicked on **Variable View**, you will see the set of variables we discuss next.

The first variable is *week*, indicating the week of the year and starts with Week 1 of January 2009. The last observation for 2009 ends with observation 52, but the variable continues to count onwards for 16 weeks in 2010. The next variable is *sales*, which indicates the weekly sales of 100 g Cadbury bars in GBP. Next, four price variables are included, *price1-price4*, which indicate the price of Cadbury, Nestlé, Guylian, and Milka in GBP. Next, *advertising1-advertising4* indicate the amount of GBP the supermarket spent on advertising each product during that week. A subsequent block of variables, *pop1-pop4*, indicate whether the products were promoted in the supermarket using a point of purchase advertising. This variable is measured as yes/no. Variables *promo1-promo4* indicate whether the product was put at the end of the supermarket aisle – where it is more noticeable. Lastly, *temperature* indicates the weekly average temperature in degrees Celsius.

You have been tasked to provide descriptive statistics for a client, using this available dataset. To help you with this task, the client has prepared a number of questions:

1. Do Cadbury's chocolate sales vary substantially across different weeks? When are Cadbury's sales at their highest? Please create an appropriate graph to illustrate any patterns.
2. Please tabulate point-of-purchase advertising for Cadbury against point-of-purchase advertising for Nestlé. Also create a few further crosstabs. What are the implications of these crosstabs?
3. How do Cadbury's sales relate to the price of Cadbury? What is the strength of the relationship?
4. Which descriptive statistics are appropriate to describe the usage of advertising? Which are appropriate to describe point-of-purchase advertising?

Questions

1. Imagine you are given a dataset on car sales in different regions and are asked to calculate descriptive statistics. How would you set up the analysis procedure?
2. What summary statistics could best be used to describe the change in profits over the last five years? What types of descriptives work best to determine the market shares of five different types of insurance providers? Should we use just one or multiple descriptives?
3. What information do we need to determine if a case is an outlier? What are the benefits and drawbacks of deleting outliers?
4. Download the US census codebook for 2007 at http://usa.ipums.org/usa/code-books/DataDict2007.pdf. Is this codebook clear? What do you think of its structure?

Further Readings

Cohen J, Cohen P, West SG, Aiken LS (2003) Applied multiple regression/correlation analysis for the behavioral sciences, 3rd cdn. Lawrence Erlbaum Associates, Mahwah, NJ

This is the seminal book on correlation (and regression) analysis which provides a detailed overview into this field. It is aimed at experienced researchers.

Field A (2009) Discovering statistics using SPSS, 3rd edn. Sage, London

In Chap. 6 of his book, Andy Field provides a very thorough introduction into the principles of correlation analysis from an application-oriented point of view.

Hair JF Jr, Black WC, Babin BJ, Anderson RE (2010) Multivariate data analysis. A global perspective, 7th edn. Prentice-Hall, Upper Saddle River, NJ

A widely used book on multivariate data analysis. Chapter 2 of this book discusses missing data issues.

Levesque R, Programming and Data Management for IBM SPSS Statistics 18. A Guide for PASW Statistics and SAS Users. Chicago, SPSS, Inc.

An advanced book demonstrating how to manage data in SPSS. Can be downloaded for free at http://www.spss.com/sites/dm-book/resources/PASW-Statistics-18-DM-Book.pdf

SPSS (PASW) On-Line Training Workshop at http://calcnet.mth.cmich.edu/org/spss/index.htm

An excellent website on which you can find movies describing different aspects of SPSS.

SPSS Learning Modules at http://www.ats.ucla.edu/stat/spss/modules/

On this website further data organization issues are discussed. This is useful if you already have a dataset, but cannot use it because of the way the data are organized.

SticiGui at http://www.stat.berkeley.edu/~stark/Java/Html/Correlation.htm

This websites interactively demonstrates how strong correlations are for different datasets.

References

Cohen J (1988) Statistical power analysis for the behavioral sciences. 2nd edn. Lawrence Erlbaum Associates, Hillsdale, NJ

Collier J (2010) Using SPSS syntax: a beginner's guide. Sage, Thousand Oaks, CA

Dillman DA (2008) Internet, mail, and mixed-mode surveys: the tailored design method. Wiley, Hoboken, NJ

Gladwell M (2008) Outliers: the story of success. Little, Brown, and Company, New York, NY

Hair JF Jr, Black WC, Babin BJ, Anderson RE (2010) Multivariate data analysis. Pearson, Upper Saddle River, NJ

Chapter 6
Hypothesis Testing & ANOVA

Learning Objectives

After reading this chapter you should understand:
- The logic of hypothesis testing.
- The steps involved in hypothesis testing.
- What test statistics are.
- Types of error in hypothesis testing.
- Common types of t-tests, one-way and two-way ANOVA.
- How to interpret SPSS outputs.

Keywords: α-Inflation · Degrees of freedom · F-test · Familywise error rate · Independent and paired samples t-test · Kolmogorov–Smirnov-test · Significance · Levene's test · Null and alternative hypothesis · One-sample and two-samples t-tests · One-tailed and two-tailed tests · One-way and two-way ANOVA · p-value · Parametric and nonparametric tests · Post hoc tests · Power of a test · Shapiro–Wilk test · Statistical significance · t-test · Type I and type II error · z-test

Does the sponsorship of cultural activities increase the reputation of the sponsoring company? To answer this question, Schwaiger et al. (2010) conducted a large-scale 1-year long experiment which included more than 3,000 consumers. Each month, members of the treatment groups received press reports with a cultural sponsoring theme, while members of the control groups received reports without any reference to culture sponsorship activities. The consumers had to rate to what extent each company supports or sponsors cultural events at the beginning and the end of the experiment. Hypothesis tests indicated that the consumers in the treatment group assessed the companies' cultural sponsorship activities significantly higher than the year before, while members of the control group did not. Further tests revealed that companies could benefit from such sponsoring activities as these had a significant positive effect on their reputation. Based on these results, companies can strengthen their positioning in the market through the sponsorship of cultural activities.

E. Mooi and M. Sarstedt, *A Concise Guide to Market Research*,
DOI 10.1007/978-3-642-12541-6_6, © Springer-Verlag Berlin Heidelberg 2011

Introduction

In the previous chapter, we learned about descriptive statistics, such as means and standard deviations, and the insights that can be gained from such measures. Often, we use these measures to compare groups. For example, we might be interested in investigating whether men or women spend more money on the Internet. Assume that the mean amount that a sample of men spends online is 200 USD per year against the mean of 250 USD for the women sample. Two means drawn from different samples are almost always different (in a mathematical sense), but are these differences also statistically significant?

To determine statistical significance, we want to ascertain whether the finding only occurred in the sample analyzed, or whether it also holds for the population (see Chap. 3 for the discussion of samples and population). If the difference between the sample and the population is so large that it is unlikely to have occurred by chance, this is statistical significance. Whether results are statistically significant depends on several factors, including variation in the sample data and the number of observations.

Practitioners, however, usually refer to "significant" in a different, non-statistical context. What they call significant refers to differences that are large enough to influence their decision making process. Perhaps the analysis discloses a significant market segment (i.e., large enough to matter), or the sample reveals such a significant change in consumer behavior that the company needs to change its behavior. Whether results are practically significant (i.e., relevant for decision making), depends on management's perception of whether the difference is large enough to require specific action.

In this chapter, we will deal with hypothesis testing which allows for the determination of statistical significance. As statistical significance is a precursor to establishing practical significance, hypothesis testing is of fundamental importance for market research.

Understanding Hypothesis Testing

Hypothesis testing is a claim about a statistic characterizing a population (such as a mean or correlation) that can be subjected to statistical testing. Such a claim is called a hypothesis and refers to a situation that might be true or false. A hypothesis may comprise a judgment about the difference between two sample statistics (e.g., the difference in the means of separate corporate reputation assessments made by customers and by non-customers). It can also be a judgment of the difference between a sample statistic and a hypothesized population parameter.

Subject to the type of claim made in the hypothesis, we have to choose an appropriate statistical test, of which there are a great number, with different tests suitable for different research situations. In this chapter, we will focus on *parametric tests* used to examine hypotheses that relate to differences in means. Parametric tests assume that the variable of interest follows a specific statistical distribution.

The most popular parametric test for examining means is the *t-test*. The t-test can be used to compare one mean with a given value (e.g., do males spend more than 150 USD a year online?). We call this type a *one-sample t-test*. Alternatively, we can test the difference between two samples (e.g., do males spend as much as females?). In this latter case, we talk about a, *two-samples t-tests* but then we need to differentiate whether we are analyzing two *independent samples* or two *paired samples*.

Independent samples t-tests consider two unrelated groups, such as males vs. females or users vs. non-users. Conversely, paired samples t-tests relate to the same set of respondents and thus, occur specifically in pre-test/post-test studies designed to measure a variable before and after a treatment. An example is the before-after design discussed in Chap. 4.

Often, we are interested in examining the differences between means found in more than two groups of respondents. For example, we might be interested in evaluating differences in sales between low, medium, and high income customer segments. Instead of carrying out several paired comparisons through separate t-tests, we should use *Analysis of Variance (ANOVA)*. ANOVA is useful for complex research questions, such as when three or more means need to be compared, as ANOVA can analyze multiple differences in one analysis. While there are many types of ANOVA, we focus on the most common types, the one-way and two-way ANOVA.

In the ⚲ Web Appendix (→ Chap. 6), we provide an introduction to popular nonparametric tests which do not require the variable of interest to follow a specific distribution and which can also be used for variables measured on a nominal or ordinal scale. There, we specifically discuss the χ^2-tests (pronounced as *chi-square*).

No type of hypothesis testing can validate hypotheses with absolute certainty. The problem is that we have to rely on sample data to make inferences and, as we have not included the whole population in our analysis, there is some probability that we have reached the wrong conclusion. However, we can (partly) control for this risk by setting an acceptable probability (called significance level) that we will accept a wrong hypothesis.

After this step of hypothesis testing, in which we choose the significance level, information is obtained from the sample and used to calculate the test statistic. Based on the test statistic, we can now decide how likely it is that the claim stated in the hypothesis is correct. Manually, this is done by comparing the test statistic with a critical value that a test statistic must exceed.

SPSS does this work for us by calculating the probability associated with the test statistic, which we only have to compare with the significance level specified earlier. For the sake of clarity, we discuss both manual and computerized ways of making a test decision in the following sections. On the basis of our final decision to either reject or support the hypothesis, we can then draw market research conclusions. Figure 6.1 illustrates the steps involved in hypothesis testing.

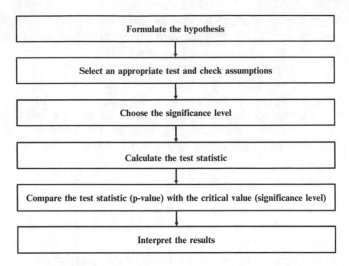

Fig. 6.1 Steps in hypothesis testing

To illustrate the process of hypothesis testing, consider the following example. Suppose that a department store chain wants to evaluate the effectiveness of three different in-store promotion campaigns (1) point of sale display, (2) free tasting stand, and (3) in-store announcements. The management decides to conduct a 1-week field experiment. The management chooses 30 stores randomly and also randomly assigns ten stores to each of the campaign types. This random assignment is important to obtain results that support generalized conclusions, because it equalizes the effect of factors that have not been accounted for in the experimental design (see Chap. 4).

Table 6.1 Sales data

	Sales (units)		
Service type	Point of sale display (stores 1–10)	Free tasting stand (stores 11–20)	In-store announcements (stores 21–30)
Personal	50	55	45
Personal	52	55	50
Personal	43	49	45
Personal	48	57	46
Personal	47	55	42
Self service	45	49	43
Self service	44	48	42
Self service	49	54	45
Self service	51	54	47
Self service	44	44	42

Table 6.1 shows the number of products sold in each store/campaign in 1 week. These sales data are normally distributed, which is a necessary condition for correctly applying parametric tests. We will discuss what this means and how we

can evaluate whether the data are normally distributed later in this chapter. The table also contains information on the service type (personal or self service). We will need this information to illustrate the concept of a two-way ANOVA later in this chapter, so let us ignore this column for now.

In what follows, we want to use these data to carry out different mean comparisons using parametric tests. We illustrate these tests by means of basic formulae. Although we will use SPSS to execute the tests, a basic knowledge of the test formulae will help you understand how the tests work. Ultimately, you will find out that the formulae are not at all as complicated as you might have thought... Most of these formulae contain Greek characters with which you might not be familiar. That's why we have included a table with a description of these characters in the ⤷ Web Appendix (→Additional Material).

Testing Hypotheses About One Mean

Formulate the Hypothesis

Hypothesis testing starts with the formulation of a null and alternative hypothesis. A null hypothesis (indicated as H_0) is a statement expecting no difference or no effect. Conversely, an alternative hypothesis (represented as H_1) is one in which some difference is expected – it is the opposite of the null hypothesis and supplements it. Examples of potential null and alternative hypotheses on the campaign types are:

- H_0: There's no difference in the mean sales between stores that installed a point of sale display and those that installed a free tasting stand (statistically, average sales of the point of sale display = average sales of the free tasting stand)
  H_1: There's a difference in the mean sales between stores that installed a point of sale display and those that installed a free tasting stand (statistically, average sales of the point of sale display $\neq$ average sales of the free tasting stand).
- H_0: The mean sales in stores that installed a point of sale display are less than (or equal to) 45 units (Note that in this hypothesis, H_0 postulates a specific direction of the effect).
  H_1: The mean sales in stores that installed a point of sale display are more than 45 units.

When carrying out a statistical test, we always test the null hypothesis. This test can have two outcomes:

The first outcome may be that we reject the null hypothesis, thus finding support for the alternative hypothesis. This outcome is, of course, desirable in most analyses, as we generally want to show that something (such as a promotion campaign) has an effect on a certain outcome (e.g., sales). This is why we generally frame the effect that we want to show in the alternative hypothesis.

The second outcome may be that we do not reject the null hypothesis. However, it would be incorrect to conclude then that the null hypothesis is true, as it is not possible to show the non-existence of a certain effect or condition. For example, one can examine any number of crows and find that they are all black, yet that would not make the statement "There are no white crows" true. Also, it is impossible statistically to show that there is no Yeti or that the Loch Ness Monster Nessie does not exist. Conversely, discovering one Yeti will demonstrate its existence. Thus, we can only reject the null hypothesis.

To make the point again: you can never prove that a hypothesis is true! Each hypothesis test inevitably has a certain degree of uncertainty so that even if we reject a null hypothesis, we can never be fully certain that this was the correct decision. Therefore, knowledgeable market researchers use terms such as "reject the null hypothesis," or "find support for the alternative hypothesis" when they discuss the findings. Terms like "prove the hypothesis" should never be part of any discussion on statistically tested hypotheses.

Returning to our example, department store managers might be interested in evaluating whether the point of sale display has a positive effect on product sales. Management may consider the campaign a success if sales are higher than the 45 units normally sold (you can likewise choose any other value – the idea is to test the sample against a given standard). But what does "generally higher" mean? Just looking at the data clearly suggests that sales are higher than 45. However, we are not interested in the sample result as much as to assess whether this result is likely to occur in the whole population (i.e., given that the sample is representative, does this result also hold for other stores?).

The appropriate way to formulate the hypotheses is:

$$H_0 : \mu \leq 45$$

(in words, the population mean – indicated by μ – is equal to or smaller than 45)

$$H_1 : \mu > 45$$

(in words, the population mean is larger than 45)

It is important to note that the hypothesis always refers to a population parameter, in this case μ (pronounced as *mu*). It is convention that Greek characters always represent population parameters and not a sample statistic (e.g., the sample mean indicated by $\bar{x}$). In the end, we want to make inferences regarding the population, not the sample, given the basic assumption that the sample is representative!

If the null hypothesis H_0 is rejected, then the alternative hypothesis H_1 will be accepted and the promotion campaign can be considered a success. On the other hand, if H_0 is not rejected, we conclude that the campaign did not have a positive impact on product sales in the population. Of course, with *conclude*, we still mean that this is what the test indicates and not that this is an absolute certainty.

In this example, we consider a *one-tailed test* (specifically, a right-tailed test) as the two hypotheses are expressed in one direction relative to the standard of 45 units: we presume that the campaign has a positive effect on product sales, which is expressed in hypothesis H_1. More precisely, we consider a right-tailed test because H_1 presumes that the population mean is actually higher than a given standard. On the other hand, suppose that we were interested in determining whether the product sales differ from the 45 units, either being higher or lower. In this case, a *two-tailed test* would be required, leading to the following hypotheses:

$$H_0 : \mu = 45$$

$$H_1 : \mu \neq 45$$

The difference between the two general types of tests is that a one-tailed test looks for an increase or, alternatively, a decrease in the parameter relative to the standard, whereas a two-tailed test looks for any difference in the parameter from the selected standard. Usually, two-tailed tests are applied because the notion of looking for any difference is more reasonable. Furthermore, two-tailed tests are stricter (and generally considered more appropriate) when it comes to revealing significant effects. Nevertheless, we will stick to our initial set of hypotheses for now.

Select an Appropriate Test and Check Assumptions

To choose an appropriate statistical test, we have to consider the purpose of the hypothesis test as well as the conditions under which the test is applied. This choice depends on the sample size and whether the data are normally distributed.

In this section, we focus on parametric tests to test differences in means. That is, we may want to compare a single sample's mean against some given standard, or evaluate whether the means of two independent or paired samples differ significantly in the population. The *parametric tests* we discuss in this chapter assume that the test variable – which needs to be measured on at least an interval scale – is normally distributed. In our numerical example of the promotion campaign, we already know that the sales are normally distributed. However, in real-world applications, we usually lack this information. To test whether the data are normally distributed, we can use two tests, the *Kolmogorov–Smirnov test (with Lilliefors correction)*, and the *Shapiro–Wilk test*. We describe these in more detail in Box 6.1 and provide an example, executed in SPSS, toward the end of this chapter. If the Kolmogorov–Smirnov or Shapiro–Wilk test suggests that the test variable is not normally distributed, you should use nonparametric tests, which do not make any distributional assumption ($\Im$ Web Appendix $\rightarrow$ Chap. 6).

The good news is that parametric tests we discuss in this chapter are generally quite robust against a violation of the normality assumption. That is, if the test statistic obtained is much below the critical value, deviations from normality matter little. If the test statistic is close to the critical value, for example the obtained p-value (introduced later) is 0.04, and n is smaller than 30, deviations from normality could matter. Still, such deviations are usually no more than a p-value of 0.01 units apart, even if severe deviations from normality are present (Boneau 1960).

Thus, even if the Kolmogorov–Smirnov or Shapiro–Wilk test suggests that the data are not normally distributed, we don't have to be concerned that the parametric test results are grossly wrong. Specifically, where we compare means, we can simply apply one of the parametric tests with a low risk of error, provided we have sample sizes greater than 30.

Box 6.1 Normality tests

An important (nonparametric) test is the one-sample Kolmogorov–Smirnov test. We can use it to test the null hypothesis that a certain variable follows a specific distribution. In most instances, we use it to examine whether a variable is normally distributed. However, in theory, we can use this test to assess any other type of distribution, such as exponential or uniform.

Somewhat surprisingly, the test's null hypothesis is that the variable follows a specific distribution (e.g., the normal distribution). This means that only if the test result is insignificant, i.e. the null hypothesis is not rejected, can we assume that the data are drawn from the specific distribution against which it is tested. Technically, when assuming a normal distribution, the Kolmogorov–Smirnov test compares the sample scores with an artificial set of normally distributed scores that has the same mean and standard deviation as the sample data. However, this approach is known to yield biased results which can be corrected for by adopting the Lilliefors correction (Lilliefors 1967). The Lilliefors correction considers the fact that we do not know the true mean and standard deviation of the population. An issue with the Kolmogorov–Smirnov test is that it is very sensitive when used on very large samples and often rejects the null hypothesis if very small deviations are present.

The Shapiro–Wilk test also tests the null hypothesis that the test variable under consideration is normally distributed. Thus, rejecting the Shapiro–Wilk test provides evidence that the variable is not normally distributed. It is best used for sample sizes of less than 50. A drawback of the Shapiro–Wilk test however, is that it works poorly if the variable you are testing has many identical values, in which case you should use the Kolmogorov–Smirnov test with Lilliefors correction.

To conduct the Kolmogorov–Smirnov test with Lilliefors correction and the Shapiro–Wilk test in SPSS, we have to go to ► Analyze ► Descriptive Statistics ► Explore ► Plots and choose the **Normality plots with tests** option (note that the menu option ► Analyze ► Nonparametric Tests ► Legacy Dialogs ► 1-Sample K-S will yield the standard Kolmogorov–Smirnov test whose results oftentimes diverge heavily from its counterpart with Lilliefors correction).

We will discuss these tests using SPSS in this chapter's case study.

When conducting a one-sample (or independent samples) t-test, we need to have independent observations (see Chap. 3 on independence of observations). Note that this does not apply when using the paired samples t-test and its nonparametric counterparts (i.e. the *McNemar test* and the *Wilcoxon signed rank test*, see ↗ Web Appendix → Chap. 6), in which we are specifically interested regarding evaluating the mean differences between the same respondents' assessments at two different points in time!

Figure 6.2 provides a guideline for choosing the appropriate parametric test for comparing means, including the associated SPSS menu options. We will discuss all of these in the remainder of the chapter.

In the present example, we know that the test variable is normally distributed and we are interested in comparing a sample mean with a given standard (e.g., 45). Thus, the one-sample t-test is appropriate.

Choose the Significance Level

As discussed previously, each statistical test is associated with some degree of uncertainty, as we want to make inferences about populations by using sample data. In statistical testing, two types of errors can occur: (1) a true null hypothesis can be incorrectly rejected (*type I* or α *error*), and (2) a false null hypothesis is not rejected (*type II* or β *error*). These two types of errors are defined in Table 6.2.

Table 6.2 Type I and type II errors

Decision based on sample data	True state of H_0	
	H_0 true	H_0 false
H_0 rejected	Type I error ✗	Correct decision
H_0 not rejected	Correct decision	Type II error ✗

In our example, a type I error would occur if using hypothesis testing we find that the point of sale display increased sales, when in fact it did not affect, or may even have decreased sales. Accordingly, a type II error would occur if we did not reject the null hypothesis, which would suggest that the campaign was not successful, even though, in reality, it did significantly increase sales.

A problem with hypothesis testing is that we don't know the true state of H_0. At first sight, there doesn't seem to be an easy way around this problem; however, we can establish a level of confidence that a true null hypothesis will not be erroneously rejected when carrying out a test that is tolerable given the circumstances that apply.

In other words, before carrying out a test, we should decide on the maximum probability that a type I error can occur that we want to allow. This probability is represented by the Greek character α (pronounced as *alpha*) and is called the *significance level*. In market research reports, this is indicated by phrases such as, "this test result is significant at a 5% level." This means that the researcher allowed for a maximum risk of 5% of mistakenly rejecting a true null hypothesis and that the actual risk, based on the data analysis, turned out to be lower than this.

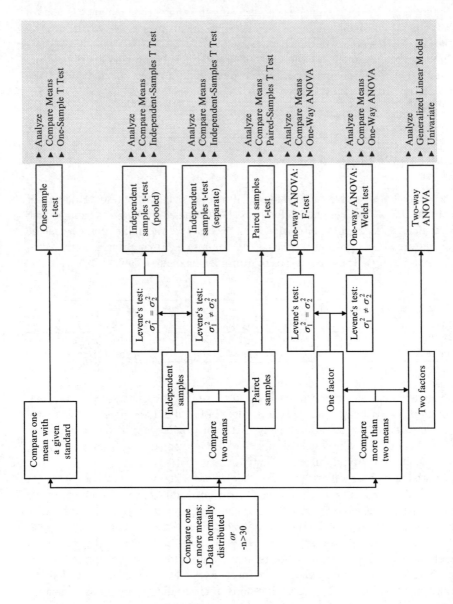

Fig. 6.2 Parametric tests for comparing means

The selection of a particular α value depends on the research setting and the costs associated with a type I error. Usually, α is set to 0.01, 0.05, or 0.10, which some researchers indicate as 1%, 5%, or 10%. Most often, an α-level of 0.05 is used, but when researchers want to be very conservative or strict in their testing, α is set to 0.01. Especially in experiments, α is often set to lower levels. In studies that are exploratory, an α of 0.10 is appropriate. An α-level of 0.10 means that if you carry out ten tests and reject the null hypothesis every time, your decision in favor of the alternative hypothesis was, on average, wrong once. This might not sound too high a probability, but when much is at stake (e.g., withdrawing a product because of low satisfaction ratings as indicated by hypothesis testing) then 10% is a high α-level.

Why don't we just set α to 0.0001% to really minimize the probability of a type I error? Obviously, setting α to such a low level would make the erroneous rejection of H_0 very unlikely. Unfortunately, this approach introduces another problem; the probability of a type I error is inversely related to that of a type II error, so that the smaller the risk of one type of error, the higher the risk of the other! However, since a type I error is considered more severe than a type II error, we directly control the former by setting α to a desired level.

Another important concept related to this is the *power of a statistical test* (defined by $1 - \beta$, where β is the probability of a type II error), which represents the probability of rejecting a null hypothesis when it is in fact false (i.e. not making a type II error). Obviously, you would want the power of a test to be as high as possible. However, as indicated before, when α is small, the occurrence of a type I error is much reduced, but then β, the probability of a type II error, is large.[1] This is why α is usually set to the levels described above, which ensures that β is not overly inflated. The good news is that both α and β, the probability of incorrect findings, can be controlled for by increasing the sample size: for a given level of α, increasing the sample size will decrease β. See Box 6.2 for further information on statistical power.

Box 6.2 Statistical power

A common problem that market researchers encounter is calculating the sample size required to yield a certain test power, given a predetermined level of α. Unfortunately, computing the required sample size (*power analyses*) can become very complicated, depending on the test or procedure we use. However, SPSS provides an add-on module called "Sample Power," which can be used to carry
(continued)

---

[1]Note that the power of a statistical test may depend on a number of factors which may be particular to a specific testing situation. However, power nearly always depends on (1) the chosen significance level, and (2) the magnitude of the effect of interest in the population.

out such analyses. In addition, the Internet offers a wide selection of download-able applications and interactive Web programs for this purpose. Just google "power analysis calculator" and you will find numerous helpful sites. In most sites you can enter the α and sample size and calculate the resulting level of power. By convention, 0.80 is an acceptable level of power.

Nevertheless, power analyses are beyond the scope of basic market research training and you should make use of certain rules of thumb. As a rough guideline, Cohen (1992) provides a convenient presentation of required sample sizes for different types of tests. For example, in order to detect the presence of large differences between two independent sample means for $\alpha = 0.05$ and a power of $\beta = 0.80$, requires n = 26 (with n = 64 for medium differences and n = 393 for small differences) observations in each group.

Calculate the Test Statistic

After having decided on the appropriate test as well as the significance level, we can proceed by calculating the test statistic using the sample data at hand. In our example we make use of a *one-sample t-test*, whose test statistic is simply computed as follows:

$$t = \frac{\bar{x} - \mu}{s_{\bar{x}}}$$

Here $\bar{x}$ and μ are the sample and assumed population means, respectively, and $s_{\bar{x}}$ is the standard error.

Let's first take a look at the formula's numerator, which describes the difference between the sample mean $\bar{x}$ and the hypothesized population mean μ. If the point of sale display was highly successful, we would expect $\bar{x}$ to be much higher than μ, leading to a positive difference between the two in the formula's numerator.

Comparing the calculated sample mean (47.30) with the hypothesized mean (45), we find that they are mathematically different:

$$\bar{x} - \mu = 47.30 - 45 = 2.30$$

At first sight, therefore, it appears as if the campaign was successful; sales during the time of the campaign were higher than those that the store normally encounters.

However, we have not yet accounted for the variation in the dataset, which is taken care of by $s_{\bar{x}}$. The problem is that if we had taken another sample from the population, for example, by using data from a different period, the new sample mean would most likely have been different from that which we first encountered. To correct this problem, we have to divide the mean difference $\bar{x} - \mu$ by the *standard error* of $\bar{x}$ (indicated as $s_{\bar{x}}$), which represents the uncertainty of the sample estimate.

This sounds very abstract, so what does this mean? The sample mean is usually used as an estimator of the population mean; that is, we assume that the sample and population means are identical. However, when we draw different samples from the same population, we will most likely obtain different means. The standard error tells us how much variability there is in the mean across different samples from the same population. Therefore, a large value for the standard error indicates that a specific sample mean may not adequately reflect the population mean.

The standard error is computed by dividing the sample standard deviation (s), by the square root of the number of observations (n):

$$s_x = \frac{s}{\sqrt{n}} = \frac{\sqrt{\frac{1}{n-1} \sum_{i=1}^{10} (x_i - \bar{x})^2}}{\sqrt{n}}$$

Why do we have to divide the difference $\bar{x} - \mu$ by the standard error $s_{\bar{x}}$? Proceeding from the calculation of the test statistic above, we see that when the standard error is very low (i.e., there is a low level of variation or uncertainty in the data), the value in the test statistic's denominator is also small, which results in a higher value for the t-test statistic. Higher values favor the rejection of the null hypothesis, which implies that the alternative hypothesis is supported. The lower the standard error $s_{\bar{x}}$, the greater the probability that the population represented by the sample truly differs from the selected standard in terms of the average number of units sold.

Note that the standard error also depends on the sample size n. By increasing the number of observations, we have more information available, thus reducing the standard error. Consequently, for a certain standard deviation, a higher n goes hand in hand with lower $s_{\bar{x}}$ which is why we generally want to have high sample sizes (within certain limits, see Box 6.3).

Box 6.3 Can a sample size be too large?

In a certain sense, even posing this question is heresy! Market researchers are usually trained to think that large sample sizes are good because of their positive relationship with the goodness of inferences.

However, it doesn't seem logical that the claim for high sample sizes should never be discussed. As long as our primary interest lies in the precise estimation of an effect (which will play a greater role when we discuss regression analysis), then the larger the sample, the better. If we want to come as close as possible to a true parameter, increasing the sample size will generally provide more precise results.

(continued)

However, there are two issues. First, all else being equal, if you increase the sample size excessively, even slight or marginal effects become statistically significant. However, statistically significant does not mean managerially relevant! In the end, we might run into problems when wanting to determine which effects really matter and how priorities should be assigned.

Second, academics especially are inclined to disregard the relationship between the (often considerable) costs associated with obtaining additional observations and the additional information provided by these observations. In fact, the incremental value provided by each additional observation decreases with increasing sample size. Consequently, there is little reason to work with an extremely high number of observations as, within reason, these do not provide much more information than fewer observations.

In addition, not every study's purpose is the precise estimation of an effect. Instead, many studies are exploratory in nature, and we try to map out the main relationships in some area. These studies serve to guide us in directions that we might pursue in further, more refined studies. Specifically, we often want to find those statistical associations that are relatively strong and that hold promise of a considerable relationship that is worth researching in greater detail. We do not want to waste time and effort on negligible effects. For these exploratory purposes, we generally don't need very large sample sizes.

In summary, with a higher mean difference $\bar{x} - \mu$ and lower levels of uncertainty in the data (i.e. lower values in $s_{\bar{x}}$), there is a greater likelihood that we can assume that the promotion campaign had a positive effect on sales.

We discuss this test statistic in greater detail because, in essence, all tests follow the same scheme. First, we compare a sample statistic, such as the sample mean, with some standard or the mean value of a different sample. Second, we divide this difference by another measure (i.e., the standard deviation or standard error), which captures the degree of uncertainty in the sample data.

In summary, the test statistic is nothing but the ratio of the variation, which is due to a real effect (expressed in the numerator), and the variation caused by different factors that are not accounted for in our analysis (expressed in the denominator). In this context, we also use the terms systematic and unsystematic variation.

If you understood this basic principle, you will have no problems understanding most other test statistics that are used.

Let's go back to the example and compute the standard error as follows

$$s_{\bar{x}} = \frac{\sqrt{\frac{1}{10-1}\left[(50-47.30)^2 + \cdots + (44-47.30)^2\right]}}{\sqrt{10}} = \frac{3.199}{\sqrt{10}} = 1.012$$

Thus, the result of the test statistic is

$$t = \frac{\bar{x} - \mu}{s_{\bar{x}}} = \frac{2.30}{1.012} = 2.274.$$

Note that in this example, we used sample data to calculate the standard error $s_{\bar{x}}$. Even though this occurs rather rarely (actually, almost never) in market research studies, textbooks routinely discuss situations in which we know the population's standard deviation beforehand. From a statistical standpoint, we would have to apply a different test, called the *z-test*, in this situation where the standard deviation in the population is known. The z-test follows a different statistical distribution (in this case, a normal instead of a t-distribution), which we have to consider when determining the critical value associated with a test statistic (we do this the following step of hypothesis testing). Likewise, the z-test is typically used in situations when the sample size exceeds 30, because the t-distribution and normal distribution are almost identical in higher sample sizes.

As the t-test is slightly more accurate, SPSS only considers the t-test in its menu options. To avoid causing any confusion, we do not present the formulae associated with the z-test here, but we have included these in the ⌁ Web Appendix ($\rightarrow$ Chap. 6).

Compare the Test Statistic (p-value) with the Critical Value (Significance Level)

In the next step, we have to determine the critical value, which the test statistic must exceed in order for the null hypothesis to be rejected. When calculating test results manually, this is done using statistical tables. In our case, we have to make use of the t-distribution table (see Table A1 in the ⌁ Web Appendix $\rightarrow$ Additional Material).

An important characteristic of the t-distribution is that – unlike the normal distribution – it also explicitly considers the amount of information (called *degrees of freedom*, usually abbreviated as "df") available to estimate the test statistic's parameters. In general terms, an estimate's degrees of freedom (such as a variable's variance) are equal to the amount of independent information used (i.e., the number of observations), minus the number of parameters estimated as intermediate steps in the estimation of the parameter itself.

The concept of degrees of freedom is very abstract, so let's look at a simple example: Suppose you have a single sample with n observations to estimate a variable's variance. Then, the degrees of freedom are equal to the number of observations (n) minus the number of parameters estimated as intermediate steps (in this case, one as we need to compute the mean, $\bar{x}$) and are therefore equal to *n-1*. Field (2009) provides a vivid explanation which we adapted and present in Box 6.4.

Box 6.4 Degrees of freedom

Suppose you have a soccer team and 11 slots in the playing field. When the first player arrives, you have the choice of 11 positions in which you can place a player. By allocating the player to a position (e.g., right defense) one position is occupied. When the next player arrives, you can chose from ten positions. With every additional player that arrives, you will have fewer choices where to position each player. For the very last player, you have no freedom to choose where to put that player – there is only one spot left. Thus, there are ten degrees of freedom. For ten players you have some degree of choice, but for one player you don't. The degrees of freedom are the number of players minus one.

The degrees of freedom for the t-statistic to test a hypothesis on one mean are also $n - 1$; that is, $10 - 1 = 9$ in our example. With 9 degrees of freedom and using a significance level of, for example, 5% (i.e. $\alpha = 0.05$), the critical value of the t-statistic is 1.833 (just look at the "significance level = 0.05" column and at line "df = 9" in Table A1 in the ☝ Web Appendix ($\rightarrow$ Additional Material)).

This means that for the probability of a type I error (i.e. falsely rejecting H_0) to be less than or equal to 0.05, the value of the test statistic must be 1.833 or greater. In our case (right-tailed test), the test statistic (2.274) clearly exceeds the critical value (1.833), which suggests that we should reject the null hypothesis.[2]

Table 6.3 shows the decision rules for rejecting the null hypothesis for different types of t-tests, where t_{test} describes the test statistic and $t_{critical}$ the critical value of a significance level α. We always consider absolute test values as these may well be negative (depending on the test's formulation), while the tabulated critical values are always positive.

Important: Unlike with right and left-tailed tests, we have to divide α by two when obtaining the critical value of a two-tailed test. This means that when using a significance level of 5%, we have to look under the 0.025 column in the t-distribution table. The reason is that a two-tailed test is somewhat "stricter" than a one-tailed test, because we do not only test whether a certain statistic differs in one direction

Table 6.3 Decision rules for testing decisions

Type of test	Null hypothesis (H_0)	Alternative hypothesis (H_1)	Reject H_0 if
Right-tailed test	$\mu \leq$ value	$\mu >$ value	$\|t_{test}\| > t_{critical}(\alpha)$
Left-tailed test	$\mu \geq$ value	$\mu <$ value	$\|t_{test}\| > t_{critical}(\alpha)$
Two-tailed test	$\mu =$ value	$\mu \neq$ value	$\|t_{test}\| > t_{critical}\left(\frac{\alpha}{2}\right)$

---

[2]To obtain the critical value, you can also use the TINV function provided in Microsoft Excel, whose general form is "TINV(α, df)." Here, α represents the desired Type I error rate and *df* the degrees of freedom. To carry out this computation, open a new Excel spreadsheet and type in "=TINV(2*0.05,9)." Note that we have to specify "2*0.05" (or, directly 0.1) under α as we are applying a one-tailed instead of a two-tailed test.

from a population value, but rather test whether it is either lower *or* higher than a population value. Thus, we have to assume a tighter confidence level of $\alpha/2$ when looking up the critical value.

You might remember the above things from an introductory statistics course and the good news is that we do not have to bother with statistical tables when working with SPSS. SPSS automatically calculates the probability of obtaining a test statistic at least as extreme as the one that is actually observed. This probability is also referred to as the *p-value* (rather confusingly, it is usually denoted with **Sig.** – also in the SPSS outputs).

With regard to our example, the p-value (or probability value) is the answer to the following question: If the population mean is really lower than or equal to 45 (i.e., in reality, therefore, H_0 holds), what is the probability that random sampling would lead to a difference between the sample mean $\bar{x}$ and the population mean μ as large (or larger) as the difference observed? In other words, the p-value is the probability of erroneously rejecting a true null hypothesis.

This description is very similar to the significance level α, which describes the tolerable level of risk of rejecting a true null hypothesis. However, the difference is that the p-value is calculated using the sample, and that α is set by the researcher before the test outcome is observed.[3] Thus, we cannot simply transfer the interpretation that a long series of α-level tests will reject no more than 100·α of true null hypotheses. Note that the p-value is not the probability of the null hypothesis being true! Rather, we should interpret it as evidence against the null hypothesis. The α-level is an arbitrary and subjective value that the researcher assigns for the level of risk of making a Type I error; the p-value is calculated from the available data.

Comparison of these two values allows the researcher to reject or not reject the null hypothesis. Specifically, if the p-value is smaller than or equal to the significance level, we reject the null hypothesis. Thus, when looking at test results in SPSS, we have to make use of the following decision rule – this should become second nature!

- p-value (**Sig.** in SPSS) $\leq \alpha \rightarrow$ reject H_0
- p-value (**Sig.** in SPSS)$> \alpha \rightarrow$ do not reject H_0

No matter how small the p-value is in relation to α, these decision rules only guarantee that you will erroneously reject the null hypothesis 100·α times out of 100 repeated tests. Otherwise stated, it is only of interest whether p-value $\leq \alpha$ but not the specific value of p itself. Thus, a statement such as "this result is highly significant" is inappropriate, as the test results are binary in nature (i.e., they reject or don't reject, nothing more). Compare it with any binary condition from real life, such as pregnancies – it is not possible to be just a little bit pregnant!

---

[3]Unfortunately, there is quite some confusion about the difference between α and p-value. See Hubbard and Bayarri (2003) for a discussion.

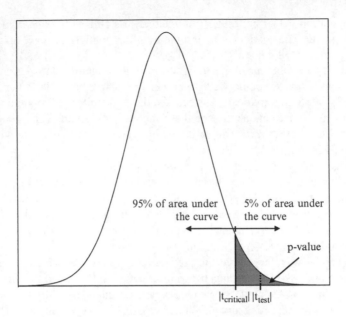

Fig. 6.3 Relationship between test value, critical value, and p-value

In our example, the actual p-value is about 0.024, which is clearly below the significance level of 0.05. Thus, we can reject the null hypothesis and find support for the alternative hypothesis.[4]

Figure 6.3 summarizes these concepts graphically. In this figure, you can see that the critical value $t_{critical}$ for an α-level of 5% divides the area under the curve into two parts. One part comprises 95% of the area, whereas the remaining part (also called the acceptance region, meaning that we accept the alternative hypothesis) represents the significance level α, that is, the remaining 5%. The test value $|t_{test}|$ defines the actual probability of erroneously rejecting a true null hypothesis, which is indicated by the area right of the dotted line. This area is nothing but the p-value, which is smaller than the 5%. Thus, we can reject the null hypothesis.

---

[4]We don't have to conduct manual calculations and tables when working with SPSS. However, we can easily compute the p-value ourselves using the TDIST function in Microsoft Excel. The function has the general form "TDIST(t, df, tails)", where t describes the test value, df the degrees of freedom and *tails* specifies whether it's a one-tailed test (tails = 1) or two-tailed test (tails = 2). For our example, just open a new spreadsheet and type in "=TDIST(2.274,9,1)". Likewise, there are several webpages with Java-based modules (e.g., http://www.graphpad.com/quickcalcs/index.cfm) that calculate p-values and test statistic values.

Interpret the Results

The conclusion reached by hypothesis testing must be expressed in terms of the market research problem and the relevant managerial action that should be taken. In our example, we conclude that there is evidence that the point of sale display significantly increased sales during the week it was installed.

Comparing Two Means: Two-samples t-test

In the previous example, we examined a hypothesis relating to one sample and one mean. However, market researchers are often interested in comparing two samples regarding their means. As indicated in Fig. 6.2, two samples can either be *independent* or *paired*, depending on whether we compare two distinct groups (e.g., males vs. females) or the same group at different points in time (e.g., customers before and after being exposed to a treatment or campaign). Let's begin with two independent samples.

Two Independent Samples

Testing the relationship between two independent samples is very common in market research settings. Some common research questions are:

- Does heavy and light users' satisfaction with products differ?
- Do male customers spend more money online than female customers?
- Do US teenagers spend more time on Facebook than German teenagers?

Each of the foregoing hypotheses aims at evaluating whether two populations (e.g., heavy and light users), represented by samples, are significantly different in terms of certain key variables (e.g., satisfaction ratings).

To understand the principles of a two independent samples t-test, let's reconsider the existing example of a promotion campaign in a department store. Specifically, we want to test whether the population mean of the sales of the point of sale display (μ_1) differs from that of the free tasting stand (μ_2). Thus, the resulting null and alternative hypotheses are now:

$$H_0 : \mu_1 = \mu_2 \text{ (or put differently} : H_0 : \mu_1 - \mu_2 = 0)$$

$$H_1 : \mu_1 \neq \mu_2 \text{ (or } H_1 : \mu_1 - \mu_2 \neq 0)$$

In its general form, the test statistic of the two independent samples t-test – which is now distributed with $n_1 + n_2 - 2$ degrees of freedom – seems very similar to the one-sample t-test:

$$t = \frac{(\bar{x}_1 - \bar{x}_2) - (\mu_1 - \mu_2)}{s_{\bar{x}_1 - \bar{x}_2}}$$

Here, $\bar{x}_1$ is the mean of the first sample (with n_1 numbers of observations) and $\bar{x}_2$ is the mean of the second sample (with n_2 numbers of observations). The term $\mu_1 - \mu_2$ describes the hypothesized difference between the population means. In this case, $\mu_1 - \mu_2$ is zero as we assume that the means are equal, but we could likewise use another value in cases where we hypothesize a specific difference in population means. Lastly, $s_{\bar{x}_1 - \bar{x}_2}$ describes the estimated standard error, which comes in two forms:

1. If we assume that the two populations have the same variance ($\sigma_1^2 = \sigma_2^2$), we compute the standard error based on the *pooled* variance estimate:

$$s_{\bar{x}_1 - \bar{x}_2} = \sqrt{\frac{[(n_1 - 1) \cdot s_1^2 + (n_2 - 1) \cdot s_2^2]}{n_1 + n_2 - 2}} \cdot \sqrt{\frac{1}{n_1} + \frac{1}{n_2}}$$

2. Alternatively, if we assume that the population variances differ (i.e. $\sigma_1^2 \neq \sigma_2^2$), things become a little bit easier as we can use a *separate* variance estimate:

$$s_{\bar{x}_1 - \bar{x}_2} = \sqrt{\frac{s_1^2}{n_1} + \frac{s_2^2}{n_2}}$$

How do we determine whether the two populations have the same variance? This is done by means of an intermediate step that consists of another statistical test. Not surprisingly, this test, known as the F-test of sample variance (also called Levene's test), considers the following hypotheses:

$$H_0 : \sigma_1^2 = \sigma_2^2$$

$$H_1 : \sigma_1^2 \neq \sigma_2^2$$

The null hypothesis is that the two population variances are the same and the alternative is that they differ.

As the computation of this test statistic is rather complicated, we refrain from discussing it in detail. If you want to learn more about Levene's test and its application to the promotion campaign example, read up on it in the ↗ Web Appendix (→ Chap. 6).

In this example, the Levene's test provides support for the assumption that the variances in the population are equal, so that we have to make use of the pooled variance estimate. First, we estimate the variances of samples 1 and 2

$$s_1^2 = \frac{1}{n_1 - 1} \sum_{i=1}^{10} (x_{1i} - \bar{x}_1)^2 = \frac{1}{10 - 1} [(50 - 47.30)^2 + \cdots + (44 - 47.30)^2]$$
$$= 10.233,$$

$$s_2^2 = \frac{1}{n_2 - 1} \sum_{i=1}^{10} (x_{2i} - \bar{x}_2)^2 = \frac{1}{10 - 1} [(55 - 52)^2 + \cdots + (44 - 52)^2] = 17.556,$$

and use these to obtain the estimated standard error:

$$s_{\bar{x}_1 - \bar{x}_2} = \sqrt{\frac{[(10 - 1) \cdot 10.233 + (10 - 1) \cdot 17.556]}{10 + 10 - 2}} \cdot \sqrt{\frac{1}{10} + \frac{1}{10}} = 1.667$$

Inserting this into the test statistic results in:

$$t = \frac{(\bar{x}_1 - \bar{x}_2) - (\mu_1 - \mu_1)}{s_{\bar{x}_1 - \bar{x}_2}} = \frac{(47.30 - 52) - 0}{1.667} = -2.819$$

As you can see, calculating these measures manually is not very difficult. Still, it is much easier to let SPSS do the calculations.

The test statistic follows a t-distribution with $n_1 + n_2 - 2$ degrees of freedom. In our case we have $10 + 10 - 2 = 18$ degrees of freedom. Looking at the statistical Table A1 in the ⌁ Web Appendix ($\rightarrow$ Additional Material), we can see that the critical value for a significance level of 5% is 2.101 (note that we are conducting a two-tailed test and, thus, have to look in the $\alpha = 0.025$ column). As the absolute value of -2.819 is greater than 2.101, we can reject the null hypothesis at a significance level of 5% and conclude that the means of the sales of the point of sale display (μ_1) and those of the free tasting stand (μ_2) differ in the population.

If we evaluated the results of the left-tailed test (i.e., $H_0 : \mu_1 \geq \mu_2$ and $H_1 : \mu_1 < \mu_2$) we find that sales of the point of sale display are significantly lower than those of the free tasting stand. Thus, the managerial recommendation would be to make use of free tasting stands when carrying out promotion campaigns, as this increases sales significantly over those of the point of sale display. Of course, in making the final decision, we would need to weigh the costs of the display and free tasting stand against the expected increase in sales.[5]

---

[5]There may be a situation in which we know the population standard deviation beforehand, for example, from a previous study. From a strict statistical viewpoint, it would be appropriate to use a z-test in this case, but both tests yield results that only differ marginally.

Two Paired Samples

In the previous example we compared the mean sales of two independent samples. Now, imagine that management wants to evaluate the effectiveness of the point of sale display in more detail. We have sales data for the week before point of sale display was installed, as well as the following week when this was not the case. Table 6.4 shows the sale figures of the ten stores under consideration for the two experimental conditions (the point of sale display and no point of sale display). Again, you can assume that the data are normally distributed.

Table 6.4 Sales data (extended)

Store	Sales (units)	
	No point of sale display	Point of sale display
1	46	50
2	51	52
3	40	43
4	48	48
5	46	47
6	45	45
7	42	44
8	51	49
9	49	51
10	43	44

At first sight, it appears that the point of sale display yielded higher sales numbers. The mean of the sales in the week during which the point of sale display was installed (47.30) is slightly higher than in the week when it was not (46.10). However, the question is whether this difference is statistically significant.

Obviously, we cannot assume that we are comparing two independent samples, as each set of two samples originates from the same store, but at different points in time under different conditions. This means we have to examine the differences by means of a *paired samples t-test*. In this example, we want to test whether the sales of the point of sale display condition are significantly higher than when no display was installed. We can express this by means of the following hypotheses, where μ_d describes the population difference in sales:

$$H_0 : \mu_d \leq 0$$

$$H_1 : \mu_d > 0$$

Obviously, we assume that the population difference is greater than zero since we suspect that the point of sale display ought to have significantly increased sales. This is expressed in the alternative hypothesis H_1, while the null hypothesis assumes that the point of sale display made no difference or even resulted in fewer sales

To carry out this test, we have to define a new variable d_i, which captures the differences in sales between the two treatment conditions (point of sale display installed and not installed) for each of the stores. Thus:

$$d_1 = 50 - 46 = 4$$

$$d_2 = 52 - 51 = 1$$

$$\ldots$$

$$d_9 = 51 - 49 = 2$$

$$d_{10} = 44 - 43 = 1$$

Based on these results, we calculate the mean difference

$$\bar{d} = \frac{1}{n} \sum_{i=1}^{10} d_i = \frac{1}{10}(4 + 1 + \cdots + 2 + 1) = 1.2$$

as well as the standard error of this difference

$$s_{\bar{d}} = \frac{\sqrt{\frac{1}{n-1} \sum_{i=1}^{10}(d_i - \bar{d})^2}}{\sqrt{n}}$$

$$= \frac{\sqrt{\frac{1}{9}[(4 - 1.2)^2 + (1 - 1.2)^2 + \cdots + (2 - 1.2)^2 + (1 - 1.2)^2]}}{\sqrt{10}} = 0.533$$

As you might suspect, the test statistic is very similar to the ones discussed before. Specifically, we compare the mean difference $\bar{d}$ in our sample with the difference expected under the null hypothesis μ_d and divide this difference by the standard error $s_{\bar{d}}$. Thus, the test statistic is

$$t = \frac{\bar{d} - \mu_d}{s_{\bar{d}}} = \frac{1.2 - 0}{0.533} = 2.250,$$

which follows a t-distribution with $n - 1$ degrees of freedom, where n is the number of pairs that we compare. Assuming a significance level of 5%, we obtain the critical value by looking at Table A1 in the ⌖ Web Appendix (→Additional Material). In our example, with 9 degrees of freedom and using a significance level of 5% (i.e. $\alpha = 0.05$), the critical value of the t-statistic is 1.833. Since the test value is larger than the critical value, we can reject the null hypothesis and presume that the point of sale display really did increase sales.

Comparing More Than Two Means: Analysis of Variance ANOVA

Researchers are often interested in examining mean differences between more than two groups. Some illustrative research questions might be:

- Do light, medium and heavy users differ with regard to their monthly disposable income?
- Do customers across four different types of demographic segments differ with regard to their attitude towards a certain brand?
- Is there a significant difference in hours spent on Facebook between US, UK and German teenagers?

Continuing with our previous example on promotion campaigns, we might be interested in whether there are significant sales differences between the stores in which the three different types of campaigns were launched.

One way to tackle this research question would be to carry out multiple pairwise comparisons of all groups under consideration. In this example, doing so would require the following comparisons (1) the point of sale display vs. the free tasting stand, (2) the point of sale display vs. the in-store announcements, and (3) the free tasting stand vs. the in-store announcements. While three comparisons seem to be easily manageable, you can appreciate the difficulty that will arise when a greater number of groups are compared. For example, with ten groups, we would have to carry out 45 group comparisons.[6]

Although such high numbers of comparisons become increasingly time consuming, there is a more severe problem associated with this approach, called α-inflation. This refers to the fact that the more tests you conduct at a certain significance level, the more likely you are to claim a significant result when this is not so (i.e., a type I error).

Using a significance level of $\alpha = 0.05$ and making all possible pairwise comparisons of ten groups (i.e. 45 comparisons), the increase in the overall probability of a type I error (also referred to as the *familywise error rate*) is found by

$$\alpha^* = 1 - (1 - \alpha)^{45} = 1 - (1 - 0.05)^{45} = 0.901.$$

That is, there is a 90.1% probability of erroneously rejecting your null hypothesis in at least some of your 45 t-tests – far greater than the 5% for a single comparison! The problem is that you can never tell which of the comparisons provide results that are wrong and which are right.

Instead of carrying out many pairwise tests and creating α-inflation, market researchers use ANOVA, which allows a comparison of averages between three

---

[6]The number of pairwise comparisons is calculated as follows: $k \cdot (k - 1)/2$, with k the number of groups to compare.

or more groups. In ANOVA, the variable that differentiates the groups is referred to as the *factor* (don't confuse this with the factors from factor analysis which we will discuss in Chap. 8!). The values of a factor (i.e., as found for the different groups under consideration) are also referred to as *factor levels*.

In the example above on promotion campaigns, we considered only one factor with three levels, indicating the type of campaign. This is the simplest form of an ANOVA and is called *one-way ANOVA*. However, ANOVA allows us to consider more than one factor. For example, we might be interested in adding another grouping variable (e.g., the type of service offered), thus increasing the number of treatment conditions in our experiment. In this case, we would use a *two-way ANOVA* to analyze the factors' effect on the units sold. ANOVA is in fact even more flexible in that you can also integrate metric independent variables and even several additional dependent variables.

For the sake of clarity, we will focus on the more fundamental form of ANOVA, the one-way ANOVA, with only a brief discussion of the two-way ANOVA.[7] For a more detailed discussion of the latter, you can turn to the ⊘ Web Appendix (→ Chap. 6).

Understanding One-Way ANOVA

As indicated above, ANOVA is used to examine mean differences between more than two groups.[8] In more formal terms, the objective of one-way ANOVA is to test the null hypothesis that the population means of the groups under consideration (defined by the factor and its levels) are equal. If we compare three groups, as in our example, the null hypothesis is:

$$H_0 : \mu_1 = \mu_2 = \mu_3$$

This hypothesis implies that the population means of all three promotion campaigns are identical (which is the same as saying that the campaigns have the same effect on mean sales). The alternative hypothesis is

$$H_1 : \text{At least two of } \mu_1, \mu_2, \text{ and } \mu_3 \text{ are different,}$$

which implies that at least two population means differ significantly. Of course, before we even think of running an ANOVA in SPSS, we have to come up with a problem formulation, which requires us to identify the dependent variable and the

---

[7]Field (2009) provides a detailed introduction to further ANOVA types such as multiple ANOVA (MANOVA) or an analysis of covariance (ANCOVA).

[8]Note that you can also apply ANOVA when comparing two groups. However, in this case, you should rather revert to the two independent samples t-test.

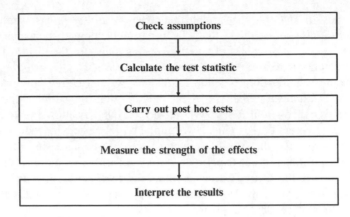

Fig. 6.4 Steps in ANOVA

factor, as well as its levels. Once this task is done, we can dig deeper into the ANOVA by following the steps described in Fig. 6.4. We will discuss each step in more detail in the following sections.

Check Assumptions

The assumptions under which ANOVA is reliable are similar as to the parametric tests discussed above. That is, the dependent variable is measured on at least an interval scale and is normally distributed in the population (see the normality tests in Box 6.1). In terms of violations of these assumptions, ANOVA is rather robust, at least in cases where the group sizes are equal. Consequently, we may also use ANOVA in situations when the dependent variable is ordinally scaled and not normally distributed, but then we should ensure that the group-specific sample sizes are equal.[9]

Thus, when carrying out experiments, it is useful to collect equal-sized samples of data across the groups (as in our example, in which we have observations in ten stores per promotion campaign type). When carrying out ANOVA the population variances in each group should also be similar. Even though ANOVA is rather robust in this respect, violations of the assumption of homogeneous variances can significantly bias the results, especially when groups are of very unequal sample size.[10] Consequently, we should always test for homogeneity of variances, which is

---

[9]Nonparametric alternatives to ANOVA are, for example, the χ^2-test of independence (for nominal variables) and the Kruskal–Wallis test (for ordinal variables). See, for example, Field (2009).

[10]In fact, these two assumptions are interrelated, since unequal group sample sizes result in a greater probability that we will violate the homogeneity assumption.

commonly done by using Levene's test. We already briefly touched upon this test and you can learn more about it in ⁻⁰ Web Appendix (→ Chap. 6).

Box 6.5 Tests to use when variances are unequal and group-specific sample sizes different

When carrying at ANOVA, violations of the assumption of homogeneity of variances can have serious consequences, especially when group sizes are unequal. Specifically, the within-group variation is increased (inflated) when there are large groups in the data that exhibit high variances. There is however a solution to this problem when it occurs. Fortunately, SPSS provides us with two modified techniques that we can apply in these situations: Brown and Forsythe (1974) and Welch (1951) propose modified test statistics, which make adjustments if the variances are not homogeneous. While both techniques control the type I error well, past research has shown that the Welch test exhibits greater statistical power. Consequently, when population variances are different and groups are of very unequal sample sizes, the application of the Welch test is generally recommended.

If Levene's test indicates that population variances are different, it is advisable to use modified F-tests such as Brown and Forsythe's test or the Welch test, which we discuss in Box 6.5 (the same holds for post hoc tests which we will discuss later in this chapter). The most severe violation of assumptions is when observations are not independent. Research has shown that when observations across groups are correlated, the probability of a type I error increases greatly. For example, when comparing ten observations across three groups, even where observations correlate only weakly at 0.05, the probability of a type I error increases to 74% instead of the 5% that is often selected. Thus, we have to make sure that the same respondents do not accidently fill out multiple surveys or that we use questionnaires collected from the same respondents at two different points in time.

Calculate the Test Statistic

The basic idea underlying the ANOVA is that it examines the dependent variable's variation across the samples and, based on this variation, determines whether there is reason to believe that the population means of the groups (or factor levels) differ significantly.

With regard to our example, each store's sales will likely deviate from the overall sales mean, as there will always be some variation. The question is whether the difference between each store's sales and the overall sales mean is likely to be caused by a specific promotion campaign or be due to a natural variation between the stores. In order to disentangle the effect of the treatment (i.e., the promotion campaign type) and the natural deviation, ANOVA splits up the total variation in the data (indicated by SS_T) into two parts (1) the between-group variation (SS_B), and (2) the within-group variation (SS_W).[11] These three types of variation are estimates of the population variation.

Conceptually, the relationship between the three types of variation is expressed as

$$SS_T = SS_B + SS_W$$

However, before we get into the maths, let's see what SS_B and SS_W are all about.

SS_B refers to the variation in the dependent variable as expressed in the variation in the group means. In our example, it describes the variation in the sales mean values across the three treatment conditions (i.e., point of sale display, free tasting stand, and in-store announcements) in relation to the overall mean. However, what does SS_B tell us? Imagine a situation in which all mean values across the treatment conditions are the same. In other words, regardless of which campaign we choose, sales are always the same. Obviously, in such a case, we cannot claim that the different types of promotion campaigns had any influence on sales. On the other hand, if mean sales differ substantially across the three treatment conditions, we can assume that the campaigns influenced the sales to different degrees.

This is what is expressed by means of SS_B; it tells us how much variation can be explained by the fact that the differences in observations truly stem from different groups. Since SS_B can be considered "explained variation" (i.e., variation explained by the grouping of data and thus reflecting different effects), we would want SS_B to be as high as possible. However, there is no given standard of how high SS_B should be, as its magnitude depends on the scale level used (e.g., are we looking at 7-point Likert scales or an income variable?). Consequently, we can only interpret the explained variation expressed by SS_B in relation to the variation that is not explained by the grouping of data. This is where SS_W comes into play.

As the name already suggests, SS_W describes the variation in the dependent variable within each of the groups. In our example, SS_W simply represents the variation in sales in each of the three treatment conditions. The smaller the variation within the groups, the greater the probability that all the observed variation can be explained by the grouping of data. It is obviously the ideal for this variation to be as small as possible. If there is much variation within some or all the groups, then this variation seems to be caused by some extraneous factor that was not accounted for in the experiment and not the grouping of data. For this reason, SS_W is also referred to as "unexplained variation." This unexplained variation can occur if we fail to account for important factors in our experimental design. For example, in some of the stores, the product might have been sold through self-service while in others personal service was available. This is a factor that we have not yet considered in our analysis, but which will be used when we look at two-way ANOVA later in the chapter. Nevertheless, some unexplained variation will always be present,

---

[11]SS is an abbreviation of "sum of squares" because the variation is calculated by means of squared differences between different types of values.

regardless of how good our experimental design is and how many factors we consider. That is why unexplained variation is frequently called (random) noise.

Therefore, the comparison of SS_B and SS_W tells us whether the variation in the data is attributable to the grouping, which is desirable, or due to sources of variation not captured by the grouping. More precisely, ideally we want SS_B to be as large as possible, whereas SS_W should be as small as possible. We'll take a closer look at this in the next section.

This relationship is described in Fig. 6.5, which shows a scatter plot, visualizing sales across stores of our three different campaign types: the point of sale display, the free tasting stand, and the in-store announcements. We indicate the group mean of each level by dashed lines. If the group means were all the same, the three dashed lines would be aligned and we would have to conclude that the campaigns have the same effect on sales. In such a situation, we could not expect the point of sale group to differ from the free tasting stand group or the in-store announcements group. Furthermore, we could not expect the free tasting stand group to differ from the in-store announcements group. On the other hand, if the dashed lines differ, we would probably conclude that the campaigns' effects differ significantly.

At the same time, we would like the variation within each of the groups to be as small as possible; that is, the vertical lines connecting the observations and the dashed lines should be short. In the most extreme case, all observations would lie on the dashed lines, implying that the grouping explains the variation in sales perfectly, something that will, however, hardly ever occur.

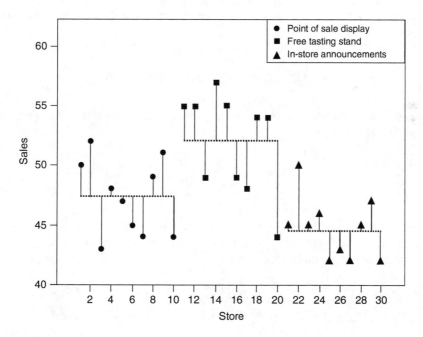

Fig. 6.5 Scatter plot of stores vs. sales

It is easy to visualize from this diagram that if the vertical bars were all, say, twice as long, then it would be difficult or impossible to draw any meaningful conclusions about the effects of the different campaigns. Too great a variation within the groups then swamps any variation across the groups.

Based on the discussion above, we can calculate the three types of variation as follows:

1. The total variation, computed by comparing each store's sales with the overall mean $\bar{x}$, which is equal to 48 in our example:

$$SS_T = \sum_{i=1}^{n} (x_i - \bar{x})^2 = (50 - 48)^2 + (52 - 48)^2 + \cdots + (47 - 48)^2 + (42 - 48)^2 = 584$$

2. The between-group variation, computed by comparing each group's mean sales with the overall mean, is:

$$SS_B = \sum_{j=1}^{k} n_j(\bar{x}_j - \bar{x})^2$$

As you can see, besides index i, as previously discussed, we also have index j to represent the group sales means. Thus, $\bar{x}_j$ describes the mean in the j-th group and n_j the number of observations in that group. The overall number of groups is denoted with k. The term n_j is used as a weighting factor: groups that have many observations should be accounted for to a higher degree relative to groups with fewer observations.

Returning to our example, the between-group variation is then given by:

$$SS_B = 10 \cdot (47.30 - 48)^2 + 10 \cdot (52 - 48)^2 + 10 \cdot (44.70 - 48)^2 = 273.80$$

3. The within-group variation, computed by comparing each store's sales with its group sales mean is:

$$SS_w = \sum_{j=1}^{k} \sum_{i=1}^{n_j} (x_{ij} - \bar{x}_j)$$

Here, we have to use two summation signs as we want to compute the squared differences between each store's sales and its group sales mean for all k groups in our set-up. In our example, this yields the following:

$$SS_W = [(50 - 47.30)^2 + \cdots + (44 - 47.30)^2] + [(55 - 52)^2 + \cdots + (44 - 52)^2] + [(45 - 44.70)^2 + \cdots + (42 - 44.70)^2]$$
$$= 310.20$$

In the previous steps, we discussed the comparison of the between-group and within-group variation. The higher the between-group variation is in relation to the within-group variation, the more likely it is that the grouping of data is responsible for the different levels in the stores' sales and not the natural variation in all sales.

A suitable way to describe this relation is by forming an index with SS_B in the numerator and SS_W in the denominator. However, we do not use SS_B and SS_W directly, as these are based on summed values and, thus, are influenced by the number of scores summed. These results for SS_B and SS_W have to be normalized, which we do by dividing the values by their degrees of freedom to obtain the true "mean square" values MSB (called between-group mean squares) and MSW (called within-group mean squares).

The resulting mean squares are:

$$MS_B = \frac{SS_B}{k-1}, \text{ and } MS_W = \frac{SS_W}{n-k}$$

We use these mean squares to compute the test statistic as follows:

$$F = \frac{MS_B}{MS_W}$$

This test statistic follows an F-distribution. Unlike the t-distribution, the F-distribution depends on two degrees of freedom: one corresponding to the between-group mean squares $(k-1)$ and the other referring to the within-group mean squares $(n-k)$. Turning back to our example, we calculate the F-value as:

$$F = \frac{MS_B}{MS_W} = \frac{SS_B/_{k-1}}{SS_W/_{n-k}} = \frac{273.80/_{3-1}}{310.20/_{30-3}} = 11.916$$

For the promotion campaign example, the degrees of freedom are 2 and 27; therefore, looking at Table A2 in the ⌐Ⴆ Web Appendix ($\rightarrow$ Additional Material), we obtain a critical value of 3.354 for $\alpha = 0.05$. Note that we don't have to divide α by two when looking up the critical value! The reason is that we always test for equality of population means in ANOVA, rather than one being larger than the others. Thus, the distinction between one-tailed and two-tailed tests does not apply in this case.

Because the calculated F-value is greater than the critical value, the null hypothesis is rejected. Consequently, we can conclude that at least two of the population sales means for the three types of promotion campaigns differ significantly.

At first sight, it appears that the free tasting stand is most successful, as it exhibits the highest mean sales $(\bar{x}_2 = 52)$ compared to the point of sale display $(\bar{x}_1 = 47.30)$ and the in-store announcements $(\bar{x}_3 = 44.70)$. However, note that rejecting the null hypothesis does not mean that all population means differ – it only means that at least two of the population means differ significantly! Market researchers often make this mistake, assuming that all means differ significantly when interpreting ANOVA results. Since we cannot, of course, conclude that all means differ from one another, this can present a problem. Consider the more complex example in which the factor under analysis does not only have three different levels, but ten. In an extreme case, nine of the population means could be the same while one is significantly different from the rest and could even be an outlier. It is clear that great care has to be taken not to misinterpret the result of our F-test.

How do we determine which of the mean values differ significantly from the others without stepping into the α-inflation trap discussed above? One way to deal with this problem is to use *post hoc tests* which we discuss in the next section.[12]

Carry Out Post Hoc Tests

The basic idea underlying post hoc tests is to perform tests on each pair of groups, but to correct the level of significance for each test so that the overall type I error rate across all comparisons (i.e. the familywise error rate) remains constant at a certain level such as $\alpha = 0.05$. The easiest way of maintaining the familywise error rate is to carry out each comparison at a statistical significance level of α divided by the number of comparisons made. This method is also known as the *Bonferroni correction*. In our example, we would use $0.05/3 = 0.017$ as our criterion for significance. Thus, in order to reject the null hypothesis that two population means are equal, the p-value would have to be smaller or equal to 0.017 (instead of 0.05!).

As you might suspect, the Bonferroni adjustment is a very strict way of maintaining the familywise error rate. While this might at first sight not be problematic, there is a trade-off between controlling the familywise error rate and increasing the type II error, which would reduce the test's statistical power. By being very conservative in the type I error rate, such as when using the Bonferroni correction, a type II error may creep in and cause us to miss out on revealing some significant effect that actually exists in the population.

The good news is that there are alternatives to the Bonferroni correction. The bad news is that there are numerous types of post hoc tests – SPSS provides no less than 18. Generally, these tests detect pairs of groups whose mean values do not differ significantly (*homogeneous subsets*). However, all these tests are based on different assumptions and designed for different purposes, whose details are clearly beyond the scope of this book. Check out the SPSS help function for an overview and references. The most widely used post hoc test in market research is Tukey's honestly significant difference test (usually simply called *Tukey's HSD*). Tukey's HSD is a very versatile test which controls for the type I error and is conservative in nature. A less conservative alternative is the *Ryan/Einot-Gabriel/Welsch Q procedure* (REGWQ), which also controls for the type I error rate but has a higher statistical power.

These post hoc tests share two important properties (1) they require an equal number of observations for each group, and (2) they assume that the population variances are equal. Fortunately, research has provided alternative post hoc tests for

---

[12]Note that the application of post hoc tests only makes sense when the overall F-test finds a significant effect.

situations in which these properties are not met. When sample sizes differ, it is advisable to use *Hochberg's GT2*, which has good power and can control the type I error. However, when population variances differ, this test becomes unreliable. Thus, in cases where our analysis suggests that population variances differ, it is best to use the *Games-Howell procedure* because it generally seems to offer the best performance.

While post hoc tests provide a suitable way of carrying out pairwise comparisons among the groups while maintaining the familywise error rate, they do not allow making any statements regarding the strength of a factor's effects on the dependent variable. This is something we have to evaluate in a separate analysis step, which is discussed next.

Measure the Strength of the Effects

To determine the strength of the effect (also *effect size*) that the factor exerts on the dependent variable, we can compute the η^2 (pronounced as *eta squared*) coefficient. It is the ratio of the between-group variation (SS_B) to the total variation (SS_T) and, as such, expresses the variance accounted for of the sample data. η^2 which is often simply referred to as effect size, can take on values between 0 and 1. If all groups have the same mean value, and we can thus assume that the factor has no influence on the dependent variable, η^2 is 0. Conversely, a high value implies that the factor exerts a pronounced influence on the dependent variable. In our example η^2 is:

$$\eta^2 = \frac{SS_B}{SS_T} = \frac{273.80}{584} = 0.469$$

The outcome indicates that 46.9% of the total variation in sales is explained by the promotion campaigns. Note that η^2 is often criticized as being inflated, for example, due to small sample sizes, which might in fact apply to our analysis.

To compensate for small sample sizes, we can compute ω^2 (pronounced *omega squared*) which adjusts for this bias:

$$\omega^2 = \frac{SS_B - (k-1) \cdot MS_W}{SS_T + MS_W} = \frac{273.80 - (3-1) \cdot 11.489}{584 + 11.489} = 0.421$$

In other words, 42.1% of the total variation in sales is accounted for by the promotion campaigns.

Generally, you should use ω^2 for small sample sizes (say 50 or less) and η^2 for larger sample sizes. It is difficult to provide firm rules of thumb regarding when η^2 or ω^2 is appropriate, as this varies from research area to research area. However, since η^2 resembles the Pearson's correlation coefficient (Chap. 5) of linear relationships, we follow the suggestions provided in Chap. 5. Thus, we can consider values below 0.30 weak, values from 0.31 to 0.49 moderate and values of 0.50 and higher as strong.

Unfortunately, the SPSS one-way ANOVA procedure does not compute η^2 and ω^2. Thus, we have to do this manually, using the formulae above.

Interpret the Results

Just as in any other type of analysis, the final step is to interpret the results. Based on our results, we can conclude that the promotion campaigns have a significant effect on sales. An analysis of the strength of the effects revealed that this association is moderate. Carrying out post hoc tests manually is difficult and, instead, we have to rely on SPSS to do the job. We will carry out several post hoc tests later in this chapter when dealing with an example application.

Going Beyond One-way ANOVA: The Two-Way ANOVA

A logical extension of one-way ANOVA is to add a second factor to the analysis. For example, we could assume that, in addition to the different promotion campaigns, management also varied the type of service provided by providing either self-service or personal service (see column "Service type" in Table 6.1). In principle, a two-way ANOVA works the same way as a one-way ANOVA, except that the inclusion of a second factor necessitates the consideration of additional types of variation. Specifically, we now have to account for two types of between-group variations (1) the between-group variation in factor 1 (i.e., promotion campaigns), and (2) the between-group variation in factor 2 (i.e., service type).

In its simplest usage, the two-way ANOVA assumes that these factors are mutually unrelated. However, in real-world market research applications this is rarely going to be the case, thereby requiring us to use the more complex case of related factors.

When we take two related factors into account, we not only have to consider each factor's direct effect (also called *main effect*) on the dependent variable, but also the factors' *interaction effect*. Conceptually, an interaction effect is the additional effect due to combining two (or more) factors. Most importantly, this extra effect cannot be

Box 6.6 A different type of interaction

http://tinyurl.com/interact-coke

observed when considering each of the factors separately and thus reflects a concept known as *synergy*. There are many examples in everyday life where the whole is more than simply the sum of the parts as we know from cocktail drinks, music or paintings (for a very vivid example of interaction, see the link provided in Box 6.6).

In our example, the free tasting stand might be the best promotion campaign when studied separately, but it could well be that when combined with personal service, the point of sale display is much more effective. A significant interaction effect indicates that the combination of the two factors is particularly effective or, on the other hand, ineffective, depending on the direction of the interaction effect. Conversely, an insignificant interaction effect suggests that we should choose the best level of the two factors and then use them in combination. The calculation of these effects as well as discussion of further technical aspects go beyond the scope of this book but are discussed in the ⁀ Web Appendix ($\rightarrow$ Chap. 6).

Table 6.5 provides an overview of steps involved when carrying out the following tests in SPSS: One-sample t-test, independent samples t-test, paired samples t-test, and the one-way ANOVA.

Table 6.5 Steps involved in carrying out t-tests and one-way ANOVA in SPSS

Theory	Action
One-sample t-test	
Compare mean value with a given standard	▶ Analyze ▶ Compare Means ▶ One-Sample T Test
Assumptions:	
Is the test variable measured on an interval or ratio scale?	Check Chap. 3 to determine the measurement level of the variables.
Are the observations independent?	Consult Chap. 3 to determine if the observations are independent.
Is the test variable normally distributed or is n>30?	If necessary, carry out normality tests: ▶ Analyze ▶ Descriptive Statistics ▶ Explore ▶ Plots. Check Normality plots with tests. For $n < 50$, interpret the Shapiro–Wilk test. If test variable exhibits many identical values or for higher sample sizes, use the Kolmogorov–Smirnov test (with Lilliefors correction).
Specification:	
Select the test variable	Enter the variable in the **Test Variable(s)** box
Specify the standard of comparison	Specify the test value in the **Test Value** box.
Results interpretation:	
Look at test results	Look at the t-value and its significance level.
Independent samples t-test	
Compare the differences in the means of the independent samples	▶ Analyze ▶ Compare Means ▶ Independent-Samples T Test
Assumptions:	
Is the test variable measured on at least an interval scale?	Check Chap. 3 to determine the measurement level of your variables.
Are the observations independent?	Consult Chap. 3 to determine if the observations are independent.

(*continued*)

Table 6.5 (continued)

Theory	Action
Is the test variable normally distributed or is $n > 30$?	If necessary, carry out normality tests: ▶ Analyze ▶ Descriptive Statistics ▶ Explore ▶ Plots. Check Normality plots with tests. For $n < 50$, interpret the Shapiro–Wilk test. If test variable exhibits many identical values or for higher sample sizes, use the Kolmogorov–Smirnov test (with Lilliefors correction).
Specification:	
Select the test variable and the grouping variable	Enter these in the **Test Variable(s)** and **Grouping Variable** boxes.
Results interpretation:	
Look at test results	If the Levene's test suggests equal population variances, interpret the t-value and its significance level based on the pooled variance estimate (upper row in SPSS output); if Levene's test suggests unequal population variances, interpret the t-value and its significance level based on the separate variance estimate (lower row in SPSS output).
Paired samples t-test	
Compare the differences in the means of the paired samples	▶ Analyze ▶ Compare Means ▶ Paired-Samples T Test
Assumptions:	
Are the test variables measured on an interval or ratio scale?	Check Chap. 3 to determine the measurement level of your variables.
Are the observations dependent?	Consult Chap. 3 to determine if the observations are dependent.
Are the test variable normally distributed or is $n > 30$?	If necessary, carry out normality tests: ▶ Analyze ▶ Descriptive Statistics ▶ Explore ▶ Plots. Check Normality plots with tests. For $n < 50$, interpret the Shapiro–Wilk test. If test variable exhibits many identical values or for higher sample sizes, use the Kolmogorov–Smirnov test (with Lilliefors correction).
Specification:	
Select the paired test variables	Enter these in the **Paired Variables** box.
Results interpretation:	
Look at test results	Look at the t-value and its significance level.
One-way ANOVA	
Compare the means of three or more groups	▶ Analyze ▶ Compare Means ▶ One-Way ANOVA
Specification:	
Select the dependent variable and the factor (grouping variable)	Enter these in the Dependent List and Factor box.
Assumptions:	
Is the dependent variable measured on an interval or ratio scale?	Check Chap. 3 to determine the measurement level of your variables.
Are the observations independent?	Consult Chap. 3 to determine if the observations are independent.
Is the dependent variable normally distributed?	Carry out normality tests: ▶ Analyze ▶ Descriptive Statistics ▶ Explore ▶ Plots. Check Normality plots with tests. For $n < 50$, interpret the Shapiro–Wilk test.

(continued)

Example   149

Table 6.5 (continued)

Theory	Action
	If test variable exhibits many identical values or for higher sample sizes, use the Kolmogorov–Smirnov test (with Lilliefors correction).
Are the population variances equal?	Carry out Levene's test: ▶ Analyze ▶ Compare Means ▶ One-Way ANOVA ▶ Options ▶ Homogeneity of variance test
Results interpretation:	
Look at test results	Check the F-value and its significance level; if Levene's test suggests different population variances and the group sizes differ significantly, interpret using Welch test. ▶ Analyze ▶ Compare Means ▶ One-Way ANOVA ▶ Options ▶ Welch
Look at the strength of the effects	Use SPSS output to compute η^2 and ω^2 manually
Carry out pairwise comparisons	Carry out post hoc tests: ▶ Analyze ▶ Compare Means ▶ One-Way ANOVA ▶ Post Hoc Equal population variances assumed: - Use R-E-G-WQ if group sizes are equal - Use Hochberg's GT2 if group sizes differ If unequal population variances assumed, use the Games-Howell procedure.

Example

Founded in 2001, vente-privee.com organizes exclusive sales events for international designer brands covering a broad range of product categories, ranging from fashion to home wares, sports products to electronics. Sales events last from 2 to 4

http://en.vente-privee.com

days offering 50–70% discounts exclusively to its 9.5 million members. vente-privee.com therefore offers a new distribution channel, which complements of traditional channels. Here, companies are given the opportunity to sell their stock in a quick, discreet, and qualitative way while still protecting and enhancing their brand image. In 2008, vente-privee.com sold 38 million products through 2,500 sales, achieving a turnover of 610 million GBP.

In 2008, vente-privee.com successfully launched its new online appearance for the UK. After 2 years of operations, the company decided to consult a market research firm to explore the customers' buying behavior and their perception of the website. In a small-scale ad hoc study, the firm gathered data from a sample of 30 randomly selected customers on the following variables (variable names in parentheses):

- Identification number (*id*)
- Respondent's gender (*gender*)
- Perceived image of vente-privee.com (*image*)
- Perceived ease-of-use of vente-privee.com (*ease*)
- Sales per respondent per year in GBP (*sales*)

Using these data, the market research firm sought to identify potential areas of improvement for the website design and ideas on how to further explore relevant target groups in future advertising campaigns. Specifically, the firm wanted to answer the following research questions:

- Is there a significant difference in sales between male and female customers?
- Does the website's perceived ease-of-use influence the customers' buying behavior?

The dataset used is *vente_privee.sav* (✇ Web Appendix → Chap. 6).[13]

Before conducting any testing procedure, we have to examine whether the variable of interest (i.e. sales in GBP) is normally distributed, as this determines whether we should consider parametric or nonparametric tests. This is done using normality test, which we can access by clicking ▶ Analyze ▶ Descriptive Statistics ▶ Explore. This will open a dialog box similar to Fig. 6.6.

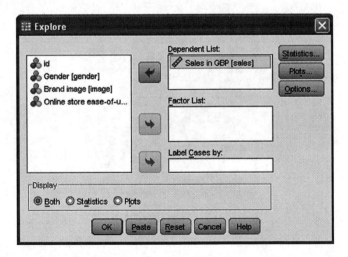

Fig. 6.6 One-sample Kolmogorov–Smirnov test dialog box

---

[13]Note that the data are artificial.

Example   151

Table 6.6 Normality tests results

Tests of Normality

	Kolmogorov-Smirnov[a]			Shapiro-Wilk		
	Statistic	df	Sig.	Statistic	df	Sig.
Sales in GBP	.077	30	.200*	.985	30	.931

a. Lilliefors Significance Correction

*. This is a lower bound of the true significance.

Simply enter the variable *sales* in the **Dependent List** box. Under **Plots**, we need to check **Normality plots with tests**. Next, click on **Continue** and then **OK** to run the analysis.

The output in Table 6.6 shows the results for both, the Kolmogorov–Smirnov as well as the Shapiro–Wilk test. As we only have 30 observations in this example, we should interpret the Shapiro–Wilk test as it exhibits more statistical power in situations with small sample sizes. Remember that the p-value is the probability of obtaining a test statistic at least as extreme as the one actually observed, assuming that the null hypothesis is true. This means that if the p-value is smaller than or equal to our level of tolerance of the risk of rejecting a true null hypothesis (i.e., α), we should reject the null hypothesis.

In this analysis, we follow the general convention by using a 5% significance level.

Because the p-value (0.931) is much larger than 0.05, the null hypothesis that the data are normally distributed should not be rejected at a 5% level. Consequently, we may assume the sales data are normally distributed in the population.

The next question that we want to address is whether there is a difference in sales based on gender. Using the previous test's results, we know that the sales variable is normally distributed and since it is also measured on an interval scale, we have to use a parametric test. In this case, we examine two distinct groups of customers (i.e., males and females). Thus, looking at our guideline in Fig. 6.2, we have to use the independent samples t-test. To run this test, go to ▶ Analyze ▶ Compare Means ▶ Independent-Samples T Test to display a dialog box similar to Fig. 6.7.

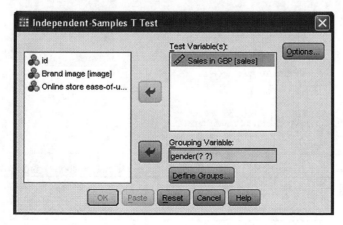

Fig. 6.7 Independent-samples t-test dialog box

Move *sales* to the **Test Variable(s)** box and move *gender* to the **Grouping Variable** box.

Click **Define Groups** and a menu similar to that shown in Fig. 6.8 will appear in which you have to specify the grouping variable's values that identify the two groups you wish to compare.

You can also specify a **Cut point**, which is particularly useful when you want to compare two groups based on an ordinal or continuous grouping variable. For example, if you want to compare younger vs. older members you could arbitrarily put all members below 30 years of age into one category and all who are 30 or above into the other category. When you indicate a cut point, observations with values less than the cut point form one group, while observations with values greater than or equal to the cut point form the other group. However, we will stick to the first option, using 1 for group 1 (males) and 2 for group 2 (females). Click on **Continue** and then on **OK** in the main menu. This will yield the outputs shown in Tables 6.7 and 6.8.

Looking at the descriptive statistics in Table 6.7, we can see that female customers have a higher mean in sales (310 GBP) than male customers (270 GBP). At first sight, it appears that the sales are really different between these two groups, but, as we learned before, we have to take the variation in the data into account to test whether this difference is also present in the population.

The output of this test appears in Table 6.8. On the left of the output, we can see the test results of Levene's test for the equality of population variances. The very low F-value of 0.001 already suggests that we cannot reject the null hypothesis that the population variances are equal. This is also mirrored in the large p-value of 0.974 (**Sig.** in Table 6.8), which lies far above our α-level of 0.05. Looking at the central and right part of the output, we can see that SPSS carries out two tests, one

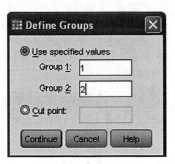

Fig. 6.8 Definition of groups

Table 6.7 Descriptive statistics (group statistics)

Group Statistics

	Gender	N	Mean	Std. Deviation	Std. Error Mean
Sales in GBP	male	15	270.00	50.723	13.097
	female	15	310.00	52.299	13.503

Example   153

Table 6.8 Independent samples t-test result

Independent Samples Test

		Levene's Test for Equality of Variances		t-test for Equality of Means						
		F	Sig.	t	df	Sig. (2-tailed)	Mean Difference	Std. Error Difference	95% Confidence Interval of the Difference	
									Lower	Upper
Sales in GBP	Equal variances assumed	.001	.974	−2.126	28	.042	−40.000	18.811	−78.533	−1.467
	Equal variances not assumed			−2.126	27.974	.042	−40.000	18.811	−78.535	−1.465

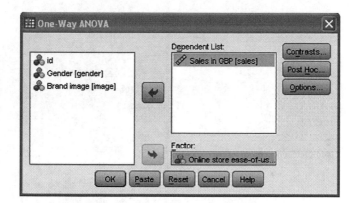

Fig. 6.9 One-way ANOVA dialog box

based on the pooled variance estimate (upper row) and the other based on separate variance estimates (lower row). Since we assume that the population variances are equal, we have to consider the pooled variance estimate. The resulting t-test statistic of −2.126 is negative due to the negative mean difference of −40 (sample mean of group 1 – sample mean of group 2). This yields a p-value of 0.042, which is barely below the threshold value of 0.05. Therefore, we can still reject the independent samples t-test's null hypothesis, namely that there is no difference in the population mean sales between male and female consumers. We can therefore conclude that the sales for men and women differ significantly.

In the next analysis, we want to examine whether the customers' perceived ease-of-use of vente-privee.com's online appearance has a significant effect on sales. Reconsidering the guideline in Fig. 6.2, we can easily see that a one-way ANOVA is the method of choice for answering this research question. Clicking on ▶ Analyze ▶ Compare Means ▶ One-Way ANOVA will open a dialog box similar to Fig. 6.9.

We start off by moving the *sales* variable to the **Dependent List** box and the ease-of-use variable (*ease*) to the **Factor** box (remember that in ANOVA, factor refers to the grouping variable). Under **Options**, we can request several statistics.

As discussed above, we have to determine whether the assumption of homogenous variances is met. For this purpose – just as in the independent samples t-test – we have to consider Levene's test, which we can request by choosing the **Homogeneity of variance test**. Because we do not yet know whether the population variances are equal or not, we should choose the statistic **Welch** (for the Welch test). Also, make sure you tick the boxes next to **Descriptive** as well as **Means plot** (Fig. 6.10). Click **Continue**.

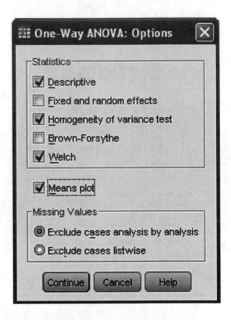

Fig. 6.10 Options for one-way ANOVA

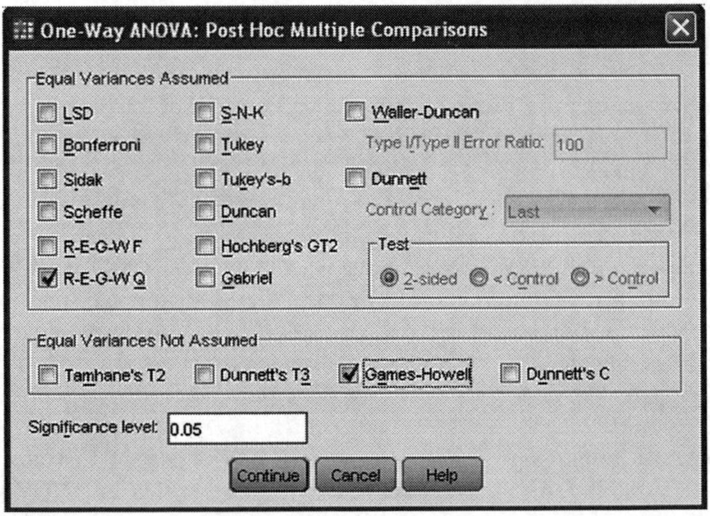

Fig. 6.11 Post hoc tests

Example   155

Under **Post Hoc** (Fig. 6.11) we can specify a series of post hoc tests for multiple group comparisons. Since we do not yet know the result of Levene's test, let's choose the Ryan/Einot-Gabriel/Welsch Q procedure (**R-E-G-W Q**) if we can assume equal variances, as well as **Games-Howell** if we have to reject Levene's test's null hypothesis that population variances are equal. Since group sizes are equal, there is no need to select Hochberg's GT2. Next, click on **Continue** to get back to the main menu.

In the main menu, click on **OK** to run the analysis. Table 6.9 shows the descriptive results. Not unexpectedly, the higher the customers rate the perceived ease-of-use of the online store, the greater the sales. This is also illustrated in the means plot in Fig. 6.12.

Table 6.9 Descriptive statistics

Descriptives

Sales in GBP

	N	Mean	Std. Deviation	Std. Error	95% Confidence Interval for Mean		Minimum	Maximum
					Lower Bound	Upper Bound		
easy	10	318.90	49.660	15.704	283.38	354.42	256	413
neutral	10	291.80	41.464	13.112	262.14	321.46	230	348
difficult	10	259.30	58.532	18.509	217.43	301.17	178	330
Total	30	290.00	54.555	9.960	269.63	310.37	178	413

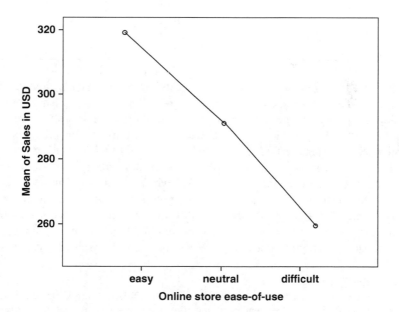

Fig. 6.12 Means plot

Table 6.10 Levene's test output (test of homogeneity of variances)

Test of Homogeneity of Variances

Sales in GBP

Levene Statistic	df1	df2	Sig.
.924	2	27	.409

Table 6.11 ANOVA results

ANOVA

Sales in GBP

	Sum of Squares	df	Mean Square	F	Sig.
Between Groups	17809.400	2	8904.700	3.510	.044
Within Groups	68502.600	27	2537.133		
Total	86312.000	29			

Table 6.12 Ryan/Einot–Gabriel/Welsch Q-procedure's result

Sales in GBP

	Online store ease-of-use		Subset for alpha = 0.05	
		N	1	2
Ryan-Einot-Gabriel-	difficult	10	259.30	
Welsch Range	neutral	10	291.80	291.80
	easy	10		318.90
	Sig.		.161	.239

Before we can evaluate the ANOVA's results, we have to take a closer look at the results of Levene's test as shown in Table 6.10. Levene's test clearly suggests that the population variances are equal, as the test's p-value is well above 0.05. Thus, to decide whether at least one group mean differs from the others, we should consider using the regular F-test, rather than the Welch test.

Table 6.11 shows that we can reject the null hypothesis that the sales of the three groups of customers are equal (**Sig. = 0.044** which is smaller than 0.05). More precisely, this result suggests that at least two group means differ significantly.[14]

To evaluate whether all groups are mutually different or only two, we take a look at the post hoc test results. As Levene's test showed that the population variances are equal, we are primarily interested in the Ryan/Einot-Gabriel/Welsch Q-procedure's

---

[14]Contrary to this, the Welch test suggests that there are no differences between the three groups (p-value 0.081 > 0.05). This divergent result underlines the importance of carefully considering the result of the Levene's test.

Example   157

Table 6.13 Games–Howell test result

Multiple Comparisons

Dependent Variable:Sales in GBP

	(I) Online store ease-of-use	(J) Online store ease-of-use	Mean Difference-(I-J)	Std. Error	Sig.	95% Confidence Interval Lower Bound	Upper Bound
Games-Howell	easy	neutral	27.100	20.458	.401	−25.26	79.46
		difficult	59.600	24.274	.061	−2.49	121.69
	neutral	easy	−27.100	20.458	.401	−79.46	25.26
		difficult	32.500	22.683	.348	−25.95	90.95
	difficult	easy	−59.600	24.274	.061	−121.69	2.49
		neutral	−32.500	22.683	.348	−90.95	25.95

result (Table 6.12). This table is a summary of the differences in the means. It organizes the means of the three groups into "homogeneous subsets" – subsets of means that do not differ at $p \leq 0.05$ are grouped together, and subsets that do differ are placed in separate columns. According to the Ryan/Einot-Gabriel/Welsch Q-procedure, groups that do not appear in the same column differ significantly at $p \leq 0.05$. Notice how the difficult and the easy groups show up in separate columns. This indicates that those groups differ significantly. The neutral group shows up in each column, indicating that it is not significantly different from either of the other two groups. Means for groups in homogeneous subsets are displayed.

Even though the population variances are assumed to be equal, let us take a look at the results of the Games-Howell procedure (Table 6.13) for the sake of comprehensiveness. There are several comparisons listed in the table. In the first row, you can see the comparison between the easy group and neutral group. The difference between the means of these two groups is 27,100 units. Following this row across, we see that this difference is statistically insignificant (p-value $= 0.401$). Similarly, in the row below this, we can see that the difference between the easy and difficult group (59.600) is also insignificant, as the p-value (0.061) lies above 0.05. Lastly, the comparison of the neutral and difficult group (two rows below) also renders a insignificant result. This difference in results compared to those of the Ryan/Einot-Gabriel/Welsch Q-procedure underlines the importance of closely considering Levene's test before interpreting the analysis results.

Finally, we want to examine the strength of the effect by computing η^2 and ω^2 manually (remember that SPSS does not provide us with these measures). Using the information from Table 6.11, we can easily compute the measures as follows:

$$\eta^2 = \frac{SS_B}{SS_T} = \frac{17,809.40}{86,312.00} = 0.206$$

$$\omega^2 = \frac{SS_B - (k-1) \cdot MS_W}{SS_T + MS_W} = \frac{17,809.40 - (3-1) \cdot 2,537.133}{86,312.00 + 2,537.133} = 0.143$$

As one can see, the strength of the effect is rather weak. Taken jointly, these results suggest that the buying behavior of customers is little influenced by their perceived ease-of-use of vente-privee.com's online store. Of course, improving the online store's navigation or layout might boost sales across all three groups jointly, but it will not necessarily introduce differences in sales between the groups.

So far, we have considered only one factor in the ANOVA but we could easily extend this example by simultaneously considering a second factor, say one which captures the customers' perceived image of vente-privee.com as a company. This would then require the application of a two-way ANOVA, which we discuss in the Web Appendix ($\sqrt[\circ]{\theta}$ Web Appendix → Chap. 6).

Case Study

In the spring of 2010, the German unit of Citibank was sold to Crédit Mutuel, a French bank. After the purchase, the former Citibank was renamed Targobank and a massive re-branding campaign was launched. The new Targobank's product range was also restructured and service and customer orientation were stressed. In addition, a comprehensive marketing campaign was launched, aimed at increasing the bank's customer base by one million new customers in 2015.

In an effort to control the campaign's success and to align the marketing actions, the management decided to conduct an analysis of newly acquired customers. Specifically, it is interested in evaluating the segment of young customers aged 30 and below. To do so, the marketing department has surveyed the following characteristics of 251 randomly drawn new customers (variable names in parentheses):

- Gender (*gender*)
- Bank deposit in Euro (*deposit*)
- Does the customer still attend school/university? (*training*)
- Customer's age specified in three categories (*age_cat*)

Use the data provided in *bank.sav* ($\sqrt[\circ]{\theta}$ Web Appendix → Chap. 6) to answer the following research questions.[15]

1. Which test do we have to apply to find out whether there is a significant difference in bank deposits between male and female customers? Do we meet the assumptions necessary to conduct this test? Also use an appropriate normality test and interpret the result. Does the result give rise to any cause for concern? Carry out an appropriate test to answer the initial research question.
2. Is there a significant difference in bank deposits between customers who are still studying and those that are not?
3. Which type of test or procedure would you use to evaluate whether bank deposits differ significantly between the three age categories? Carry out this procedure and interpret the results.

---

[15]Note that the data are artificial.

4. Reconsider the previous question and, using post hoc tests, evaluate whether there are significant differences between the three age groups.
5. Is there a significant interaction effect between the variables *training* and *age_cat* on *deposit*?
6. On the basis of your analysis results, please provide recommendations on how to align future marketing actions for Targobank's management.

Questions

1. Describe the steps involved in hypothesis testing in your own words.
2. Explain the concept of the p-value and explain how it relates to the significance level α.
3. What level of α would you choose for the following types of market research studies? Give reasons for your answers.
   (a) An initial study on the preferences for mobile phone colors
   (b) The production quality of Rolex watches
   (c) A repeat study on differences in preference for either Coca Cola or Pepsi
4. Write two hypotheses for each of the example studies in question 3, including the null and alternative hypotheses.
5. Describe the difference between independent and paired samples t-tests in your own words and provide two examples of each type.
6. Use the data from the vente-privee.com example to run a two-way ANOVA, including the factors (1) ease-of-use and (2) brand image, with sales as the dependent variable. To do so, go to Analyze ▶ General Linear Model ▶ Univariate and enter *sales* in the Dependent Variables box and *image* and *online_store* in the Fixed Factor(s) box. Interpret the results.

Further Readings

Field A (2009) Discovering statistics using SPSS, 3rd edn. Sage, London
   Good reference for advanced types of ANOVA.
Hubbard R, Bayarri MJ (2003) Confusion over measure of evidence (p's) versus errors (α's) in classical statistical testing. Am Stat 57(3):171–178
   The authors discuss the distinction between p-value and α and argue that there is general confusion about these measures' nature among researchers and practitioners. A very interesting read!
Kanji GK (2006) 100 statistical tests, 3rd edn. Sage, London
   If you are interested in learning more about different tests, we recommend this best-selling book in which the author introduces various tests with information on how to calculate and interpret their results using simple datasets.

Sawyer AG, Peter JP (1983) The significance of statistical significance tests in marketing research. J Mark Res 20(2):122–133
  Interesting article in which the authors discuss the interpretation and value of classical statistical significance tests and offer recommendations regarding their usage.

References

Boneau CA (1960) The effects of violations of assumptions underlying the t test. Psychol Bull 57(1):49–64
Brown MB, Forsythe AB (1974) Robust tests for the equality of variances. J Am Stat Assoc 69(346):364–367
Cohen J (1992) A power primer. Psychol Bull 112(1):155–159
Field A (2009) Discovering statistics using SPSS, 3rd edn. Sage, London
Hubbard R, Bayarri MJ (2003)[AU4] Confusion over measure of evidence (p's) versus errors (α's) in classical statistical testing. Am Stat 57(3):171–178
Lilliefors HW (1967) On the Kolmogorov–Smirnov test for normality with mean and variance unknown. J Am Stat Assoc 62(318):399–402
Schwaiger M, Sarstedt M, Taylor CR (2010) Art for the sake of the corporation: Audi, BMW Group, DaimlerChrysler, Montblanc, Siemens, and Volkswagen Help Explore the Effect of Sponsorship on Corporate Reputations. Journal of Advertising Research 50(1):77–90
Welch BL (1951) On the comparison of several mean values: an alternative approach. Biometrika 38(3/4):330–336

Chapter 7
Regression Analysis

Learning Objectives

After reading this chapter, you should understand:
- What regression analysis is and what it can be used for.
- How to specify a regression analysis model.
- How to interpret basic regression analysis results.
- What the issues with, and assumptions of, regression analysis are.
- How to validate regression analysis results.
- How to conduct regression analysis in SPSS.
- How to interpret regression analysis output produced by SPSS.

Keywords Regression analysis · Errors · Residuals · Ordinary least squares · R^2 · Adjusted R^2 · F-test · Sample size · Linearity · Outliers · Heteroskedasticity · (Multi)collinearity · Autocorrelation · Durbin-Watson test · Kolmogorov-Smirnov test · Shapiro-Wilk test

> Many organizations, including Procter & Gamble, McKinsey & Company, and Nestlé use regression analysis to help make key marketing decisions. They can, for example, support decisions on pricing, trade promotions, advertising, and distribution with regression analysis. Regression analysis helps these organizations by providing precise quantitative information on which managers can base their decisions. In this chapter, we explain how you can use regression analysis for market research.

Introduction

Regression analysis is one of the most frequently used tools in market research. In its simplest form, regression analysis allows market researchers to analyze relationships between one independent and one dependent variable. In marketing applications, the dependent variable is usually the outcome we care about (e.g., sales), while the independent variables are the instruments we have to achieve those outcomes with

E. Mooi and M. Sarstedt, *A Concise Guide to Market Research*,
DOI 10.1007/978-3-642-12541-6_7, © Springer-Verlag Berlin Heidelberg 2011

(e.g., advertising). Regression analysis can provide insights that few other techniques can. The key benefits of using regression analysis are that it can:

1. Indicate if independent variables have a significant relationship with a dependent variable.
2. Indicate the relative strength of different independent variables' effects on a dependent variable.
3. Make predictions.

Knowing about the effects of independent variables on dependent variables can help market researchers in many different ways. For example, it can help direct spending if we know promotional activities significantly increases sales.

Knowing about the relative strength of effects is useful for marketers because it may help answer questions such as if sales depend more strongly on price or on advertising. Most importantly, regression analysis allows us to compare the effects of variables measured on different scales such as the effect of price changes (e.g., measured in USD) and the number of promotional activities.

Regression analysis can also help make predictions. For example, if we have data on sales, prices, and promotional activities, regression analysis could provide a precise answer to what would happen to sales if prices were to increase by 5% and promotional activities were to increase by 10%. Such precise answers can help (marketing) managers make sound decisions. Furthermore, by providing various scenarios, such as calculating the sales effects of price increases of 5%, 10%, and 15%, managers can evaluate marketing plans and create marketing strategies.

Understanding Regression Analysis

In the previous paragraph, we briefly discussed what regression can do and why it is a useful market research tool. But what is regression analysis all about? Regression analysis is a way of fitting a "best" line through a series of observations. Figure 7.1 plots a dependent (y) variable (weekly supermarket sales in USD) against an independent (x) variable (an index of promotional activities). With "best" line we mean that it is fitted in such a way that it results in the lowest sum of squared differences between the observations and the line itself. It is important to know that the best line fitted with regression analysis is not necessarily the true line (i.e., the line that holds in the population). Specifically, if we have data issues, or fail to meet the regression assumptions (discussed later), the estimated line may be biased in a certain way.

Before we start explaining regression analysis further, we should discuss regression notation. Regression models are generally described as follows:

$$y = \alpha + \beta_1 x_1 + e$$

What does this mean? The y represents the dependent variable, which is the variable you are trying to explain. In Fig. 7.1, we plot the dependent variable on

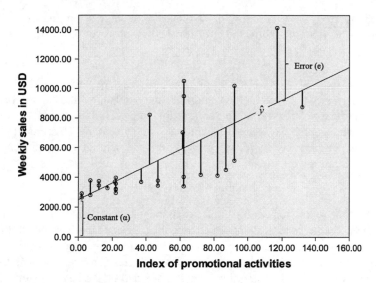

Fig. 7.1 A visual explanation of regression analysis

the vertical axis. The α represents the *constant* (sometimes called *intercept*) of the regression model, and indicates what your dependent variable would be if all of the independent variables were zero. In Fig. 7.1, you can see the constant indicated on the y-axis. If the index of promotional activities is zero, we expect sales of around 2,500 USD. It may of course not always be realistic to assume that independent variables are zero (just think of prices, these are rarely zero) but the constant is always included to make sure that the regression model has the best possible fit with the data.

The independent variable is indicated by x_1. As we have only one independent variable, we only see one x in our model. β_1 (pronounced as *beta*) indicates the (regression) coefficient of the independent variable. This coefficient represents the gradient of the line and is also referred to as the *slope*. A positive β_1 coefficient indicates an upward sloping regression line while a negative β_1 indicates a downward sloping line. In our example, the gradient slopes upward. This makes sense since sales tend to increase as promotional activities increase. In our example, we estimate β_1 as 55.968, meaning that if we increase promotional activities by one unit, sales will go up by 55.968 USD on average. In regression analysis, we can calculate whether this value (the β_1 parameter) differs significantly from zero by using t-tests.

The last element of the notation, the e denotes the *error* or *residual* of the equation. The term error is commonly used in research. However, SPSS refers to errors as residuals. If we use the word error, we discuss errors in a general sense. If we use residuals, we refer to specific output created by SPSS. The error is the distance between each observation and the best fitting line. To clarify what a regression error (or residual) is, consider Fig. 7.1 again. The error is the difference between the regression line (which represents our regression prediction) and the actual observation. The predictions made by the "best" regression line are indicated by $\hat{y}$ (pronounced *y-hat*). Thus, the error for the first observation is:[1]

$$e_1 = y_1 - \hat{y}_1$$

In the example above, we have only one independent variable. We call this *bivariate regression*. If we include multiple independent variables, we call this *multiple regression*. The notation for multiple regression is similar to that of bivariate regression. If we were to have three independent variables, say index of promotional activities (x_1), price of competitor 1 (x_2), and the price of competitor 2 (x_3), our notation would be:

$$y = \alpha + \beta_1 x_1 + \beta_2 x_2 + \beta_3 x_3 + e$$

We need one regression coefficient for each independent variable (i.e., β_1, β_2, and β_3). Technically the βs indicate how a change in an independent variable influences the dependent variable if all other independent variables are held constant.[2]

Now that we have introduced some basics of regression analysis, it is time to examine how to execute a regression analysis. We outline the key steps in Fig. 7.2. We first introduce the data requirements for regression analysis that determine if regression analysis can be used. After this first step, we specify and estimate the regression model. In this step, we discuss the basics, such as which independent variables to select. Thereafter, we discuss the assumptions of regression analysis. Next, we interpret and validate the model. The last step is to use the regression model to make predictions.

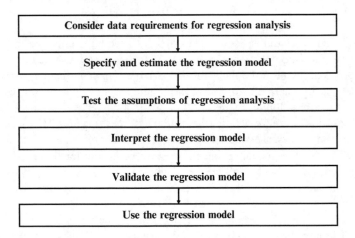

Fig. 7.2 Steps to conduct a regression analysis.

---

[1]Strictly speaking, the difference between predicted and observed y-values is $\hat{e}$.
[2]This only applies to the standardized βs.

Conducting a Regression Analysis

Consider Data Requirements for Regression Analysis

Several data requirements have to be considered before we undertake a regression analysis.

A first data requirement is that we need a sufficiently large sample size. Acceptable sample sizes relate to a minimum sample size where you have a good chance of finding significant results if they are actually present, and not finding significant results if these are not present. There are two ways to calculate "acceptable" sample sizes.

The first approach is the formal one in which we use power analysis to calculate the minimum sample size required to accept the regression outcomes with a particular level of confidence. As mentioned in Chap. 6 (Box 6.2), these calculations are difficult. Fortunately, the Internet offers a wide selection of downloadable applications and interactive Web programs that will simplify your work. Just google "power analysis calculator regression" and you will find numerous helpful sites. Most require you to specify several parameters, such as the number of independent variables or the sample size, to calculate the resulting level of power. By convention, 0.80 is an acceptable level of power. Kelley and Maxwell (2003) also discuss sample size requirements in this context.

The second approach is through rules of thumb. These rules are not specific to a situation and are easy to apply. Green (1991) proposes a rule of thumb for sample sizes in regression analysis. Specifically, he proposes that if you want to test the overall relationships between the independent and dependent variable, the number of observations is at least $50 + 8 \cdot k$ (where k are the number of independent variables). Thus, for a model with ten independent variables, you need $50 + 8 \times 10 = 130$ observations, or more. If you want to test for individual parameters' effect (i.e., if one coefficient is significant or not), Green proposes a sample size of $104 + k$. Thus, if you have ten independent variables, you need $104 + 10 = 114$ observations. If you are interested in both the general relationship, and the individual coefficients, you should take the higher number of required observations of the two formulas.[3]

A related data requirement is that the sample used is representative of the population (see Chap. 3 for a discussion on samples and populations). Imagine that we want to understand what drives the satisfaction of US car owners. If our sample is collected just from executives (who typically earn high incomes), our results may be biased, as high-income consumers usually own more expensive cars, such as a BMW, Lexus, or Mercedes, than the total population of US car owners. If

---

[3]Rules of thumb are almost never without drawbacks and caveats. For Green's formula, these are that you need a larger sample size than he proposes if you expect small effects (thus a low expected R^2 such as 0.10 or smaller). In addition, if the variables are poorly measured, or if you want to use a stepwise method, you need a larger sample size. With "larger" we mean around three times the required sample size if the expected R^2 is low, and about twice the required sample size in case of measurement errors or if stepwise methods are used.

we run regression analysis using such data, our results reflect those for executives, and not those of the population.

A third data requirement is that no regression model works if the variables have no variation. Specifically, if there is no variation in the dependent variable (i.e., it is a constant), we also do not need regression, as we already know what the dependent variable's outcome is. Likewise, if an independent variable has no variation, it cannot explain any variation in the dependent variable.

A fourth regression analysis data requirement is that the dependent variable needs to be interval or ratio scaled. To determine if data are interval or ratio scaled, consult Chap. 2. If the data are not interval or ratio scaled, alternative types of regression need to be used. You should use binary logistic regression if the dependent variable is binary and only takes on two values (e.g., zero and one). If the dependent variable consists of nominal variable with more than two levels, you can use multinomial logistic regression although OLS is also used for this purpose in practice. This should, for example, be used if you want to explain why people prefer product A over B or C. Finally, if the dependent variable is ordinally scaled (e.g., to predict first, second, and third choice) you should use ordinal regression. We do not discuss these different methods in this chapter, but they are intuitively similar to regression. For a comprehensible discussion of regression methods with dependent variables measured on a nominal or ordinal scale, see Field (2009).

The last data requirement is that no or little *collinearity* is present. Collinearity is a data issue that arises if two independent variables are highly correlated. If more than two independent variables are highly correlated, we talk about *multicollinearity*. *Perfect (multi)collinearity* occurs if we enter two (or more) independent variables with exactly the same information in them (i.e., they are perfectly correlated). This may happen because you entered the same independent variable twice, or because one variable is a linear combination of the other (e.g., one variable is a multiple of another variable such as sales in units and sales in thousands of units). If this occurs, regression analysis cannot estimate one of the two coefficients and SPSS will automatically drop one of the independent variables.

In practice, however, weaker forms of collinearity are common. For example, if we study how satisfied customers are with a restaurant, satisfaction with the waiter/waitress and satisfaction with the speed of service may be highly related. If this is so, there is little uniqueness in each variable, since both provide much the same information. The problem with these weaker forms of collinearity is that they tend to decrease the significance of independent variables.

Fortunately, collinearity is relatively easy to detect by calculating the *tolerance* or *VIF (Variance Inflation Factor)*. A tolerance of below 0.10 indicates that (multi) collinearity is a problem.[4] The VIF is just the reciprocal value of the tolerance. Thus, VIF values above ten indicate collinearity issues. We can produce these

---

[4]The tolerance is calculated using a completely separate regression analysis. In this regression analysis, the variable for which the tolerance is calculated is taken as a dependent variable and all other independent variables are entered as independents. The R^2 that results from this model is deducted from 1, thus indicating how much is *not explained* by the regression model. If very little is not explained by the other variables, (multi) collinearity is a problem.

statistics in SPSS by clicking on **Collinearity diagnostics** under the **Options** button found in the main regression dialog box of SPSS.

You can remedy collinearity in several ways. If perfect collinearity occurs, SPSS will automatically delete one of the perfectly overlapping variables. If weaker forms of collinearity occur, it is up to you to decide what to do. Firstly, if you have multiple overlapping variables, you could conduct a factor analysis first (see Chap. 8). Using factor analysis, you create a small number of factors that have most of the original variables' information in them but which are mutually uncorrelated. For example, through factor analysis you may find that satisfaction with the waiter/waitress and satisfaction with the speed of service fall under a factor called *service satisfaction*. If you use factors, collinearity between the original variables is no longer an issue. Alternatively, you could re-specify the regression model by removing highly correlated variables. Which variables should you remove? If you create a correlation matrix (see Chap. 5) of all the independent variables entered in the regression model, you should focus first on the variables that are most strongly correlated. Initially, try removing one of the two most strongly correlated variables. Which one you should remove is a matter of taste and depends on your analysis set-up. Another good way of identifying variables that cause multicollinearity is by looking at the condition index output in SPSS. Since this output is quite advanced, we refrain from discussing it in greater detail here. On Garson's Statnotes regression page (Box 7.1) you will find a brief explanation of this additional table.

Box 7.1 Advanced collinearity diagnostics

http://faculty.chass.ncsu.edu/garson/PA765/regressa.htm

Specify and Estimate the Regression Model

To conduct a regression analysis, we need to select the variables we want to include, decide on how they are included, and decide on how the model is estimated. Let's first show the main regression dialog box in SPSS to provide some idea of what we need to specify for a basic regression analysis. First open the dataset called *Sales data.sav* (⌐ Web Appendix → Chap. 7). These data contain information on supermarket sales per week in USD (*Sales*), the (average) price level (*Price*), and an index of promotional activities (*Promotion*), amongst other variables. After having opened the dataset, click on ▶ Analyze ▶ Regression ▶ Linear. This opens a box similar to Fig. 7.3.

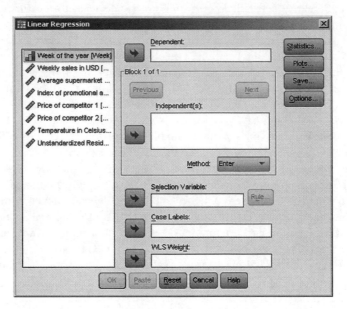

Fig. 7.3 The main regression dialog box in SPSS

For a basic regression model, we need to specify the **Dependent** variable and choose the **Independent(s)**. As discussed before, the dependent variable is the variable we care about as the outcome.

How do we select independent variables? Market researchers usually select independent variables on the basis of what the client wants to know and on prior research findings. For example, typical independent variables explaining the supermarket sales of a particular product include the price, promotional activities, level of in-store advertising, the availability of special price promotions, packaging type, and variables indicating the store and week. Market researchers may, of course, select different independent variables for other applications. A few practical suggestions to help you select variables:

– Never enter all the available variables at the same time. Carefully consider which independent variables may be relevant. Irrelevant independent variables may be significant due to chance (remember the discussion on hypothesis testing in Chap. 6) or can reduce the likelihood of determining relevant variables' significance.
– If you have a large number of variables that overlap in terms of how they are defined, such as satisfaction with the waiter/waitress and satisfaction with the speed of service, try to pick the variable that is most distinct. Alternatively, you

could conduct a factor analysis first and use the factor scores as input for the regression analysis (factor analysis is discussed in Chap. 8).

– Take the sample size rules of thumb into account. If practical issues limit the sample size to below the threshold recommended by the rules of thumb, use as few independent variables as possible. With larger sample sizes, you have more freedom to add independent variables, although they still need to be relevant.

For this example, we use *sales* as the dependent variable and *price* as well as the *index of promotional activities* as independent variables.

Once we know which variables we want to include, we need to specify if all of them should be used, or if – based on the significance of the findings – the analysis procedure can further select variables from this set. There are two general options to select variables under **Method** in Fig. 7.3. Either you choose the independent variables to be in the model yourself (the *enter* method) or you let a process select the best subset of variables available to you (a *stepwise* method). There are many different types of stepwise methods such as the *forward* and *backward* methods.

Starting with the constant (α) only, the forward method runs a very large number of separate regression models. Then it tries to find the best model by adding just one independent variable from the remaining variables. Subsequently it compares the results between these two models. If adding an independent variable produces a significantly better model, it proceeds by adding a second variable from the variables that remain. The resulting model (which includes the two independent variables) is then compared to the previous model (which includes one independent variable). This process is repeated until adding another variable does not improve the model significantly. The backward method does something similar but initially enters all variables that it may use and removes the least contributing independent variable until removing another makes the model significantly worse.

Choosing between the enter and stepwise methods means making a choice between letting the researcher or a procedure choose the best independent variables. We recommend using the enter method. Why? Because stepwise methods often result in adding variables that are only significant "by chance," rather than truly interesting or useful. Another problem with forward and backward methods is related to how regression deals with missing values. Regression can only estimate models when it has complete information on all the variables. If a substantial number of missing values are present, using backward or forward methods may result in adding variables that are only relevant for a subset of the data for which complete information is present. Generally, backward or forward models result in finding highly significant models that only use a small number of observations from the total number of available observations. In this case, a regression model results that fits a small set of the data well but not the whole data set or population. Finally, as a market researcher, you want to select variables that are meaningful for the decision-making process. You also need to think about the actual research problem, rather than choosing the variables that produce the "best model." Does this mean that the forward and backward methods are completely useless? Certainly not!

Market researchers commonly use stepwise methods to find their way around the data quickly and to develop a feel for relationships in the data.

After deciding on the variable selection process, we need to choose an estimation procedure. *Estimation* refers to how the "best line" we discussed earlier is calculated. SPSS estimates regression models by default, using *ordinary least squares (OLS)*. As indicated before, OLS estimates a regression line so that it minimizes the squared differences between each observation and the regression line. By squaring distances, OLS avoids negative and positive deviations from the regression line cancelling each other out. Moreover, by squaring the distances, OLS also puts greater weight on observations that are far away from the regression line. The sum of all these squared distances is called the *sum of squares* and is indicated in the SPSS output. While minimizing the sum of squares, OLS also ensures that the mean of all errors is always zero. Because the error is zero on average, researchers sometimes omit the *e* from the regression notation. Nevertheless, errors do occur in respect of individual observations (but not *on average*). Figure 7.1 illustrates this. Almost all observations fall above or below the regression line. However, if we calculate the mean of all the distances of regression points above and below the line, the result is exactly zero. In certain situations, OLS, does not work very well and we need to use alternative procedures such as *Weighted Least Squares (WLS)*. We briefly discuss when WLS should be used. Greene's (2007) work on WLS is a good source of further information. Greene also discusses other estimation procedures such as *Two-staged least squares* that are beyond the scope of this book.

A last point related to specifying and estimating the regression model is if we conduct just one regression analysis, or if we run multiple models. Market researchers typically choose to run many different models. A standard approach is to start with relatively simple models, such as with one, two, or three independent variables. These independent variables should be those variables you believe are the most important ones. You should start with just a few variables because adding further variables may cause the already entered variables to lose significance. If important decisions are made with a regression model, we need to be aware that sometimes variables that are significant in one model may no longer be significant if we add (or remove) variables. As discussed earlier, this is often due to collinearity. Once you have determined a number of key basic variables, you could (depending on the research purpose) add further independent variables until you have a model that satisfies your needs and does a good job of explaining the dependent variable. Generally, regression models have between 3 and 10 independent variables but bivariate regression models are also common. In specific applications, such as regression models that try to explain economic growth, regression models can have dozens of independent variables.

Test the Assumptions of Regression Analysis

We have already discussed several issues that determine if it is useful to run a regression analysis. We now turn to discussing regression analysis assumptions. If a regression analysis fails to meet the assumptions, regression analysis can provide invalid results. Four regression analysis assumptions are required to provide valid results:

- The regression model can be expressed in a linear way.
- The expected mean error of the regression model is zero.
- The variance of the errors is constant (homoskedasticity).
- The errors are independent (no autocorrelation).

A fifth assumption is optional. If we meet this assumption, we have information on how the regression parameters are distributed, thus allowing straightforward conclusions on their significance. If we fail to meet this assumption, the regression model will still be accurate but it becomes more difficult to determine the regression parameters' significance.

- The errors need to be approximately normally distributed.

We next discuss these assumptions and how we can test each of them.

The first assumption means that we can write the regression model as $y = \alpha + \beta_1 x_1 + e$. Thus, relationships such as $\beta_1^2 x_1$ are not permissible. On the other hand, expressions such as x_1^2 or $\log(x_1)$ are possible as the regression model is still specified in a linear way. As long as you can write a model where the regression parameters (the βs) are linear, you satisfy this assumption. You can, however, transform the x variables any way that is necessary to produce a best fitting regression line. For example, if you take the log of the x variable, the relationship between the y and x variables becomes non-linear, but you still satisfy this assumption because the β is linear. In practice, most relationships between x and y variables are linear but there are also many exceptions, sometimes quite dramatic ones.

Checking the linearity between y and x variables can be done by plotting the independent variables against the dependent variable. Using this scatter plot, we can then assess whether there is some type of non-linear pattern. Figure 7.4 shows such a plot. The straight line indicates a linear relationship. For illustration purposes, we have also added a dashed, upward sloping, and another downward sloping line. The upward sloping line corresponds to an x_1^2 transformation, while the downward sloping line corresponds to a $\log(x_1)$ transformation. For this particular data, it appears however that a linear line fits the data best. It is important to correctly specify the relationship, because if we specify a relationship as linear when it is in fact non-linear, the regression analysis results will be biased.

The second assumption is that the expected (not the estimated!) mean error is zero. If we do not expect the sum of the errors to be zero, we obtain a line that is biased. That is, we have a line that consistently over- or under-estimates the true relationship. This assumption is not testable by means of statistics, as OLS always renders a best line where the mean error is exactly zero. If this assumption is challenged, this is done on theoretical grounds. Imagine that we want to explain the weekly sales in USD of all US supermarkets. If we were to collect our data only in downtown areas, we would mostly sample smaller supermarkets. Thus, a regression model fitted using the available data would differ from those models obtained if we were to include all

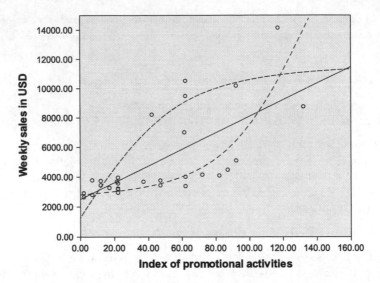

Fig. 7.4 Different relationships between promotional activities and weekly sales

supermarkets. Our error in the regression model (estimated as zero) therefore differs from the population as a whole (where the estimate should be truly zero). Furthermore, omitting important independent variables could cause the expected mean not to be zero. Simply put, if we were to omit a relevant variable x_2 from a regression model that only includes x_1, we induce a bias in the regression model. More precisely, β_1 is likely to be inflated, which means that the estimated value is higher than it should actually be. Thus, β_1 itself is biased because we omit x_2!

The third assumption is that the errors' variance is constant, a situation we frequently call *homoskedasticity*. Imagine that we want to explain the weekly sales of various supermarkets in USD. Clearly, large stores have a much larger spread in sales than small supermarkets. For example, if you have average weekly sales of 50,000 USD, you might see a sudden jump to 60,000 USD or a fall to 40,000 USD. However, a very large supermarket could see sales move from an average of 5,000,000–7,000,000 USD. This issue causes weekly sales' error variance to be much larger for large supermarkets than for small supermarkets. We call this non-constant variance *heteroskedasticity*. We visualize the increasing error variance of supermarket sales in Fig. 7.5, in which we can see that the errors increase as weekly sales increase.

If we estimate regression models on data in which the variance is not constant, they will still result in errors that are zero on average (i.e., our predictions are still correct), but this may cause some βs not to be significant, whereas, in reality, they are.

Unfortunately, there is no easy (menu-driven) way to test for heteroskedasticity in SPSS. Thus, understanding whether heteroskedasticity is present, is (if you use the SPSS menu functions) only possible on theoretical grounds and by creating graphs.

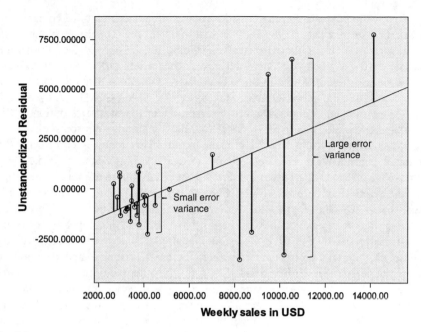

Fig. 7.5 The heteroskedasticity issue

On theoretical grounds, try to understand whether it is likely that the errors increase as the value of the dependent variable in(de)creases. If you want to visualize heteroskedasticity, it is best to plot the errors against the dependent variable, as in Fig. 7.5. As the dependent variable in(de)creases, the variance should not in(de)crease. If heteroskedasticity is an issue, the points are often funnel shaped, becoming more, or less, spread out across the graph. This funnel shape is typical of heteroskedasticity and indicates increasing variance across the errors.

If you think heteroskedasticity is an issue, SPSS can deal with it by using weighted least squares (WLS). Simply use the variable that you think causes the variance not to be constant (e.g., store size) and "weight" the results by this variable. Only use WLS if heteroskedasticity is a real concern. If WLS is used, and heteroskedasticity is no problem or the weight variable has not been chosen correctly, the regression results may be invalid.

The fourth assumption is that the regression model errors are independent; that is, the error terms are uncorrelated for any two observations.

Imagine that you want to explain the sales of a particular supermarket using that supermarket's previous week sales. It is very likely that if sales increased last week, they will also increase this week. This may be due to, for example, a growing economy, or other reasons that underlie supermarket sales growth. This issue is called *autocorrelation* and means that regression errors are correlated positively, or negatively, over time. Fortunately, we can identify this issue using the Durbin–Watson test. The *Durbin–Watson test* assesses whether there is autocorrelation by testing a null hypothesis of no autocorrelation. If this is rejected, we find support for an alternative hypothesis that there is some degree of autocorrelation. To carry out this test, first sort the data on the variable that indicates the time dimension in your data, if you have this. Otherwise, the test should not be carried out. With time dimension, we mean that you have at least two observations collected from a single respondent at different points in time. Do this by going to ▶ Data ▶ Sort Cases. Then enter your time variable under **Sort by:** and click on **OK**. To carry out the actual test, you need to check **Durbin–Watson** under the **Statistics** option of the main regression dialog box in SPSS. SPSS calculates a Durbin–Watson statistic, but does not indicate if the test is significant or not. This requires comparing the calculated Durbin–Watson value with the critical Durbin–Watson value. These Durbin–Watson values lie between 0 and 4. Essentially, there are three situations. First, the errors may be positively related (called *positive autocorrelation*). This means that if we take observations ordered according to time, we observe that positive errors are typically followed by positive errors and that negative errors are typically followed by negative errors. For example, supermarket sales usually increase over certain periods in time (e.g., before Christmas) and decrease in other periods (e.g., the summer holidays). If, on the other hand, positive errors are commonly followed by negative errors and vice-versa, we have *negative autocorrelation*. Negative autocorrelation is less common than positive autocorrelation, but also occurs. If we study, for example, how much time salespeople spend on shoppers, we may see that if they spend much time on one shopper, they spend less time on the next, allowing the salesperson to stick to his/her schedule or simply go home on time. If no systematic pattern of errors occurs, we have no autocorrelation. These Durbin–Watson values are used to test a null hypothesis of no autocorrelation. Depending on the calculated Durbin–Watson test statistic values, we can draw three different conclusions:

– The calculated Durbin–Watson value falls below the lower critical value. In this case, we have negative autocorrelation.
– The calculated Durbin–Watson value falls above the upper critical value. In this case, we have positive autocorrelation.
– The calculated Durbin–Watson value falls in between the lower and higher critical value. In this case, we have no autocorrelation.

The critical values can be found on the website accompanying this book (⌁ Web Appendix → Chap. 7). From this table, you can see that the lower critical value of a model with five independent variables and 200 observations is 1.718 and the upper critical value is 1.820. If the Durbin–Watson test concludes that there is no autocorrelation, you can proceed with the regression model. If the Durbin–Watson test indicates autocorrelation, you may have to use models that account for this problem, such as panel and time-series models. We do not discuss these in this book, but a useful source of further information is Hill et al. (2008).

The fifth, optional, assumption is that the regression model errors are approximately normally distributed. If this is not the case, the t-values may be incorrect. However, even if the errors of the regression model are not normally distributed, the regression model still provides good estimates of the coefficients, particularly if the sample size used is reasonably large (above the recommended minimum sample size discussed previously). Therefore, we consider this assumption as optional.

Potential reasons for non-normality include outliers (discussed in Box 7.2) and a non-linear relationship between an independent and a dependent variable.

Box 7.2 Outliers

Outliers can influence regression results dramatically. When running regression analysis, it is important to be aware of outliers in the data. Study Fig. 7.6. The observation in the upper left corner (indicated with the solid circle) is probably an outlier as it differs very much from all the other observations. Without the outlier, the slope of the regression line (indicated by the dashed line) is positive. If we include the outlier, the slope becomes negative. Including the outlier produces an effect that is opposite to the results without it!

We can detect outliers in several ways. We can try to detect outliers by looking at one variable at a time, by looking at the relationship between two variables, or by looking at a regression model's errors. Next, we discuss several ways to identify outliers, which should always be used as each method has its advantages and disadvantages.

If we investigate one variable at a time, we can calculate the minimum and maximum of each variable and see if unexpectedly high or low values occur. If the minimum or maximum falls outside the expected range, for example, because we have made a typing error, we can identify that observation and subsequently run a regression model without that observation. Researchers often consider values more than three standard deviations away from the mean as potential outliers.

Scatter plots are another good way to identify outliers that are the result of a combination of extreme values for two variables. For example, if we look at Fig. 7.6, we can see that the observation in the upper right corner is very different in that it is both very high on the y-axis and on the x-axis. These kinds of observations can strongly influence the results, much more so than if the outlier only had very high x or y values.

We can also check if the regression errors of some observations are very large. This is particularly important if the regression model has multiple independent variables. SPSS can do this using **Casewise Diagnostics**, which is included in the **Statistics** option included in the main regression dialog box. Casewise diagnostics indicate if large errors occur. Remember that errors are very large if the particular observation is very far away from the regression line. If a particular observation's error is large, that observation "pulls" the regression line upwards (if the error is positive) or downwards (if the error is negative). Regression errors that occur at extreme values for the independent variable are particularly influential, because these have a great deal of "leverage," meaning they may shift the entire line up (or down) and change the slope of the line (from

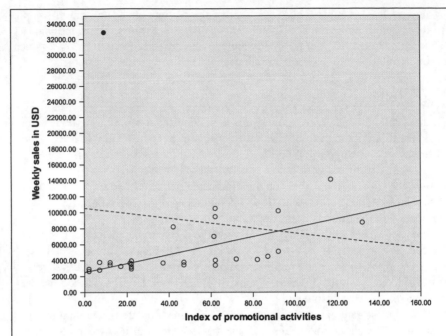

Fig. 7.6 Outliers

positive to negative and vice versa). In Chap. 5, we further discuss how to identify outliers and how to deal with them.

The critical decision with outliers is whether they should be retained, transformed, or deleted. This decision is somewhat arbitrary as there are no fixed recommendations on what to do. The only fixed recommendation is that if outliers are deleted, you should clearly indicate why you have chosen to do so.

There are two main ways of checking for normally distributed errors, either you use plots or you can perform a formal test. The plots are easily explained and interpreted and may suggest the source of non-normality (if present). The formal test may indicate non-normality and provide absolute standards. However, the formal test results reveal little about the source of non-normality.

To test for non-normality using plots, first save the unstandarized errors by going to the **Save** dialog box in the regression menu. Then create a histogram of these errors and plot a normal curve in it to understand if any deviations from normality are present. We can make histograms by going to ▶ Graphs ▶ Legacy Dialogs ▶ Histogram. Make sure to check **Display normal curve**. The result may look something like Fig. 7.7. How do we interpret this figure? If we want the errors to be approximately normally distributed, the bars should end very "close" to the normal curve, which is the black bell-shaped curve. What "close" means exactly, is open to different interpretations, but Fig. 7.7 suggests that the errors produced by the estimated regression model are almost normally distributed.

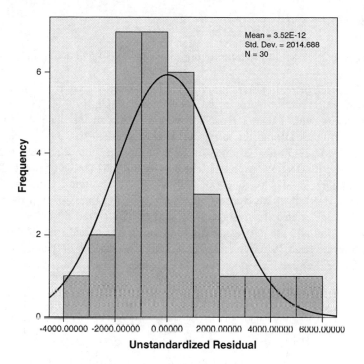

Fig. 7.7 Histogram of the errors

Table 7.1 Output produced by the Shapiro–Wilk test

Tests of Normality

	Kolmogorov-Smirnov[a]			Shapiro-Wilk		
	Statistic	df	Sig.	Statistic	df	Sig.
Unstandardized Residual	.131	30	.200[*]	.939	30	.084

a. Lilliefors Significance Correction

*. This is a lower bound of the true significance.

Since we have less than 50 observations in our dataset, we should use the Shapiro–Wilk test (see Chap. 6) as a formal test of normality. As we can easily see, the Shapiro–Wilk test result indicates that the errors are normally distributed as we cannot reject the null hypothesis at a significance level of 5% (p-value = 0.084) (Table 7.1).

Interpret the Regression Model

In the previous sections, we discussed how to specify a basic regression model and how to test regression assumptions. We now turn to discussing the fit of the regression model.

Overall Model Fit

We can assess the overall model fit using the (adjusted) R^2 and significance of the F-value.

The R^2 (or *coefficient of determination*) indicates the degree to which the model explains the observed variation in the dependent variable. In Fig. 7.8, we explain this graphically with a scatter plot. The y-axis relates to the dependent variable (weekly sales in USD) and the x-axis to the independent variable (price). In the scatter plot, we see 30 observations of sales and price (note that we use a small sample size for illustration purposes). The horizontal line (at about 5,000 USD sales per week) refers to the average sales of all 30 observations. This is also our benchmark. After all, if we were to have no regression line, our best estimate of the weekly sales is also the average. The sum of all squared differences between each observation and the average is the total variation or total sum of the squares (usually referred to as SS_T). We indicate the total variation for only one observation on the right of the scatter plot.

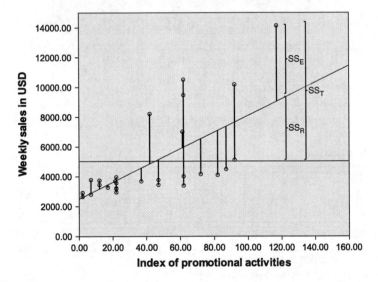

Fig. 7.8 Explanation of the R^2

The upward sloping line (starting at the y-axis at about 2,500 USD sales per week) is the regression line that is estimated using OLS. If we want to understand what the regression model adds beyond the average (the benchmark), we can calculate the difference between the regression line and the average. We call this the regression sum of the squares (usually abbreviated SS_R) as it is the variation in the data that is explained by the regression analysis. The final point we need to understand regarding how well a regression line fits the available data, is the unexplained sum of squares. This refers to the regression error that we discussed previously and which is consequently denoted as SS_E. In more formal terms, we can describe these types of variation as follows:

$$SS_T = SS_R + SS_E$$

This is the same as:

$$\sum_{i=1}^{n} (y_i - \bar{y})^2 = \sum_{i=1}^{n} (\hat{y}_i - \bar{y})^2 + \sum_{i=1}^{n} (y_i - \hat{y}_i)^2$$

Here, n describes the number of observations, y_i is the value of the independent variable for observation i, $\hat{y}_i$ is the predicted value of observation i and $\bar{y}$ is the mean value of y. As you can see, this description is very similar to the one-way ANOVA, discussed in Chap. 6. A good regression line should explain a substantial amount of variation (have a high SS_R) relative to the total variation (SS_T). This is the R^2 and we can calculate this as:

$$R^2 = \frac{SS_R}{SS_T}$$

The R^2 always lies between 0 and 1, where a higher R^2 indicates a better model fit. When interpreting the R^2, higher values indicate that more of the variation in y is explained by variation in x, and therefore that the SS_E is low. The R^2 is the total relationship between the independent variables and the dependent variable. It is difficult to provide rules of thumb regarding what R^2 is appropriate, as this varies from research area to research area. For example, in longitudinal studies R^2s of 0.90 and higher are common. In cross-sectional designs, values of around 0.30 are common while for exploratory research, using cross-sectional data, values of 0.10 are typical.

If we use the R^2 to compare different regression models (but with the same dependent variable), we run into problems. If we add irrelevant variables that are slightly correlated with the dependent variable, the R^2 will increase. Thus, if we use the R^2 as the only basis for understanding regression model fit, we are biased towards selecting regression models with many independent variables. Selecting a model only based on the R^2 is plainly not a good strategy, as we want regression models that do a good job of explaining the data (thus a low SS_E), but which also have few independent variables (these are called *parsimonious models*). We do not want too many independent variables because this makes the regression model results less actionable. It is easier to recommend that management changes a few key variables to improve an outcome than to recommend a long list of somewhat related variables. Of course, relevant variables should always be included. To quote Albert Einstein: "Everything should be made as simple as possible, but not simpler!"

To avoid a bias towards complex models, we can use the *adjusted R^2* to select regression models. The adjusted R^2 only increases if the addition of another independent variable explains a substantial amount of variance. We calculate the adjusted R^2 as follows:

$$R^2_{adj} = 1 - (1 - R^2) \cdot \frac{n - 1}{n - k - 1}$$

Here, n describes the number of observations and k the number of independent variables (not counting the constant α). This adjusted R^2 is a relative measure and should be used to compare different regression models with the same dependent variable. You should pick the model with the highest adjusted R^2 when comparing regression models.

However, do not blindly use the adjusted R^2 as a guide, but also look at each individual variable and see if it is relevant (practically) for the problem you are researching. Furthermore, it is important to note that we cannot interpret the adjusted R^2 as the percentage of explained variance in the sample used for regression analysis. The adjusted R^2 is only a measure of how much the model explains while controlling for model complexity.

Besides the (adjusted) R^2, the F-test is an important determinant of model fit. The test statistic's F-value is the result of a one-way ANOVA (see Chap. 6) that tests the null hypothesis that all regression coefficients together are equal to zero. Thus, the following null hypothesis is tested:

$$H_0 : \beta_1 = \beta_2 = \beta_3 = \ldots = 0$$

The alternative hypothesis is that at least one β differs from zero. Thus, if we reject this null hypothesis, we conclude that the model is most likely useful. However, if the regression coefficients were all equal to zero, then the effect of all the independent variables on the dependent variable is zero. In other words, there is no (zero) relationship between the dependent variable and the independent variables. If we do not reject the null hypothesis, we need to change the regression model or, if this is not possible, report that the regression model is insignificant.

The test statistic's F-value closely resembles the F-statistic, as discussed in Chap. 6 and is also directly related to the R^2 we discussed previously. We can calculate the F-value as follows:

$$F = \frac{\frac{SS_R}{k}}{\frac{SS_E}{n} - k - 1} = \frac{R^2}{1 - R^2} \cdot \frac{n - k - 1}{k}$$

The F-statistic follows an F-distribution with k and $(n - k - 1)$ degrees of freedom. Finding that the p-value of the F-test is below 0.05 (i.e., a significant model), does not, however, automatically mean that all of our regression coefficients are significant or even that one of them is, when considered in isolation, significant. This is due to testing differences – the F-test is used for the entire model, and the t-test for individual parameters – and due to issues such as multicollinearity.

However, if the F-value is significant, it is highly likely that at least one or more regression coefficients are significant.

When we interpret the model fit, the F-test is the most critical, as it determines if the overall model is significant. If the model is insignificant, we do not interpret the model further. If the model is significant, we proceed by interpreting individual variables.

Effects of Individual Variables

After having established that the overall model is significant and that the R^2 is satisfactory, we need to interpret the effects of the various independent variables used to explain the dependent variable. First, we need to look at the t-values reported for each individual parameter. These t-values are similar to those discussed in Chap. 6 in the context of hypothesis testing. If a regression coefficient's p-value (indicated in SPSS by the column headed by **Sig.**) is below 0.05, we generally say that that particular independent variable has a significant influence on the dependent variable

To be precise, the null and alternative hypotheses tested for an individual parameter (e.g., β_1) are:

$$H_0 : \beta_1 = 0$$

$$H_1 : \beta_1 \neq 0$$

If a coefficient is significant (meaning we reject the null hypothesis), we also need to look at the unstandardized β coefficient and the standardized β coefficient. The unstandardized β coefficient indicates the effect of a 1-unit increase in the independent variable (on the scale in which the original independent variable is measured) on the dependent variable. Thus it is the partial relationship between a single independent variable and the dependent variable. At the very beginning of this chapter, we learned that there is a positive relationship between promotional activities and the weekly sales in USD with a β_1 coefficient of 55.968. This means that if we increase promotional activities by one unit, weekly sales will go up by 55.968 USD. In other cases, the effect could of course also be negative (e.g., increasing prices reduces sales). Importantly, if we have multiple independent variables, the unstandardized β_1 coefficient is the effect of an increase of that independent variable by one unit, keeping the other independent variables constant.

While this is a very simple example, we might run a multiple regression in which the independent variables are measured on different scales, such as in USD, units sold, or on Likert scales. Consequently, the independent variables' effects cannot be directly compared with one another as their influence also depends on the type of scale used. Comparing the (unstandardized) β coefficients would in any case amount to comparing apples with oranges!

Fortunately, the standardized βs allow us to compare the relative effect of differently measured independent variables. This is achieved by expressing β as standard deviations with a mean of zero. The standardized βs coefficient expresses the effect of a single standardized deviation change of the independent variable on the dependent variable. All we need to do is to look at the highest absolute value. This value indicates which variable has the strongest effect on the dependent variable. The second highest absolute value indicates the second strongest effect, etc. Only consider the significant βs in this respect, as insignificant βs do not (statistically) differ from zero! Practically, the standardized β is important, because it allows us to ask questions on what, for example, the relative effect of promotional activities is relative to decreasing prices. It can therefore guide management decisions.

However, while the standardized βs are helpful from a practical point of view, there are two problems associated with their usage. First, standardized β allow comparing the coefficients only within and not between models! Even if you add just a single variable to your regression model, standardized βs may change substantially. Second, standardized βs are not meaningful when the independent variable is a binary variable. Standardized βs provide insight into the unique (as opposed to total) relationship with the dependent variable. In certain situations, however, it may seem that one independent variable has a slight relationship with the dependent variable (low standardized β), even if the actual (total) effects are strong. This happens if this variable exhibits high correlations with other independent variables (multicollinearity) which exert a stronger influence on the dependent than itself.

When interpreting (standardized) β coefficients, you should always keep the effect size in mind. If a β coefficient is significant, it indicates some effect that differs from zero. However, this does not necessarily mean that it is managerially relevant. For example, we may find that increasing promotional activities' unstandardized effect on sales in USD is just 0.01, yet statistically significant. Statistically we could conclude that the effect of a single increase in promotional activities increases sales by an average of 0.01 USD (just one dollar cent). While this effect differs significantly from zero, in practice we would probably not recommend increasing promotional activities (we would lose money at the margin) as the effect size is just too small. An interesting perspective on significance and effect sizes is offered by Cohen's (1994) classical article "The Earth is Round (p $<.05$)."

Validate the Regression Model

After we have checked for the assumptions of regression analysis and interpreted the results, we need to check for the *stability* of the regression model. Stability means that the results are stable over time, do not vary across different situations, and do not depend heavily on the model's specification. We can check for the stability of a regression model in several ways.

First, we could validate the regression results by splitting our data into two parts (called *split-sample validation*) and run the regression model again on each subset of data. 70% of the randomly chosen data are often used to estimate the regression model and the remaining 30% are used for comparison purposes. We can only split the data if the remaining 30% still meets the sample size rules of thumb discussed earlier. If the use of the two samples results in similar effects, we can conclude that the model is stable.

Second, we can also cross-validate our findings on a new dataset and see if those findings are similar to the original findings. Again, similarity in the findings indicates stability and that our regression model is properly specified. This, naturally, assumes that we have a second dataset.

Lastly, we could add a number of alternative variables to the model. But we would need to have more variables available than included in the regression model to do so. For example, if we try to explain weekly supermarket sales, we could use a number of "key" variables (e.g., the breadth of the assortment or downtown/non-downtown location) in our regression model to help us. Once we have a suitable regression model, we could use these variables. If the basic findings of, for example, promotional activities are the same for stores with a differing assortment width or store location (i.e. the assortment width and location are not significant), we conclude that the effects are stable. However, it might also be the opposite, but whatever the case, we want to know.

Note that not all regression models need to be identical when you try to validate the results. The signs of the individual parameters should at least be consistent and significant variables should remain so, except if they are marginally significant, in which case changes are expected (e.g., p = 0.045 becomes p = 0.051).

Table 7.2 summarizes (on the left side) the major theoretical decisions we need to make if we want to run a regression model. On the right side, these decisions are then "translated" into SPSS actions, which are related to these theoretical decisions.

Table 7.2 Key steps involved in carrying out a regression analysis

Theory	Execution in SPSS
Issues with regression analysis	
Is the sample size sufficient?	Check if sample size is 50 + 8 k or 104 + k, where *k* indicates the number of independent variables.
Is the sample representative?	Check the recommendations made in Chap. 3.
Do the dependent and independent variables show variation?	Calculate the standard deviation of the variables by going to ▶ Analyze ▶ Descriptive Statistics ▶ Descriptives ▶ Options (check **Std. Deviation**). At the very least, the standard deviation should be a positive value.
Is the dependent variable interval or ratio scaled?	Use Chap. 2 to determine the measurement level.
Is (multi)collinearity present?	Check for tolerance and VIF. Do this with ▶ Analyze ▶ Regression ▶ Linear ▶ Statistics (check **Collinearity diagnostics**). The tolerance should be above 0.10. VIF should be below 10.
Specifying and estimating the regression model	
Select variables based on theory or based on strength of effects	Preferably use the enter method. If stepwise methods are used (such as the forward method), only add

(continued)

Table 7.2 (continued)

Theory	Execution in SPSS
	variables that could have a relationship with the dependent variable. Do not add all variables regardless.
Testing the assumptions of regression analysis	
Is the relationship between the independent and dependent variables linear?	Consider whether you can write the regression model as $y = \alpha + \beta_1 x_1 + \ldots + e$. To understand if the independent variables are linearly related to the dependent variable, plot the y variables separately against the dependent variable of the regression model. Create scatter plots using ▶ Graphs ▶ Legacy Dialogs ▶ Scatter/ Dot (choose **Simple Scatter**). If you see a non-linear pattern showing up, non-linearity is an issue. To specify a different relationship, see the *transform variables* section in Chap. 5.
Is the expected mean error of the regression model zero?	No actions in SPSS. Choice made on theoretical grounds.
Are the errors constant (no heteroskedasticity)?	Plot the residual of the regression model on the y-axis and the dependent variable on the x-axis, using a scatter plot by means of ▶ Graphs ▶ Legacy Dialogs ▶ Scatter/Dot (choose **Simple Scatter**). If you see that the errors in/decrease as the dependent variable increases, the variance of the errors is not constant. You can use WLS to remedy this.
Test whether the errors are not correlated with one another	First assess if there is a time component to the data (i.e., multiple observations, across time, from one respondent/object). If there is, sort the data according to the time variable and conduct the Durbin–Watson test. Compare the calculated Durbin–Watson value with the critical values. If autocorrelation is present and panel or time-series models need to be used: ▶ Analyze ▶ Regression ▶ Linear ▶ Statistics and check the **Durbin–Watson** box.
Are the errors normally distributed?	Create a histogram of the errors with a standard normal curve in it: ▶ Graphs ▶ Legacy Dialogs ▶ Histogram and enter the saved errors. Also check Display normal curve. Calculate the Kolmogorov-Smirnov test (for $n \geq 50$) or Shapiro–Wilk test (for $n < 50$). ▶ Analyze ▶ Descriptive Statistics ▶ Explore ▶ Plots and check the **Normality plots with tests** box.
Interpret the regression model Consider the overall model fit.	Check the R^2 and adjusted R^2 and significance of the F-value.
Consider the effects of the independent variables separately.	Check the (standardized) β. Also check the sign of the β. Consider significance of the t-value.
Validate the model Are the results robust?	Split the file into subsets or run the regression model against another sample to check for robustness. Add additional variables that may be useful and check if a similar regression model results.

Use the Regression Model

When we have found a useful regression model that satisfies the assumptions of regression analysis, it is time to use the regression model. A key use of regression models is *prediction*. Essentially, prediction entails calculating the values of the dependent variable based on assumed values of the independent variables and their related but previously calculated unstandardized β coefficients. Let us illustrate this by returning to our opening example. Imagine that we are trying to predict weekly supermarket sales (in USD) (y) and have estimated a regression model with two independent variables: the average price (x_1) and an index of promotional activities (x_2). The regression model for this is as follows:

$$y = \alpha + \beta_1 x_1 + \beta_2 x_2 + e$$

Table 7.3 Table containing sample regression coefficients[a]

Coefficients[a]

Model		Unstandardized Coefficients		Standardized Coefficients	t	Sig.
		B	Std. Error	Beta		
1	(Constant)	29011.585	18448.456		1.573	.127
	Price of product	−24003.037	16694.676	−.241	−1.438	.162
	Index of promotional activities	44.227	13.567	.547	3.260	.003

a. Dependent Variable: Weekly sales in USD

If we estimate this model on a dataset, the estimated coefficients using regression analysis could be similar to those in Table 7.3.

We can also use these coefficients to make predictions of sales in different situations. Imagine, for example, that we have set the price at 1.10 USD and promotional activities at 50. Our expectation of the weekly sales would then be:

$\hat{y} = 29{,}011.585 - 24{,}003.037 \times 1.10 \text{ USD} + 44.227 \times 50 \text{ promotional activities}$
$= 4{,}819.594 \text{ USD sales per week.}$

We could also build several scenarios to plan for different situations, by, for example, increasing the price to 1.20 and reducing promotional activities to 40. Regression models can be used like this to, for example, automate stocking and logistical planning or develop strategic marketing plans.

Another way in which regression can help is by providing insight into variables' specific effects. For example, if the effect of price is not significant, it may tell managers that the supermarket's sales are relatively insensitive to pricing decisions. Alternatively, the strength of promotional activities' effect may help managers understand whether promotional activities are useful and worth the expenditure.

Example

In the example, we take a closer look at the American Customer Satisfaction Index (*ACSI Data.sav*, ⏏ Web Appendix → Chap. 7). Every year, the American Customer Satisfaction Index (ACSI) surveys about 80,000 Americans about their level of satisfaction with a number of products and services. These satisfaction scores are used to benchmark competitors and to rate industries. For example, towards the end of 2007, the H.J. Heinz Company, Hershey Company, and Mars Incorporated were rated as the three food manufacturers with the highest scores. If you go to http://www.theacsi.org, you will find the current scores for various industries.[5] The ACSI data contain several variables, but we only focus on the following (variable names in parentheses):

- *Overall Customer Satisfaction (lvsat)* is measured by statements put to consumers about their overall satisfaction, expectancy disconfirmation (degree to which performance falls short of, or exceeds, expectations) and performance versus the customer's ideal product or service in the category.
- *Customer Expectations (lvexpect)* is measured by statements put to consumers about their overall expectations of quality (prior to purchase), their expectation regarding to how well the product fits the customer's personal requirements (prior to purchase), and expectation regarding reliability, or how often things will go wrong (prior to purchase).
- *Perceived Value (lvvalue)* is the consumers' rating of quality given price, and price given quality.
- *Customer Complaints (lvcomp)* captures whether or not the customer has complained formally or informally about the product or service (1 = yes, 0 = no).

The data included is a set of n = 1,640 responses provided by customers, but due to non-response, the actual number of responses for each variable is lower.

Consider Data Requirements for Regression Analysis

First we need to check if our sample size is sufficient. By calculating descriptive statistics (▶ Analyze ▶ Descriptive Statistics ▶ Descriptives; see Chap. 5) of the four above mentioned variables we can see that we have 1,640 valid listwise observations. This means that we have complete information for 1,640 observations. This is far above the minimum sample sizes as recommended by Green

---

[5]For an application of the ACSI, see, for example, Ringle et al. (2010).

Example 187

(1991). Although we have no further information on the sampling process, we assume that this has been correctly done. Looking at the dependent and independent variables' variance, we can also see that all variables show variation. Finally, as our dependent variable is also ratio scaled, we can proceed with regression analysis. Multicollinearity might be an issue, but we can only check this thoroughly after running a regression analysis. We will therefore discuss this later.

Specify and Estimate the Regression Model in SPSS

Although it is useful to know who comes out on top, from a marketing perspective, it is more useful to know how organizations can increase their satisfaction. We can use regression for this and explain how a number of independent variables relate to satisfaction. Simply click on ▶ Analyze ▶ Regression ▶ Linear and then enter *Overall Customer Satisfaction* into the **Dependent** box and *Customer Expectations, Perceived Value*, and *Customer Complaints* into the **Independent(s)** box. Figure 7.9 shows the regression dialog box in SPSS.

SPSS provides us with a number of options. Under **Method** choose **Enter**. The enter option includes all variables added into the **Independent(s)** box and does not remove any of the variables on statistical grounds (as opposed to the stepwise methods). Under **Statistics** in the main regression dialog box (see Fig. 7.10), SPSS

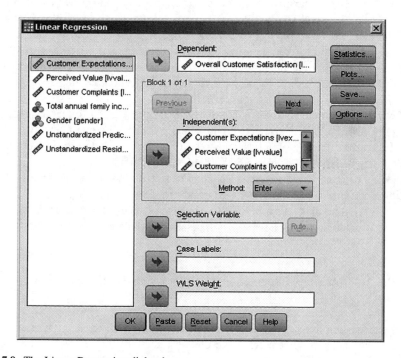

Fig. 7.9 The Linear Regression dialog box

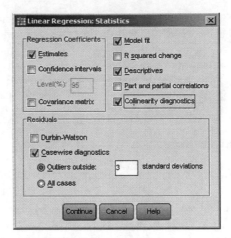

Fig. 7.10 The statistics dialog box

offers several options on the output that you may want to see. The **Estimates** and **Model fit** options are checked by default and are essential. The **Confidence intervals** and **Covariance matrix** options are not necessary for standard analysis purposes, so we skip these. The **R squared change** option is only useful if you select any of the stepwise methods but is irrelevant if you use the (recommended) enter option. The **Descriptives** option does what it says and provides the mean, standard deviation, and number of observations for the dependent and independent variables. The **Part and partial correlations** option produces a correlation matrix, while the **Collinearity diagnostics** option checks for (multi)collinearity. The **Durbin–Watson** option checks for autocorrelation, while **Casewise diagnostics** provides outlier diagnostics. In this case, there is no time component to our data and thus the Durbin–Watson test is not applicable.

Next, make sure the **Estimates**, **Model fit**, **Descriptives**, **Collinearity diagnostics**, and **Casewise diagnostic** options are checked. Then click on **Continue**. In the main regression dialog box, click on **Save**. This displays a dialog box similar to Fig. 7.11. Here, you can save predicted values and residuals.

Check the boxes **Unstandardized** under **Predicted Values** and **Residuals**. After clicking on **Continue** in the **Linear Regression: Save** dialog box and **OK** in the **Linear Regression** dialog box, SPSS runs a regression analysis and saves the residuals as a new variable in your dataset. We will discuss all the output in detail below.

Test the Assumptions of Regression Analysis Using SPSS Regression Output

To test the assumptions, we need to run three separate analyses.

First, we check for linearity. If we create a scatter plot of *Overall Customer Satisfaction* against *Customer Expectations*, SPSS produces Fig. 7.12. This plot

Example   189

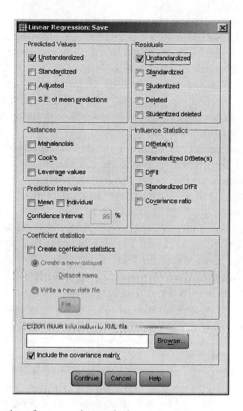

Fig. 7.11 The Save options for regression analysis

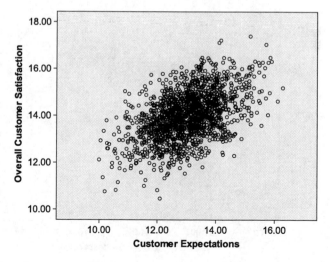

Fig. 7.12 Overall customer satisfaction against customer expectations

seems to suggest a linear relationship between the two variables. For a full analysis, we should plot every separate independent variable against the dependent variable. Try this yourself and you will see that the other independent variables are also linearly related to *Overall Customer Satisfaction*. Note that *Perceived Value* includes a clear outlier but with or without this outlier the relationship is still linear. Also note that if we include variables that take on few different values, such as *Customer Complaints* that only takes on the values of 0 and 1, linearity is hard to spot. Overall, the first assumption is fulfilled.

Next, we have to check if the regression model's expected mean error is zero (second assumption). Remember, this choice is made on theoretical grounds. We have a randomly drawn sample from the population and a model is similar in specification to other models explaining customer satisfaction. This makes it highly likely that the regression model's expected mean error is zero.

The third assumption is that of homoskedasticity. To test for this, we plot the errors against the dependent variable. Do this by going to ▶ Graphs ▶ Legacy Dialogs ▶ Scatter/Dot (choose **Simple Scatter**). Enter the *Unstandardized Residual* to the **Y-axis** and put *Overall Customer Satisfaction* to the **X-axis**. Then click on **OK**.

SPSS then produces a plot similar to Fig. 7.13. The results do not suggest heteroskedasticity. Note that it clearly seems that there is an outlier present. By looking at the **Casewise Diagnostics** in Table 7.4, we can further investigate this issue (note we have set Casewise diagnostics to "Outliers outside: 2 standard deviations" to be conservative).

Cases where the errors are high indicate that those cases influence the results. SPSS assumes by default (see Fig. 7.10 under **Outliers outside: 3 standard deviations**) that observations that are three standard deviations away from the

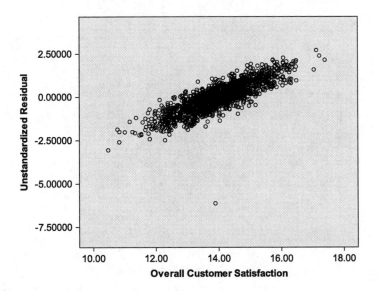

Fig. 7.13 A plot of the errors against the predicted values

Example   191

Table 7.4 Casewise diagnostics[a]

Casewise Diagnostics[a]

Case Number	Std. Residual	Weekly sales in USD	Predicted Value	Residual
8	2.466	14134.00	8984.7644	5149.23563
18	2.241	10512.00	5832.2042	4679.79581

a. Dependent Variable: Weekly sales in USD

mean are potential outliers. The results in Table 7.4 suggest that there are four potential outliers. Case 257 has the strongest influence on the results (the standardized error is the highest). Should we delete these four cases? If we have many observations (as in this example) and only few outliers, we should avoid deleting these. However, case 257 seems to be very far away from the other observations (also see Fig. 7.13) and should be deleted. The other potential outliers appear to be simply part of the data, and don't much influence results, thus they should be included.

If we delete a case from the initial dataset, we have to re-run the model. When doing so, we have to re-consider the assumptions we just discussed based on the newly estimated unstandardized residuals. However, we refrain from displaying the results twice – just try it yourself! Let's instead continue by discussing the remaining two (partly optional) assumptions using the dataset without the outlier.

If we had data with a time component, we would also perform the Durbin–Watson test to test for potential autocorrelation (fourth assumption). However, since the data do not include any time component, we should not conduct this test.

Lastly, we should explore how the errors are distributed. Do this by going to ▶ Graphs ▶ Legacy Dialogs ▶ Histogram. Enter the *Unstandardized Residual* under **Variable**. Also make sure that you check **Display normal curve**. In Fig. 7.14, we show a histogram of the errors.

Figure 7.14 suggest that our data are normally distributed as the bars indicating the frequency of the errors generally follow the normal curve. However, we can check this further by conducting the Kolmogorov-Smirnov test (with Lilliefors correction) by going to ▶ Analyze ▶ Descriptive Statistics ▶ Explore. Table 7.5 shows the output.

The results of this test (Table 7.5) suggest that the errors are normally distributed as we do not reject the test's null hypothesis. Thus, we can assume that the errors are normally distributed.

Now we turn to testing for multicollinearity. There are two tables in which SPSS indicates if multicollinearity issues are present. The first table is Table 7.11, in which the regression coefficient estimates are displayed. This table output also shows each variable's **Tolerance** in the second to last column and **VIF** in the last column. In this example, the tolerance values clearly lie above 0.10, and VIF values below 10, indicating that multicollinearity is of no concern.

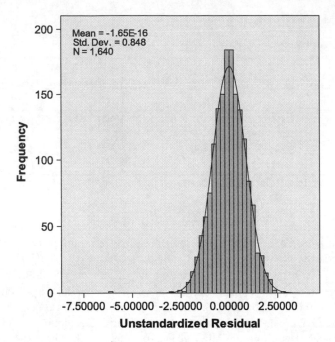

Fig. 7.14 Histogram of the errors with a standard normal curve

Table 7.5 Output produced by the Kolmogorov–Smirnov test

Tests of Normality

	Kolmogorov-Smirnov[a]			Shapiro-Wilk		
	Statistic	df	Sig.	Statistic	df	Sig.
Unstandardized Residual	.016	1639	.200[*]	.998	1639	.041

a. Lilliefors Significance Correction

*. This is a lower bound of the true significance.

Interpret the Regression Model Using SPSS Regression Output

The results of the regression analysis that we just carried out are presented below. We will discuss each element of the output that SPSS created in detail.

Tables 7.6 and 7.7 describe the dependent and independent variables in detail and provide several descriptives discussed in Chap. 5. Notice that the deletion of the outlier reduced the overall number of observations from 1,640 to 1,639. These are the observations for which we have complete information for the dependent and independent variables. Table 7.7 shows the correlation matrix and gives an idea how the different variables are related to each other.

Example   193

Table 7.6 Descriptive statistics table

Descriptive Statistics

	Mean	Std. Deviation	N
Overall Customer Satisfaction	13.9999	1.00219	1639
Customer Expectations	13.0009	.99957	1639
Perceived Value	9.9990	1.01018	1639
Customer Complaints	.2288	.42019	1639

Table 7.7 Correlation matrix

Correlations

		Overall Customer Satisfaction	Customer Expectations	Perceived Value	Customer Complaints
Pearson Correlation	Overall Customer Satisfaction	1.000	.492	.766	−.144
	Customer Expectations	.492	1.000	.478	−.073
	Perceived Value	.766	.478	1.000	−.137
	Customer Complaints	−.144	−.073	−.137	1.000
Sig. (1-tailed)	Overall Customer Satisfaction	.	.000	.000	.000
	Customer Expectations	.000	.	.000	.001
	Perceived Value	.000	.000	.	.000
	Customer Complaints	.000	.001	.000	.
N	Overall Customer Satisfaction	1639	1639	1639	1639
	Customer Expectations	1639	1639	1639	1639
	Perceived Value	1639	1639	1639	1639
	Customer Complaints	1639	1639	1639	1639

SPSS also produces Table 7.8, which indicates the variables used as dependent and independent variables and how they were entered in the model. It confirms that we use the **Enter** option (indicated under **Method**). All independent variables included in the model are mentioned under **Variables Entered** and under **b.** Furthermore, under **Dependent Variable**, the name of the dependent variable is indicated.

We interpret Tables 7.9 and 7.10 jointly, as they provide information on the model fit; that is, how well the independent variables relate to the dependent variable. The R^2 provided in Table 7.9 seems highly satisfactory and is above the value of 0.30 that is common for cross-sectional research. Usually, as is the case in our analysis, the R^2 and adjusted R^2 are similar. If the adjusted R^2 is substantially lower, this could indicate that you have used too many independent variables and that some could possibly be removed. Next, consider the significance of

Table 7.8 Variables used and regression method

Variables Entered/Removed[b]

Model	Variables Entered	Variables Removed	Method
1	Customer Complaints, Customer Expectations, Perceived Value[a]	.	Enter

a. All requested variables entered.

b. Dependent Variable: Overall Customer Satisfaction

Table 7.9 The model summary[a]

Model Summary[b]

Model	R	R Square	Adjusted R Square	Std. Error of the Estimate
1	.780[a]	.609	.608	.62756

a. Predictors: (Constant), Customer Complaints, Customer Expectations, Perceived Value

b. Dependent Variable: Overall Customer Satisfaction

Example   195

Table 7.10 ANOVA[a]

ANOVA[b]

Model		Sum of Squares	df	Mean Square	F	Sig.
1	Regression	1001.261	3	333.754	847.453	.000[a]
	Residual	643.914	1635	.394		
	Total	1645.175	1638			

a. Predictors: (Constant), Customer Complaints, Customer Expectations, Perceived Value

b. Dependent Variable: Overall Customer Satisfaction

Table 7.11 The estimated coefficients

Coefficients[a]

Model		Unstandardized Coefficients		Standardized Coefficients	t	Sig.	Collinearity Statistics	
		B	Std. Error	Beta			Tolerance	VIF
1	(Constant)	5.124	.016		23.863	.000		
	Customer Expectations	.164	.018	.163	9.257	.000	.771	1.296
	Perceived Value	.677	.018	.683	38.484	.000	.761	1.314
	Customer Complaints	-.092	.037	-.038	-2.458	.014	.981	1.019

a. Dependent Variable: Overall Customer Satisfaction

the F-test. The result in Table 7.10 indicates that the regression model is significant (p-value ≤ 0.05).

After assessing the overall model fit, it is time to look at the individual parameters. We find these in Table 7.11. First, you should look at the individual parameters' t-values, which test if the regression coefficients are individually equal to zero. If this is the case, the parameter is insignificant. In the model above, we find three significant variables, those with p-values (under **Sig.**) are below the commonly used level of 0.05. Although the constant is also significant, this is not a variable and is usually excluded from further interpretation. The significant variables require further interpretation.

First look at the sign (plus or minus) in the **Standardized Coefficients** column. Here, we find that *Customer Expectations* and *Perceived Value* are significantly and positively related to *Overall Customer Satisfaction*. *Customer Complaints* is significant and negatively related to *Overall Customer Satisfaction*. This means that if people complain, their customer satisfaction is significantly lower on average. By looking at the standardized coefficients' values you can assess if *Customer*

Expectations, *Perceived Value*, or *Customer Complaints* is most strongly related to *Overall Customer Satisfaction*. You only look at the absolute value (without the minus or plus sign therefore) and choose the highest value. In this case, *Perceived Value* (0.683) has clearly the strongest relationship with overall customer satisfaction. Therefore, this might be the first variable you want to increase if you aim to increase customer satisfaction. However, this assessment is not accurate since standardized βs cannot be meaningfully compared when an independent variable is binary (as it is the case with *Customer Complaints*). Nevertheless, the comparison gives us a rough idea regarding the relative strengths of the independent variables' effects on the dependent variable.

The **Unstandardized Coefficients** column gives you an indication of what would happen if you were to increase one of the independent variables by exactly one unit. For example, if *Customer Expectations* were to increase by one unit, we would expect *Overall Customer Satisfaction* to increase by 0.164 units. The standard errors are used to calculate the t-values. If we take the unstandardized coefficient of *Customer Expectations* (0.164) and divide this by its standard error (0.018), we obtain a value that is approximately the t-value of the 9.257 indicated in the table (see Chap. 6 for a description of the t-test statistic). The slight differences are due to rounding. As indicated before, *Customer Complaints* is a binary variable which can only take the value of 0 or 1. More precisely, for those customers who have not complained thus far, *Customer Complaints* takes the value 0. On the contrary, if a customer has already complained, the variable's value is 1 for this observation. Thus, the corresponding coefficient (-0.092) is the difference in $\hat{y}$ for customers who complained compared to those who have not complained.

Overall, it seems that we have found a useful model that seems to satisfy the key assumptions of regression analysis.

Validate the Regression Model using SPSS

Next, we need to validate the model. Let's first split-validate our model. Do this by going to ▶ Data ▶ Select Cases. This displays a dialog box similar to Fig. 7.15.

In this dialog box, go to **Select Cases: Range**. This displays a dialog box similar to Fig. 7.16.

Select the first 1,150 cases, which is approximately 70%. Then run the regression analysis again. Afterwards, return to **Select Cases: Range** and select observations 1,151–1,639. Compare the results of this model to those of the previous model. This approach is simple to execute but *only* works if the ordering of the data is random.

Next, we can add a few key additional variables to our model and see if the basic results change. Key variables with which to check the stability (the so-called *covariates*) could be the total annual family income and the respondent's gender. Then interpret the basic model again to see if the regression results change.

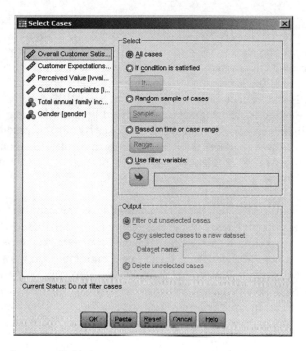

Fig. 7.15 The select cases dialog box

Fig. 7.16 The select cases: range dialog box

Case Study

AgriPro is a firm based in Colorado, USA, which does research on and produces genetically modified wheat seed. Every year AgriPro conducts thousands of experiments on different varieties of wheat seeds in different locations of the USA. In these experiments, the agricultural and economic characteristics, regional adaptation, and yield potential of different varieties of wheat seeds are investigated. In addition, the benefits of the wheat produced, including the milling and baking quality, are examined. If a new variety of wheat seed with superior characteristics is identified, AgriPro produces and markets it throughout the USA and Canada.

AgriPro's product is sold to farmers through their distributors, known in the industry as growers. Growers buy wheat seed from AgriPro, grow wheat, harvest the seeds, and sell the seed to local farmers, who plant them in their fields. These growers also provide the farmers who buy their seeds with expert local knowledge on management and the environment.

AgriPro sells its products to these growers in several geographically defined markets. These markets are geographically defined because different local conditions (soil, weather, and local plant diseases) force AgriPro to produce different products. One of these markets, the heartland region of the USA is an important market for AgriPro, but the company has been performing below management expectations in these markets. The heartland region includes the states of Ohio, Indiana, Missouri, Illinois, and Kentucky.

To help AgriPro understand more about farming in the heartland region, they commissioned a marketing research project among farmers in these states. AgriPro, together with a marketing research firm, designed a survey, which included questions on what farmers who decide to plant wheat find important, how they obtain information on growing and planting wheat, what is important in their purchasing decision, and their loyalty to and satisfaction with the top five wheat suppliers (including AgriPro). In addition, questions were asked about how many acres of farmland the respondents possessed, how much wheat they planted, how old they were, and their level of education.

http://www.agriprowheat.com

This survey was mailed to 650 farmers selected from a commercial list that includes nearly all farmers in the heartland region. In all, 150 responses were received, resulting in a 23% response rate. The marketing research firm also assisted AgriPro to assign variable names and labels. They did not delete any questions or observations due to nonresponse to items.

Your task is to analyze the dataset further and provide the management of AgriPro with advice based on the dataset. This dataset is labeled *Agripro.sav* and is available in the ᗡ Web Appendix (→ Chap. 7). Note that the dataset (under **Variable View** at the bottom of the SPSS screen) contains the variable names and labels and these match those in the survey. In the ᵛ⁰ Web Appendix (→ Chap. 7), we also include the original survey.[6]

To help you with this task, a number of questions have been prepared by AgriPro that they would like to see answered:

1. Produce appropriate descriptive statistics for each item in the dataset. Consider descriptive statistics that provide useful information in a succinct way. In addition, produce several descriptive statistics on the demographic variables in the dataset, using appropriate charts and/or graphs.
2. Are there any outliers in the data? What (if any) observations do you consider to be outliers and what would you do with these?
3. What are the most common reasons for farmers to plant wheat? From which source are farmers most likely to seek information on wheat? Is this source also the most reliable one?
4. Consider the five brands included in the dataset. Describe how these brands compare on quality, advice provided, and farmer loyalty.
5. How satisfied are the farmers with the brand's distributors?
6. AgriPro expects that farmers who are more satisfied with their products devote a greater percentage of the total number of acres available to them to wheat. Please test this assumption by using regression analysis. In addition, check the assumptions of regression analysis.
7. Is there a relationship between farmers' satisfaction with AgriPro and the respondent's educational level, age, and number of acres of farmland? Conduct a regression analysis with all these four variables. How do these results relate to question 6?
8. Are all assumptions satisfied? If not, is there anything we can do about it or should we ignore the assumptions if they are not satisfied?
9. What is the relationship between the quality of AgriPro seed and the satisfaction with AgriPro?
10. As AgriPro's consultant, and based on the empirical findings of this study, what marketing advice would you have for AgriPro's marketing team? Provide four or five carefully thought through suggestions as bullet points.

Questions

1. Try to explain what regression analysis is in your own words.
2. Imagine you are asked to use regression analysis to explain the profitability of new supermarket products, such as the introduction of a new type of jam or yoghurt, in the first year of the launch. What independent variables would you use to explain the profitability of these new products?

---

[6]We would like to thank Dr. D.I. Gilliland and AgriPro for making the data and case available.

3. Imagine you are going to a client to present the findings of a regression model. The client believes that the regression model is a "black box" and that anything can be made significant. What would your reaction be?
4. I do not care about the assumptions – just give me the results! Please evaluate this statement. Do you agree?
5. Are all regression assumptions equally important? Please discuss assumptions
6. Using standardized βs, we can compare effects between different variables. Can we really compare apples and oranges after all? Please discuss.
7. Run the ACSI example without deleting the outlier observation (i.e. using the full dataset with 1,640 observations) and compare the results with those presented above. Explain why deviations occur.

Further Readings

American Customer Satisfaction index at http://www.theacsi.org
  This website contains scores of the American Satisfaction Index.
Garson's Statnotes page at http://www2.chass.ncsu.edu/garson/pa765/statnote.htm
  This website provides an excellent overview on regression analysis from a technical perspective.
Hair JF, Black WC, Babin BJ, Anderson RE (2010) Multivariate data analysis. A global perspective, 7th edn. Pearson Prentice Hall, Upper Saddle River, NJ
  This is an excellent book, which discusses many statistical terms from a theoretical perspective in a highly accessible manner.
Nielsen at http://www.nielsen.com
  This is the website for Nielsen, one of the world's biggest market research companies. They publish many reports that use regression analysis.
The Food Marketing Institute at http://www.fmi.org
  This website contains data, some of which can be used for regression analysis.

References

Cohen J (1994) The Earth is round (P <.05). Am Psychol 49(912):997–1003
Field A (2009) Discovering statistics using SPSS, 3rd edn. Sage, London
Green SB (1991) How many subjects does it take to do a regression analysis? Multivariate Behav Res 26:499–510
Greene WH (2007) Econometric analysis, 6th edn. Prentice Hall, Upper Saddle River, NJ
Hill C, Griffiths W, Lim GC (2008) Principles of econometrics, 3rd edn. Wiley, Hoboken, NJ
Kelley K, Maxwell SE (2003) Sample size for multiple regression: obtaining regression coefficients that are accurate, not simply significant. Psychol Methods 8(3):305–321
Ringle CM, Sarstedt M, Mooi EA (2010) Response-based segmentation using FIMIX-PLS. Theoretical foundations and an application to ACSI data. Ann Inf Syst 8:19–49

Chapter 8
Factor Analysis

Learning Objectives

After reading this chapter, you should understand:
- The principles of exploratory and confirmatory factor analysis.
- The difference between principal components analysis and principal axis factoring.
- Key terms such as Eigenvalues, communality, factor loadings and factor scores.
- How to determine whether data are suitable for carrying out an exploratory factor analysis.
- How to interpret SPSS factor analysis output.
- The principles of reliability analysis and how to carry it out in SPSS.
- The basic idea behind structural equation modeling.

Keywords Anti-image · Bartlett's test of sphericity · Communality · Exploratory and confirmatory factor analysis · Principal axis factoring · Principal components analysis · Eigenvalue · Factor loadings · Factor scores · Kaiser criterion · Kaiser–Meyer–Olkin (KMO) criterion · Measure of sampling adequacy (MSA) · Scree plot · Orthogonal and oblique rotation · Varimax and direct oblimin rotation · Reliability analysis · Cronbach's Alpha · Structural equation modeling · LISREL · PLS path modeling

The increasingly complex media environment provides media planners with more options to reach their target audiences. However, it also makes media planning more difficult, as consumers react to the abundance of media by being selective and paying less attention to it. In their market research study, Bronner and Neijens (2006) investigate how the media context influences the effects of advertisements. Over 1,000 respondents were asked to rate their experience with advertisements using ten survey items. Factor analysis revealed that five factors underlie these ten items. Using the resulting factor scores, the authors show that, for example, advertising on TV and radio are perceived as irritating, whereas newspaper and cinema ads appear stimulating. Furthermore, advertisements on the Internet are considered informative but somewhat irritating. These factor analysis results help media planners to better target their audiences by choosing the appropriate medium to create awareness and persuasion, or to establish a relationship between the brand and the consumer.

E. Mooi and M. Sarstedt, *A Concise Guide to Market Research*,
DOI 10.1007/978-3-642-12541-6_8, © Springer-Verlag Berlin Heidelberg 2011

Introduction

Factor analysis identifies unobserved variables (factors) that explain patterns of correlations within a set of observed variables. It is often used to identify a small number of factors that explain most of the variance embedded in a larger number of variables. Thus, factor analysis is about data reduction. It can also be used to generate hypotheses regarding the composition of factors. Furthermore, factor analysis is often used to screen variables for subsequent analysis (e.g., to identify collinearity prior to performing a linear regression analysis as discussed in Chap. 7).

There are three types of factor analyses we discuss, namely *exploratory factor analysis, confirmatory factor analysis*, and *structural equation modeling*. The first two techniques are identical from a statistical point of view; however, they are used in different ways. Exploratory factor analysis is used to reveal the number of factors and the variables that belong to specific factors. When we conduct a confirmatory factor analysis, we have clear expectations regarding the factor structure (e.g., because we make use of a previously used survey) and we want to test if the expected structure is indeed present. Structural equation modeling differs from those two techniques, both statistically and practically. It is used to evaluate how well variables relate to factors and what the relationships between the factors are. This technique will be briefly discussed at the end of this chapter.

In this chapter, we primarily deal with exploratory factor analysis, as it conveys the principles that underlie all factor analytic procedures. Two exploratory factor analytic procedures are commonly used in market research: *principal components analysis* and *principal axis factoring*. When the purpose is to summarize information (variance) represented by the variables using a small number of factors, principal components analysis is used. Alternatively, if the aim is to identify underlying factors or dimensions that reflect what communalities variables share, principal axis factoring is used. We will discuss this distinction in greater detail later in this chapter. Principal components and principal axis factoring essentially require the same analysis steps and involve the same interpretation. However, as the concept of principal components analysis is easier to understand, we focus on this approach, but briefly highlight differences.

Understanding Principal Components Analysis

In many situations, researchers are faced with the problem of working with large questionnaires that comprise a multitude of questions (i.e., *items*, see Chap. 3). In order to evaluate all aspects of a specific marketing research problem, researchers often have to consider how the questions in these questionnaires are related.

For example, in a survey of a major German soccer club's marketing department, the management was particularly interested in identifying and evaluating performance features that relate to soccer fans' satisfaction. Features that could be of importance include the stadium, the composition of the team and their success, the trainer and the management. The marketing department therefore commissioned a questionnaire comprising 99 items that had been previously identified using literature databases and focus groups with various fans. All the items were measured on Likert scales ranging from 1 ("very dissatisfied") to 7 ("very satisfied"). Table 8.1 shows an overview of selected items considered in the study.

Table 8.1 Items in the soccer fan satisfaction study

Satisfaction with...	
Condition of the stadium	Public appearances of the players
Interior design of the stadium	Number of stars in the team
Outer appearance of the stadium	Interaction of players with fans
Signposting outside the stadium	Volume of the loudspeakers in the stadium
Signposting inside the stadium	Choice of music in the stadium
Roofing inside the stadium	Entertainment program in the stadium
Comfort of the seats	Stadium speaker
Video score boards in the stadium	Newsmagazine of the stadium
Condition of the restrooms	Price of annual season ticket
Tidiness within the stadium	Entry fees
Size of the stadium	Offers of reduced tickets
View onto the playing field	Design of the home jersey
Number of restrooms	Design of the away jersey
Sponsors' advertisements in the stadium	Assortment of merchandise
Location of the stadium	Quality of merchandise
Name of the stadium	Prices of merchandise
Determination and commitment of the players	Pre-sale of tickets
Current success regarding matches	Online-shop
Identification of the players with the club	Opening times of the fan-shops
Quality of the team composition	Accessibility of the fan-shops
Presence of a player with whom fans can identify	Behavior of the sales persons in the fan shops

Imagine you are a market researcher and were asked to evaluate the data from this survey to answer the management's research question which is to identify and evaluate performance features that relate to soccer fans' satisfaction. What would be the first thing to do? Obviously, the first step would be to compute descriptive statistics to gain an overview of the dataset. You could compute the mean values of each item and rank these. You could then identify features with which fans are very dissatisfied and take measures to address these deficiencies. Even though this approach may prove useful to gain a first overview, it is certainly not very helpful in evaluating the research question. The differences in the fans' satisfaction with features might only be marginal and carrying out pairwise t-tests to evaluate whether these differences are significant or not will prove problematic in the light of the large number of items involved (see discussion on the familywise error rate in Chap. 6). In our example, comprising 99 items, we would have to carry out exactly 4,851 pairwise t-tests.[1]

---

[1]This number is calculated as $k \cdot (k-1)/2$, with k being the number of items to compare.

Furthermore, this approach does not help explain which features contribute most to the respondents' overall satisfaction. In order to address the latter question, you may use the item "Overall, how satisfied are you with your soccer club?" as a criterion variable and regress it on all remaining performance items. However, this is likely to create the collinearity problem discussed in Chap. 7. Just by looking at the formulation of the items, we expect that several of the items are highly correlated. For example, satisfaction with the condition (x_1), outer appearance (x_2), and interior design (x_3) of the stadium cover similar aspects relating to the respondents' satisfaction with the stadium. If a soccer fan is generally very satisfied with the stadium, he/she will most likely answer all three items positively. Conversely, if a respondent is generally dissatisfied with the stadium, he/she is most likely to be rather dissatisfied with all the performance aspects of the stadium, such as the outer appearance and interior design. Consequently, these three items are most likely to be highly correlated, as they cover related aspects of the respondents' overall satisfaction with the stadium. In other words, with regard to their core meaning, these items are to a certain degree redundant. This is where the principal components analysis comes into play.

The basic idea of principal components analysis is to make use of these correlations to summarize sets of items within latent variables. As the name already suggests, these latent variables are not directly observable but each is inferred and based on several items. A latent variable is also called a factor or component – essentially, all three terms mean the same but the more generic term factor is most commonly used in the context of principal components analysis. Figure 8.1 displays

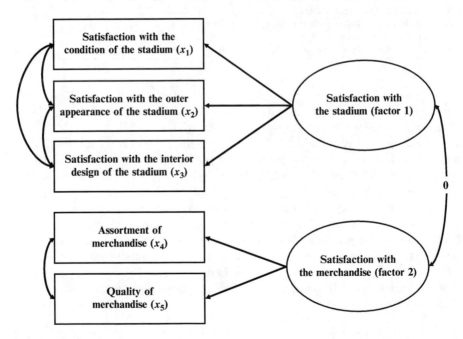

Fig. 8.1 Example of a factor model

the coherence between two factors and a set of items. It is standard practice for factors to be illustrated by circles, whereas rectangles are used for items.

The upper part of the figure suggests that there is one factor that relates directly to the three items x_1, x_2, and x_3. These three items are likely to be highly correlated, as indicated by the arrows between them. We assume that this correlation is caused by an underlying factor, which is indicated by the arrows pointing from the factor to the items. Specifically, the items are reflecting the factor. Consequently, the items can be interpreted as manifestations of the factor with the factor capturing the joint meaning of the items related to it. In our example, the "joint meaning" of the three items could be described as *satisfaction with the stadium*, since the items represent somewhat different, yet related, aspects of this issue. Likewise, we can think of another factor that relates to another set of items as described in Fig. 8.1. This factor relates to two items (x_4 and x_5) which, similarly to the first factor, share a common meaning. This common meaning is captured by the factor which we could label *satisfaction with the merchandise*.

The basic idea of principal components analysis is to use large correlations between the items to compute factors that best represent the items in our dataset. Therefore, a certain amount of correlation is necessary to conduct a principal components analysis. Often, many items in a dataset are correlated with one another. Figure 8.1 therefore only indicates that there are high correlations between x_1, x_2, and x_3 on the one hand and x_4 and x_5 on the other. Other items, such as x_1 and x_4, are most likely somewhat correlated but to a lesser degree than the group of items x_1, x_2, and x_3 and the pair x_4 and x_5.

Using the correlations between sets of items, the principal components analysis extracts a number of factors which can be considered salient unobserved variables capturing important aspects of the complete item set. Initially, these factors are, by definition, uncorrelated so that each factor covers distinct and unrelated aspects (indicated by the 0 on the arrow linking factors 1 and 2).[2] This is a very important feature, as it means that factors are uncorrelated and thus, if we use them in regression analysis, collinearity is not an issue. Instead of using many highly correlated items as independent variables in a regression analysis, we can use only a few uncorrelated factors that represent the original item set. However, using only a few factors instead of many items comes at the expense of accuracy. Naturally, these factors cannot represent all the information inherent in the items. Consequently, there is a trade-off between simplicity and accuracy. In order to make the analysis as simple as possible, we want to extract only a few factors. At the same time, we do not want to lose too much information by having too few factors. This trade-off has to be addressed in any principal components analysis when deciding how many factors should be extracted from the data.

---

[2]Note that this changes when factors are rotated in a oblique way. We will discuss factor rotation later in this chapter.

In the example above, we do not have any prior knowledge of how the items relate to a factor or how many factors underlie the items (that's the basic idea of an exploratory factor analysis). We simply use all the items related to our research question and integrate them into one analysis. However, in practice, we usually have an idea of what the factor structure could look like and, thus, might adjust the factor solution if this is more reasonable. These adjustments might affect the number of factors extracted or the way in which items are assigned to a factor.

After having decided on the number of factors to retain from the data, we can proceed with the interpretation of the factor solution. This requires us to come up with a label for each factor that best characterizes the joint meaning of all the variables associated with it. Often, this step is very challenging but a rotation of the factors can facilitate the interpretation of the factor solution. Lastly, we have to assess how well the factors reproduce the data, which is done by examining the solution's goodness-of-fit. Figure 8.2 illustrates the steps involved in a principal components analysis; we will discuss these in more detail in the following sections.

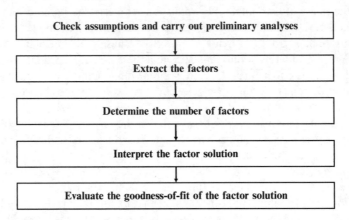

Fig. 8.2 Steps involved in conducting a principal components analysis

Conducting a Principal Components Analysis

Check Assumptions and Carry out Preliminary Analyses

Before carrying out a principal components analysis, we have to consider some basic assumptions that underlie the approach.

To conduct principal components analysis, it is best to have data measured on an interval or ratio scale level. In practical applications, however, it has become common to also use items measured on an ordinal scale level. This procedure usually leads to valid results, particularly if there is a large number of response categories (five or more) for the items. However, using ordinal data requires the items' scale steps to be equidistant. Equidistant means that the difference in the wording between scale steps is the same. Accordingly, the difference in wording between ordinal categories should capture this condition (see Chap. 3). Another point of concern is the sample size. As a rule, the number of (valid) observations should be at least ten times the number of items used for analysis. This also includes a missing value analysis. Since it is generally recommended that cases with missing values should be excluded, this can greatly reduce the number of valid observable variables in our analysis.

Furthermore, we have to ensure that the observations are independent. We discuss this issue in Chap. 3.

As indicated before, principal components analysis is based on correlations between items. Consequently, carrying out a principal components analysis only makes sense if the items are sufficiently correlated. The problem is how to decide what "sufficient" actually means.

An obvious step is to examine the *correlation matrix*. Naturally, we want correlations between different items to be as high as possible.[3] However, this will not always be the case. Regarding our previous example, we expect high correlations between x_1, x_2, and x_3, on the one hand, and x_4 and x_5 on the other. Conversely, we might expect lower correlations between, for example, x_1 and x_4 and between x_3 and x_5. Thus, not all elements of the correlation matrix necessarily have to have high values. Generally, correlations should be above absolute 0.30. However, if single correlations are lower, this is not necessarily problematic. Only when all the correlations are around zero, does principal components analysis stop being useful. In addition, the statistical significance of each correlation coefficient (indicated in the output produced by SPSS) helps decide whether it differs significantly from zero.

There are additional measures to determine whether the items are sufficiently correlated. One is the *anti-image*. The anti-image describes the portion of an item's variance that is independent of another item in the analysis. Obviously, we want all items to be highly correlated, so that an item's anti-images are as small as possible. This issue is captured in the anti-image matrices. Initially, we do not interpret these matrices directly but, instead, revert to two measures based on the concept of anti-image: *The Kaiser–Meyer–Olkin (KMO)* statistic and the *Bartlett's test of sphericity*. The KMO statistic, also called the *measure of sampling adequacy (MSA)*, indicates whether the correlations between variables can be explained by the other variables in the dataset. Kaiser (1974), who introduced the statistic, recommends a set of (very vividly labeled) threshold values for KMO and MSA, as presented in Table 8.2.

The *Bartlett's test of sphericity* can be used to test the null hypothesis that the correlation matrix is a diagonal matrix (i.e., all non-diagonal elements are zero) in the population. Since we need high correlations for principal components

---

[3]Note that variables should not be perfectly correlated (the correlation is −1 or 1), as this might lead to problems in the analysis.

Table 8.2 Threshold values
for KMO and MSA

KMO/MSA value	Adequacy of the correlations
Below 0.50	Unacceptable
0.50–0.59	Miserable
0.60–0.69	Mediocre
0.70–0.79	Middling
0.80–0.89	Meritorious
0.90 and higher	Marvelous

analysis, we want to reject the null hypothesis. A large test statistic value and a small p-value will each favor the rejection of the hypothesis. In practical applications, it is virtually impossible not to reject this null hypothesis, as some variables will always be correlated. Moreover, low test statistic values always go hand in hand with poor KMO values.

As a consequence, the final decision of whether the data are appropriate for principal components analysis should be primarily based on the KMO statistic. Likewise, the correlation matrix with the associated significance levels provides a first insight into the correlation structures. If these measures indicate sufficiently correlated variables, we can continue the analysis of the results.

How do we proceed if this is not the case? In such a situation, we can try to identify items that are only weakly correlated with the remaining items and, thus, affect the results negatively. This can be done by examining the correlation matrix and the significance levels of correlations. A better approach, however, is to take another look at the anti-image correlation matrix. The diagonal elements of this matrix describe the *variable-specific MSA values*, which are interpreted like the overall KMO statistic (see Table 8.2). In fact, the KMO statistic is nothing but the overall mean of all item-specific MSA values. Consequently, all MSA values on the anti-image correlation matrix's diagonal should also lie above the threshold level of 0.50. If this is not the case, we should consider removing this item from the analysis. An item's *communality* (we will discuss this term in the next section) can also serve as a useful indicator of how well an item is represented by the factors extracted. However, communalities are more often considered when evaluating the solution's goodness-of-fit.

Extract the Factors

In a principal components analysis, factors are extracted in such a way that the variables' initial correlation matrix is reproduced in the best possible way, which means that the discrepancy between the initial and reproduced correlation matrix should be as small as possible. Operationally, the principal components analysis selects a number of variables that are highly correlated and relates those to a certain factor. Next, another set of highly correlated variables is chosen and related to a second factor. This is repeated in a step-by-step manner until all the variables have been included.

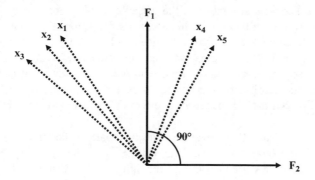

Fig. 8.3 Factor extraction

The first factor is extracted in such a way that it maximizes its variance accounted for. We can easily visualize this by looking at the vector space illustrated in Fig. 8.3. In this example, we have five variables ($x_1, \ldots, x_5$) that are represented by five vectors starting at the zero point (with its length standardized to one). To maximize the variance accounted for, the first factor F_1 is fitted into this vector space in such a way that the sum of all the angles between this factor and the five variables in the vector space is minimized. This is done because we can interpret the angle between two vectors as correlations. For example, if the factor's vector and a variable's vector are congruent, the angle between these two is zero, indicating that the factor and the variable are perfectly correlated. On the other hand, if the factor and the considered variable are uncorrelated, the angle between these two is 90°. This correlation between factor and variables is referred to as *factor loading*.

After this, a second factor (F_2) is extracted and maximizes the remaining variance accounted for. This factor is – by definition – independent from the first one and, thus, is fitted into the vector space at a 90° angle (Fig. 8.3). If we extracted a third factor, it would explain the maximum amount of the variance that has hitherto not been accounted for by factors 1 and 2. This one would also be fitted in a 90° angle from the first two factors. We don't illustrate this third factor in Fig. 8.3, as we would be looking at a three-dimensional space.[4] This procedure continues until as many factors as there are variables (i.e., five) are extracted.

One important feature of the principal components analysis is that it works with standardized variables (see Chap. 5 for an explanation of what standardized

---

[4]Note that in Fig. 8.3, we consider a special case as the five variables are scaled down into a two-dimensional space. Actually, in this set-up, it would be possible to explain all five variables by means of the two factors. However, in real-life, the five variables span a five-dimensional vector space.

variables are). The standardization of the variables is done automatically by SPSS, which means we do not have to bother with this. However, this characteristic has important implications for our analysis, since it helps us assess how much information a factor captures. This information is incorporated in a factor's *Eigenvalue*. An Eigenvalue describes how much variance is accounted for by a certain factor. Likewise, the standardization enables us to assess how much of each variable's variance is captured or reproduced by the factors extracted. This is referred to as *communality*.

How can we interpret these two measures adequately? To answer this question, think of the soccer fan satisfaction study (Fig. 8.1). In the example, there are five variables, each with a variance of one. In a simplified way, we could say that the overall information (i.e., variance) that we want to reproduce by means of factor extraction is five. Let us assume that we extract the two factors presented above.

The first factor's Eigenvalue indicates how much variance of the total variance (i.e., five units) this factor accounts for. If this factor has an Eigenvalue of, let's say 2.10, it covers the information of 2.10 variables or, put differently, accounts for 2.10/5.00 = 42% of the overall variance (Fig. 8.4).

Extracting a second factor will allow us to explain another part of the remaining variance (i.e., 5.00 − 2.10 = 2.90 units, Fig. 8.4). However, the Eigenvalue of the second factor will always be smaller than that of the first factor. Assume that the second factor has an Eigenvalue of 1.30 units. The second factor then accounts for 1.30/5.00 = 26% of the overall variance. Together, these two factors explain (2.10 + 1.30)/5.00 = 68% of the overall variance.

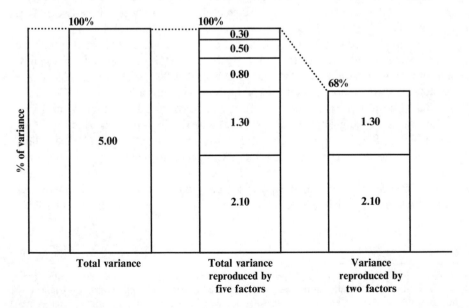

Fig. 8.4 Total variance explained by variables and factors

Every additional factor extracted, increases the variance accounted for until we have extracted as many factors as there are variables. In this case, the overall variance accounted for by the factors is 100%, which means that the complete variance is reproduced by the factors (Fig. 8.4).

Following the principal components approach, we assume that each variable's entire variance can be reproduced by means of factor extraction. In other words, we assume that each variable's variance is common, that is, it is shared with other variables. As a consequence, variables do not have any unique variance. A different, but also popular, approach to factor analysis is *principal axis factoring* (also called common factor analysis or principal factor analysis), which we briefly discuss in Box 8.1.

Box 8.1 Principal components analysis vs. principal axis factoring

Unlike with principal components analysis, the principal axis factoring approach assumes that each variable has some common as well as unique variance. However, only the variance shared with all other variables in your analysis (i.e., the communality) can be reproduced by means of factor extraction. This variance shared is usually the R^2 obtained from a regression of that variable on all remaining ones. Consequently, each variable's initial communality, which indicates the amount of variance that can be explained, is lower than one (unlike in the principal components approach in which the initial communality is always 1). The extraction of factors follows the same principles as in principal components analysis and the interpretation of statistical measures such as KMO, Eigenvalues, or factor loadings are analogous.

From a theoretical perspective, the assumption that there is a unique variance which cannot be fully accounted for by the factors is generally more realistic but, at the same time, more restrictive. Although theoretically sound, this restriction can sometimes lead to complications in the analysis which have contributed to the widespread use of principal components analysis, especially in market research practice.

Usually, researchers suggest using the principal components analysis when data reduction is the primary concern; that is, when the focus is to extract a minimum of factors that account for a maximum proportion of the variables' total variance. On the contrary, if the primary concern is to identify latent dimensions represented in the variables, principal axis factoring should be applied.[5] However, as both approaches often yield very similar results, we generally suggest using principal components analysis.

(continued)

---

[5]Researchers often argue along the lines of measurement error when distinguishing between principal components analysis and principal axis factoring (e.g., Hair et al. 2010). However, as this distinction does not really have implications for market research studies, we omitted this argument.

If you are interested in finding out more about the differences between principal components analysis and principal axis factoring, just visit Garson's Statnotes page on factor analysis:

http://faculty.chass.ncsu.edu/garson/PA765/factor.htm

Lastly, additional methods for carrying out factor analyses are available, such as the unweighted least squares, generalized least squares, or maximum likelihood approaches. However, these are statistically complex and inexperienced users should therefore not consider them. Hair et al. (2010) provide an excellent introduction to these advanced techniques.

Whereas the Eigenvalue tells us how much variance is accounted for by each factor, the *communality* indicates how much variance of each variable can be reproduced through factor extraction. There is no commonly agreed threshold for a variable's communality, as this depends strongly on the complexity of the analysis at hand. However, generally, at least 30% of a variable's variance should be accounted for through the extracted factors. Thus, the communalities should lie above 0.30. Every additional factor extracted will increase this variance and if we extract as many factors as there are items (in our example five), the communality of each variable would be 1.00. The variable will then be entirely explained by the factors extracted; that is, a certain amount of its variance will be explained by the first factor, another part by the second factor, and so on.

However, as our overall objective is to reduce the number of variables through factor extraction, we should rather extract only a few factors that account for a high degree of the overall variation. This raises the question of how to decide on the number of factors to extract from the data, which we discuss in the following section.

Determine the Number of Factors

The intuitive way to decide on the number of factors is to extract all factors with an Eigenvalue greater than one. The reason is that every factor with an Eigenvalue greater than one accounts for more variance than a single variable (remember, we are looking at standardized variables, which is why each variable's variance is exactly one). As the overall objective of principal components analysis is to reduce the overall number of variables, each factor should, of course, account for more variance than a single variable can. If this occurs, then this factor is useful for reducing the set of variables. Extracting all factors with an Eigenvalue greater than one is frequently called the *Kaiser criterion* and is by far the most frequently used criterion to decide the number of factors. However, in some situations, the inclusion (exclusion) of additional factors with a smaller (higher) Eigenvalue than one might prove beneficial for interpreting the solution in a meaningful way. Ultimately, we should not entirely rely on the data but keep in mind that the research results should be interpretable and actionable for market research practice.

There are also alternative approaches to decide on the number of factors to extract. SPSS offers the possibility to plot each factor's Eigenvalue (y-axis) against the factor with which it is associated (x-axis). This results in a so-called *scree plot* that typically has a distinct break in it, thereby showing the "correct" number of factors. This distinct break is referred to as the "elbow" and it is generally recommended that all factors should be retained above this break, as they contribute most to the explanation of the variance in the dataset. Thus, we select one factor less than indicated by elbow. In some situations, however, the distinct break is not clear-cut and we should instead rely on the Kaiser criterion.

In other situations, we might have a priori information regarding the number of factors we want to find, which might be the case in a situation in which we want to replicate a previous market research study. In this case, we should also be guided by the findings of this previous study. Thus, if we find four factors and a number of previous studies suggest that five are present, we should try to select five factors. However, strictly speaking, this is a confirmatory approach to factor analysis. Another approach is to split the dataset into two halves and carry out separate factor analyses on each dataset. Only factors with a high correspondence of factor loadings across the two samples are extracted (split-half reliability).[6] Whatever approach is used to determine the number of factors, the factors extracted should account for at least 50% of the total variance explained (75% or more is recommended).

After having decided on the number of factors to retain from the data, we can proceed with the interpretation of the factor solution.

Interpret the Factor Solution

To interpret the solution of the principal components analysis, we have to determine which variables strongly relate to each of the factors extracted. This is done by

---

[6]Note that there are further approaches to determine the number of factors such as the parallel analysis or the minimum average partial test which we discuss in the Web Appendix (⌐ Web Appendix → Chapter 8).

examining the factor loadings, which represent the correlations between the factors and the variables and, thus, can take values from -1 to $+1$. High factor loadings indicate that a variable is well represented by a certain factor. Subsequently, we always look for high absolute values as the correlation between a variable and a factor can also be negative. Using the highest absolute factor loadings, we "assign" each variable to a certain factor and then try to come up with a label for each factor that best characterizes the joint meaning of all the variables associated with it. This labeling is subjective, but nevertheless a key step in principal components analysis. An example of a label is the respondents' satisfaction with the stadium that represents the items referring to its condition, outer appearance, and interior design.

To facilitate the interpretation of the factors, we can make use of *factor rotation*. We do not have to rotate the factor solution, but it will facilitate interpreting findings, particularly if we have a reasonably large number of items (say six or more). To understand what factor rotation is all about, reconsider the factor structure described in Fig. 8.3. Here, we see that both factors relate to the variables in the set. However, the first factor appears to be generally more strongly correlated with the variables, whereas the second factor is only weakly correlated with the variables (to clarify, we look for small angles between the factors and variables). This implies that we "assign" all variables to the first factor without taking the second one into consideration. This does not appear to be very meaningful, as we want both factors to represent certain facets of the variable set. This problem can be resolved by means of factor rotation. By rotating the factor axes, we can bring about a situation in which a set of variables is loaded highly on only one specific factor, whereas another set loads highly on another. Figure 8.5 illustrates the factor rotation graphically.

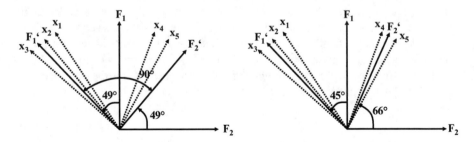

Fig. 8.5 Orthogonal and oblique factor rotation

On the left hand side of the figure, we can see that both factors are rotated $49°$ in an orthogonal way, meaning that the $90°$ angle between the factors is sustained during the rotation procedure. Consequently, the factors remain uncorrelated, which is in line with the initial objective of the principal components analysis. By rotating the first factor from F_1 to $F_{1'}$, it is now strongly related to variables x_1, x_2, and x_3 but weakly related to x_4 and x_5. Conversely, by rotating the second factor from F_2 to $F_{2'}$, it is now strongly related to x_4 and x_5 weakly related to the remaining variables. The assignment of the variables is now much clearer, which facilitates the interpretation of the factors significantly. Various orthogonal rotation methods exist which differ with regard to their treatment of the loading structure. The *varimax* procedure is the most prominent one; this procedure aims at maximizing the dispersion of loadings within factors. Other orthogonal rotation methods include the quartimax or equamax procedures. See the SPSS help option for more information on these procedures' properties.

Alternatively, we can choose an oblique rotation technique. In this approach, the 90° angle between the factors is not maintained during rotation and the resulting factors are therefore correlated. Figure 8.5 (right hand side) illustrates an example of an oblique factor rotation. *Direct oblimin* is the most commonly used oblique rotation technique. Here, researchers have to specify a constant δ (pronounced as *delta*) which determines the level of correlation allowed between the factors. The default value of zero ensures that the factors are – if at all – only moderately correlated, which is acceptable for most analyses. For example, it is very likely that the respondents' satisfaction with the stadium is unrelated to their satisfaction with other aspects of a soccer club, such as the number of stars in the team or the quality of merchandise. However, giving up the initial objective of extracting uncorrelated factors can diminish the interpretability of the factors.

We recommend using the varimax rotation to enhance the interpretability of the results. Only if the results are difficult to interpret, should an oblique rotation be applied.

Despite the factor rotation, the interpretation of the factors is usually the most challenging step in a principal components analysis, as the assignment of variables is often not clear-cut. Sometimes it is reasonable to assign a variable to another factor even though it does not load highly on this specific factor. While this can help to increase the results' face validity, we should make sure that the variable's factor loading with the designated factor still lies above an acceptable level. With very few factors extracted, the loading should be at least 0.50, but with a high number of factors, lower loadings of above 0.30 are feasible. In other situations, it might even be worthwhile eliminating a certain variable. In the end, the results should be interpretable and actionable, but keep in mind that this is first and foremost exploratory.

Following the rotation and interpretation of the factors, we can consider another important element of the analysis, the *factor scores*. These represent the degree to which each respondent exhibits the characteristic of a particular factor. While factor loadings describe the association between variables and factors, factor scores characterize the relation between observations and factors. Each factor's scores are standardized to a mean of zero. This means that if a respondent has a value greater than zero for a certain factor, he or she exhibits the characteristic described by the factor above the average. Conversely, if a factor score is below zero, then this respondent exhibits the characteristic below average. There are different procedures to produce factor scores but we suggest using the regression method, as this is the most commonly used and easily understood approach.[7]

Factor scores are used in several ways: If the objective of the principal components analysis is to reduce the number of variables, subsequent analyses can simply be based upon the factor scores. For example, instead of calculating the average for x_1, x_2, and x_3 and using this as a construct value, we can use the factor scores of *satisfaction with the stadium* in follow-up analyses. The scores of the uncorrelated factors, instead of highly correlated predictor variables, can specifically be used if the objective of the principal components analysis was to overcome collinearity problems in an OLS regression.

Evaluate the Goodness-of-fit of the Factor Solution

The overall objective of principal components analysis is to extract factors in such a way that the factors and their loadings reproduce the data in the best possible way. Consequently, we can make use of the differences between the correlations in the data and those implied by the factors to assess the obtained solution's goodness-of-fit. We require the absolute difference between the observed and reproduced correlation coefficients (the residuals) to be as small as possible. In practice, we check the proportion of the correlation matrices' residuals with an absolute value higher than 0.05. Even though there is no rule of thumb regarding the maximum proportion, a value of more than 50% should raise concern. However, low correlations and an unsatisfactory KMO measure usually go hand in hand with high residuals; consequently, this problem already emerges in the testing of assumptions.

Furthermore, we should consider each variable's communality, which should, of course, be as high as possible. However, if several communalities exhibit rather low values, we should consider removing these variables. To help make that decision, we could also take the variable-specific MSA measures into account. There is no minimum value for a variable's communality, as the values usually depend on the number of variables considered. If there are more variables in your dataset, communalities usually become smaller, however, if your factor solution accounts for less than 30% (i.e., the variable's communality is less than 0.30) of a variable's variance, it is worthwhile reconsidering your set-up.

In Table 8.3 we summarize the main steps that need to be taken when conducting a factor analysis using SPSS.

---

[7]Alternative procedures include the Bartlett method and the Anderson–Rubin method, which are designed to overcome potential problems associated with the regression technique. However, these problems are of rather theoretical nature and of little importance to market research practice.

Table 8.3 Steps involved in carrying out a factor analysis in SPSS

Theory	SPSS
Research problem	
Select variables that should be reduced to a set of underlying factors (principal factor analysis) or that should be used to identify underlying dimensions (principal axis factoring)	Enter these into the Variables box in the Factor Dialog Box: ▸ Analyze ▸ Dimension Reduction ▸ Factor.
Assumptions	
Are the variables interval or ratio scaled?	Determine the measurement level of your variables (see Chap. 3). If ordinal variables are used, make sure that the scale steps are equidistant.
Missing value analysis	Check descriptive statistics output for the number of valid cases out of the total number of cases: ▸ Analyze ▸ Dimension Reduction ▸ Factor ▸ Descriptives ▸ Univariate descriptives
Is the sample size sufficiently large?	Check that the number of valid observations is at least ten times the number of items
Are the observations independent?	Determine whether the observations are dependent or independent (see Chap. 3).
Are the variables sufficiently correlated?	▸ Analyze ▸ Dimension Reduction ▸ Factor ▸ Descriptives ▸ Coefficients | Significance levels | KMO and Bartlett's test of sphericity | Anti-image. – Are correlation coefficients ≥ 0.30? – Are correlation coefficients' p-values ≤ 0.05? – Is the KMO ≥ 0.50? – Is the p-value of the Bartlett's test ≤ 0.05? – Are the variable-specific MSA values ≥ 0.50?
Specification	
Handle missing values	Delete missing values listwise: ▸ Analyze ▸ Dimension Reduction ▸ Factor ▸ Options ▸ Exclude cases listwise
Choose the method of factor analysis	If the scope of the analysis is to reduce the number of variables: ▸ Analyze ▸ Dimension Reduction ▸ Factor ▸ Extraction ▸ Principal components. If the scope of the analysis is to identify underlying dimensions: ▸ Analyze ▸ Dimension Reduction ▸ Factor ▸ Extraction ▸ Principal axis factoring
Determine the number of factors	Extract all factors with an Eigenvalue greater than one (default) and create a scree plot ▸ Analyze ▸ Dimension Reduction ▸ Factor ▸ Extraction ▸ Scree plot Alternatives: – Pre-specify the number of factors based on a priori information: ▸ Analyze ▸ Data Reduction ▸ Factor ▸ Extraction ▸ Factors to extract

(continued)

Table 8.3 (continued)

Theory	SPSS
	– Extract factors that jointly account for at least 50% (75% recommended) of the total variance: Create plot Total Variance Explained.
	– Split-half reliability: Split up the dataset in two halves of equal size and carry out separate factor analyses.
Rotate the factors	Use the varimax procedure or, if necessary, choose the direct oblimin procedure with $\delta = 0$: ▶ Analyze ▶ Dimension Reduction ▶ Factor ▶ Rotation
Assign variables to factors	Use the rotated solution to assign each variable to a certain factor based on the highest absolute loading. To facilitate interpretation, you may also assign a variable to a different factor but check that the loading lies at a passable level (0.50 if only few factors are extracted, 0.30 if many factors are extracted).
Compute factor scores	Save factor scores as new variables using the regression method: ▶ Analyze ▶ Dimension Reduction ▶ Factor ▶ Scores ▶ Save as variables: Regression
Checking results	
Determine the number of factors	Check the factors' Eigenvalues, the % of variance and the cumulative % explained: Examine the scree plot.
Interpret the factors	Consider the rotated component matrix and find an umbrella term for pairs of items assigned to each factor.
Checking goodness-of-fit	
Check the congruence of the initial and reproduced correlations	Create reproduced correlation matrix: ▶ Analyze ▶ Dimension Reduction ▶ Factor ▶ Descriptives ▶ Reproduced
	Is the proportion of residuals greater than $0.05 \leq 50\%$?
Check how much of each variable's variance is reproduced by means of factor extraction	Examine the communalities. Check if communalities are greater than 0.30.

Confirmatory Factor Analysis and Reliability Analysis

Many researchers and practitioners acknowledge the prominent role that factor analysis plays in exploring data structures. Data can be analyzed without preconceived ideas regarding the number of factors or how they relate to the variables under consideration. Whereas this approach is exploratory in nature, the *confirmatory factor analysis* allows for testing hypothesized structures underlying a set of variables.

Consequently, in a confirmatory factor analysis, the researcher needs to first specify the factors and their associations with variables, which should be based on previous measurements or theoretical considerations. Instead of allowing the procedure to determine the number of factors, as is done in an exploratory factor analysis, the confirmatory factor analysis tells us how well the actual data fit the pre-specified structure. Reverting to our introductory example, we could, for example, assume that the construct *satisfaction with the stadium* can be measured using the three items x_1, x_2, and x_3 (without having carried out an exploratory factor analysis beforehand!). Likewise, we could hypothesize that *satisfaction with the merchandise* can be adequately measured using the items x_4 and x_5. In a confirmatory factor analysis, we set up a theoretical model (also referred to as measurement model) linking the items with the respective factor (or construct – note that in confirmatory factor analysis, we use the term construct rather than factor).

This process is also called operationalization (see Chap. 3) and usually involves drawing a visual representation (called a *path diagram*) indicating the hypothesized relationships. This path diagram is very similar to the model presented in Fig. 8.1. In a path diagram, it is common to use a notation in which constructs are represented by Greek characters, whereas measured variables are represented by Latin characters. In a confirmatory factor analysis, constructs (ξ, pronounced as *xi*) are presented as circles or ovals, and measured variables (x) are presented as square or rectangular. Other elements include the relationships between the constructs and respective items (λ, pronounced as *lambda*), the error terms (σ, pronounced as *sigma*) that capture the extent to which a construct does not explain the item, and the correlations between the constructs of interest (Φ, pronounced *theta*). Figure 8.6 shows the hypothesized relationship between the observed items and constructs.

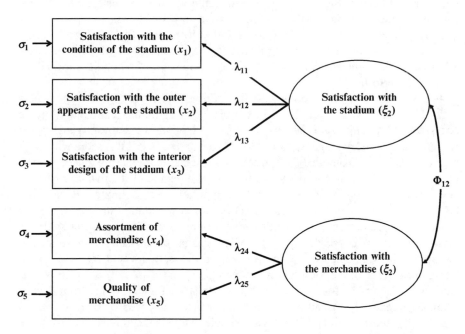

Fig. 8.6 Example of a path diagram

Having defined the individual constructs and developed the overall measurement model, the researcher needs to gather data. This allows the model parameters to be estimated. In this respect, the relationships between the constructs and items, that is, the factor loading λ, are of particular interest. There are several software programs that carry out confirmatory factor analyses (e.g., LISREL or EQS). In addition, the SPSS division of IBM offers AMOS for this task. The parameter estimates allow the researcher to assess the items' ability to measure a specific construct. This is referred to as construct validity and includes evaluating whether a measure correlates with another established scale of the same construct (convergent validity), or whether a construct is truly distinct from others in the model (discriminant validity). Furthermore, it is essential to assess each construct's reliability.

Carrying out a confirmatory factor analysis is rather demanding and requires a thorough understanding of the principles of measurement. An important element of a confirmatory factor analysis, which is crucial when working with scales, is the reliability analysis. Unlike the confirmatory factor analysis, a reliability analysis (see Chap. 3 for a discussion of reliability) can easily be carried out in SPSS. The preferred way to evaluate reliability is to make two independent measurements (using the same subjects) and to compare them by means of correlation analyses. This is also referred to as test-retest reliability (see Chap. 3).

However, in practice, researchers have often not had the opportunity to recapture their subjects for a second survey. This difficulty has been circumvented by the introduction of the split-half approach in which scale items are divided into halves and the scores of the halves are correlated to obtain an estimate of reliability. As all items should be consistent in what they indicate about the construct, the halves can be considered approximations of alternative forms of the same scale. Consequently, instead of looking at the scale's stability by means of test-retest reliability, researchers consider the scale's equivalence, which shows to which extent two measures of the same general trait agree. We call this type of reliability the *internal consistency reliability*.

In the example of "satisfaction with the stadium," we could compute this scale's split-half reliability manually by, for example, splitting up the scale into x_1 on the one side, and x_2 and x_3 on the other. We then compute the sum of x_2 and x_3 (or calculate the items' average) to form a total score and correlate this score with x_1. A high correlation indicates that the two subsets of items are measuring related aspects of the same underlying construct and, thus, a high degree of internal consistency. However, this example indicates that the computation result strongly depends on how the items are split. Cronbach (1951) proposed calculating the average of all possible split-half coefficients resulting from different ways of splitting the sample's scale items. His *Cronbach's Alpha* coefficient has become by far the most popular measure of internal consistency. In the example above, this would comprise calculating the average of the correlations between (1) x_1 and x_2+x_3, (2) x_2 and x_1+x_3, as well as (3) x_3 and x_1+x_2. The Cronbach's Alpha coefficient varies from 0 to 1, whereas a generally agreed lower limit for the coefficient is 0.70. However, in exploratory studies, a value of 0.60 is acceptable, while in the more advanced stages of research, values of 0.80 or higher are regarded as satisfactory.

SPSS not only reports one Cronbach's Alpha value for the entire scale, but also indicates how this value would be altered if a particular item was deleted. This information provides valuable suggestions on how to improve a scale's reliability if the initial estimate implies a low degree of internal consistency.

When calculating Cronbach's Alpha, ensure that all items are formulated identically. For example, in psychological measurement, it is common to use both negatively and positively worded items in a questionnaire. These need to be reversed prior to the reliability analysis. In SPSS, this can be achieved using the **Recode** option discussed in Chap. 5. Furthermore, we have to be aware of potential subscales in our item set. Some multi-item scales comprise subsets of items that measure different facets of a multidimensional construct. For example, soccer fan satisfaction is a multidimensional construct that includes aspects such as satisfaction with the stadium, the merchandise (as described above), the team, and the coach. Each of these dimensions is measured by means of different sets of items, which have to be evaluated separately with regard to internal consistency. Calculating one total Cronbach's Alpha value as a function of all 99 items in the study would certainly be inappropriate. Cronbach's Alpha is always calculated over the items belonging to one construct and not all items in the dataset!

One issue of assessing Cronbach's Alpha is its tendency to increase as the number of items in the scale increases. Consequently, researchers have to impose more stringent requirements (i.e., higher threshold values for Cronbach's Alpha) for scales with a large number of items. In particular, scales with more than ten items, should have a Cronbach's Alpha of least 0.80.

We will illustrate a reliability analysis using the standard SPSS module in the example at the end of this chapter.

Structural Equation Modeling

Whereas a confirmatory factor analysis involves testing if and how items relate to specific constructs, structural equation modeling involves the estimation of relations between these constructs. It has become one of the most important methods in the social sciences, including marketing research.

There are two approaches for estimating structural models. The covariance-based approach, which is also referred to as linear structural relations (LISREL) owing to its corresponding software application, and the variance-based approaches, of which partial least squares (PLS) path modeling is currently the most prominent procedure. Both estimation methods are based on the idea of an underlying model that allows the researcher to model, verify, and measure causal relationships between multiple items and constructs.

Figure 8.7 shows an example path model with four constructs and their respective items (note that we omitted the error terms for clarity's sake). A path model incorporates two types of constructs (1) Exogenous constructs (indicated with ξ, and pronounced as *ksi*) that do not depend on other constructs and (2) endogenous constructs (indicated with η, and pronounced as *eta*) that depend on one or more exogenous (or other endogenous) constructs. The relations between the constructs (indicated with γ, and pronounced as *gamma*) are called inner relations, while the relations between the constructs and their respective items (indicated with λ, and pronounced as *lambda*) are called outer relations. One can distinguish between the structural model (also inner model) that incorporates the relations between the constructs and the (exogenous and endogenous) measurement models (also outer models) that represent the relations between the constructs and their dedicated items. Items that measure exogenous (endogenous) constructs are labeled x (y).

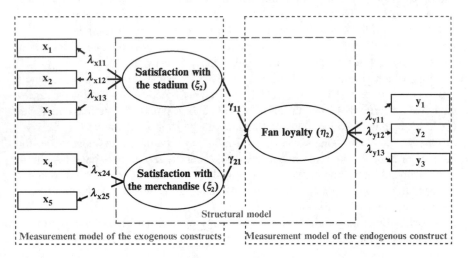

Fig. 8.7 Path model

In this model, we assume that the two exogenous constructs *satisfaction with the stadium* and *satisfaction with the merchandise* relate to the endogenous construct *fan loyalty*, which is operationalized by means of three items y_1, y_2, and y_3. Depending on the research question, we could, of course, incorporate additional exogenous and endogenous constructs. Using data from an empirical survey, we could test this model and, thus, evaluate the exogenous constructs' influence on the endogenous construct. By doing so, we could assess which of the two constructs ξ_1 or ξ_2 exerts the greater influence on η_1. This could guide us in developing marketing plans in order to increase fan loyalty by answering the research question whether we should rather concentrate on increasing the fans' satisfaction with the stadium or with the merchandise.

The results evaluation of a path model analysis requires several steps that include the assessment of both measurement models and the structural model. Janssens et al. (2008) describe covariance-based structural equation modeling. Likewise, Diamantopoulos and Siguaw (2000) and Hair et al. (2010) provide a thorough description of this approach and its application. Chin (1998), Haenlein and Kaplan (2004), as well as Henseler et al. (2009) and Hair et al. (2011) illustrate the PLS path modeling methodology and criteria for assessing results, while Hulland (1999) provides a review of sample PLS path modeling applications.

Lastly, it should be noted that confirmatory factor analysis and structural equation modeling primarily involve the testing of a hypothesized model based on theoretical reasoning, which is more the domain of academic research than business practice.[8] Consequently, these procedures currently play a limited role in market research practice, although this is expected to grow as the investigation of complex model set-ups becomes increasingly important to gain consumer insights and competitive advantages.

Example: Principal Components Analysis and Reliability Analysis

In this example, we take a closer look at some of the items from our soccer fan satisfaction study (soccer_fan_satisfaction.sav, ✍ Web Appendix → Chap. 8). For each of the following items, the respondents had to rate their degree of satisfaction from 1 ("very unsatisfied") to 7 ("very satisfied"). The performance features comprise the respondents' satisfaction with the following features (variable names in parentheses):

- Condition of the stadium (x_1),
- Outer appearance of the stadium (x_2),
- Interior design of the stadium (x_3),
- Quality of the team composition (x_4),
- Number of stars in the team (x_5),
- Price of annual season ticket (x_6), and
- Entry fees (x_7).

The complete item set was presented to various clubs' soccer fans in July 2007. The selection of the respondents comprised fans of several German soccer clubs. Invitations to participate in the study were posted on various Internet fan forums not affiliated with any particular club. Of the 953 people who participated in the study, 495 completed the survey. Since the link to the survey appeared in several club-affiliated Internet forums, the database had to be reduced further to avoid having too many fans from the same clubs. In total, the market research agency selected 251 observations for further analysis. Let us use that dataset to run a principal components analysis.

To run the principal components analysis, simply click on ▸ Analyze ▸ Dimension Reduction ▸ Factor, which will open a dialog box similar to Fig. 8.8. Next, enter all seven variables into the **Variables** box.

---

[8]In some cases, path analysis can also be used in an exploratory way, especially when using PLS path modeling. Asparouhov and Muthén (2009) provide a rather technical discussion of this subject in the context of covariance-based structural equation modeling. However, please note that using structural equation modeling in an exploratory way is still an exception.

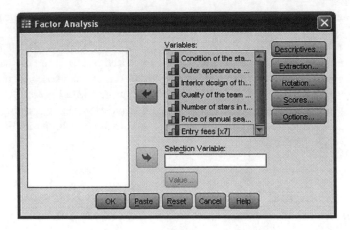

Fig. 8.8 Factor analysis dialog box

SPSS provides several options that relate to Table 8.3. Under **Descriptives**, you can choose to display univariate descriptive statistics, which is a useful way of gaining an overview of the extent of the missing values in your dataset. Furthermore, you can choose from several outputs and statistical measures that relate to the correlation matrix and help assess the data's appropriateness for the analysis. Be sure to check the **Coefficients**, **Significance levels**, **Reproduced** (which refers to the reproduced correlation matrix), **Anti-image**, as well as the **KMO and Bartlett's test of sphericity** boxes to check the assumptions previously discussed. All other options are of minor importance, so skip these and click **Continue**.

The **Extraction** option allows you to specify the analysis method. By default, SPSS sets this as the principal components; however, you can also set it to different types in the **Method** drop-down menu. Under **Extract**, you can determine the rule for factor extraction: By default, all factors with an Eigenvalue greater than one will be extracted. This default option is acceptable – except when you have previous information on the factor structure. If so, you should specify the number of factors manually.

Under **Display**, you should check the scree plot option, which provides additional help in determining the number of factors to extract. Now click **Continue** to access the main menu again.

Under **Rotation**, you can choose between several orthogonal and oblique rotation methods. Always use the **Varimax** procedure – unless your initial solution is difficult to interpret and you have strong theoretical grounds for assuming (moderately) correlated factors. Click **Continue**.

If you wish to use factor scores in subsequent analyses, you can save these in the **Scores** option. Since we strongly recommend using the Regression method, choose **Save as variables** and **Regression**, followed by **Continue**.

Lastly, under **Options**, you can decide how missing values should be handled and specify the display format of the coefficients in the component matrix. In general, we recommend excluding cases that have missing values in any of the variables used in any of the analyses (Option: **Exclude cases listwise**). Avoid replacing missing values with the mean as this will diminish the variation in the data, especially if there are many missing values in your dataset. You should always check the menu **Sorted by size** (under **Coefficient Display Format**), as this greatly increases the clarity of the display of results. If you wish, you can suppress loadings less than 0.10; however, in this example, we ignore this option.

After having specified all the options, you can proceed by clicking the **OK** button.

The descriptive statistics in Table 8.4 reveal that there are several observations with missing values in the dataset. According to our rule of thumb, we would need 7 × 10 = 70 observations. As there are 195 observations without any missing values in the dataset (last column on the right in Table 8.4), we can proceed with checking the variables' correlations. The correlation matrix in Table 8.5 indicates that there are several pairs of variables that are highly correlated. For example, condition of the stadium (x_1) is highly correlated with the outer appearance $(x_2$, correlation = 0.783), as well as the interior design $(x_3$, correlation = 0.754) of the stadium. Likewise, x_2 and x_3 are also highly correlated (correlation = 0.762). As these variables' correlations with the remaining ones are less pronounced, we may suspect that these three variables constitute one factor. As you can see, by just looking at the correlation matrix, we can already hypothesize about a potential factor structure.

Table 8.4 Descriptive statistics

Descriptive Statistics

	Mean	Std. Deviation	Analysis N
x1	5.39	1.962	195
x2	5.50	1.795	195
x3	5.02	1.905	195
x4	4.65	1.718	195
x5	4.56	1.864	195
x6	4.43	1.614	195
x7	4.22	1.509	195

However, at this point of the analysis, we are more interested in checking whether the variables are sufficiently correlated to conduct a principal components analysis. Most correlation coefficients lie above the threshold value of 0.30. When we look at the lower part of Table 8.5, we see that the p-values are extremely low. These results indicate that the variables are sufficiently correlated. However, for a concluding evaluation, we need to take the anti-image and related statistical measures into account. These are presented in Tables 8.6 and 8.7.

The analysis results in Table 8.6 reveal that the KMO value is 0.721, which is middling (see Table 8.2) but still satisfactory. Likewise, the variable-specific MSA values (Table 8.7) on the diagonal of the anti-image correlation matrix are all above the threshold value of 0.50. Furthermore, the Bartlett's test is significant (p < 0.05), which means that we can reject the null hypothesis that, in the population, all

Table 8.5 Correlation matrix

Correlation Matrix

		x1	x2	x3	x4	x5	x6	x7
Correlation	x1	1.000	.783	.754	.395	.338	.246	.172
	x2	.783	1.000	.762	.445	.350	.238	.224
	x3	.754	.762	1.000	.445	.329	.287	.235
	x4	.395	.445	.445	1.000	.829	.311	.241
	x5	.338	.350	.329	.829	1.000	.304	.214
	x6	.246	.238	.287	.311	.304	1.000	.696
	x7	.172	.224	.235	.241	.214	.696	1.000
Sig. (1-tailed)	x1		.000	.000	.000	.000	.000	.008
	x2	.000		.000	.000	.000	.000	.001
	x3	.000	.000		.000	.000	.000	.000
	x4	.000	.000	.000		.000	.000	.000
	x5	.000	.000	.000	.000		.000	.001
	x6	.000	.000	.000	.000	.000		.000
	x7	.008	.001	.000	.000	.001	.000	

Table 8.6 KMO and Bartlett's test measures

KMO and Bartlett's Test

Kaiser-Meyer-Olkin Measure of Sampling Adequacy.		.721
Bartlett's Test of Sphericity	Approx. Chi-Square	809.353
	df	21
	Sig.	.000

variables are uncorrelated. Consequently, we know that the data are appropriate for principal components analysis.

We can now take a look at the factor extraction process table, shown in Table 8.8.

Table 8.8 lists the Eigenvalues associated with each factor before extraction, after extraction, and after rotation. In the columns labeled **Initial Eigenvalues**, we see the results before extraction. SPSS lists all seven factors (we know that there are potentially as many factors as there are variables) in this column. Most of these factors are of course only of minor importance. This is reflected in each factor's Eigenvalue, which is displayed in the table's second column. Here, we see that the first factor has an Eigenvalue of 3.520. As there are seven variables in our dataset, this factor accounts for $3.520/7.00 = 50.290\%$ of the overall variance, which is indicated in the third column. It is quite remarkable that by using only one factor instead of seven variables, we can account for over 50% of the overall variance! The second factor has an Eigenvalue of 1.415 and, thus, still covers more variance than a single variable (remember: since we are looking at standardized variables,

Table 8.7 Anti-image matrices

Anti-image Matrices

		x1	x2	x3	x4	x5	x6	x7
Anti-image Covariance	x1	.321	-.153	-.127	.023	-.032	-.032	.039
	x2	-.153	.308	-.120	-.033	.007	.033	-.042
	x3	-.127	-.120	.337	-.054	.038	-.031	-.008
	x4	.023	-.033	-.054	.275	-.229	-.007	-.011
	x5	-.032	.007	.038	-.229	.304	-.036	.012
	x6	-.032	.033	-.031	-.007	-.036	.479	-.329
	x7	.039	-.042	-.008	-.011	.012	-.329	.507
Anti-image Correlation	x1	.787[a]	-.488	-.385	.077	-.101	-.082	.096
	x2	-.488	.798[a]	-.373	-.113	.024	.086	-.105
	x3	-.385	-.373	.824[a]	-.177	.119	-.076	-.018
	x4	.077	-.113	-.177	.672[a]	-.793	-.018	-.028
	x5	-.101	.024	.119	-.793	.638[a]	-.094	.031
	x6	-.082	.086	-.076	-.018	-.094	.647[a]	-.668
	x7	.096	-.105	-.018	-.028	.031	-.668	.807[a]

a. Measures of Sampling Adequacy(MSA)

Table 8.8 Results of factor extraction

Total Variance Explained

Component	Initial Eigenvalues			Extraction Sums of Squared Loadings			Rotation Sums of Squared Loadings		
	Total	% of Variance	Cumulative %	Total	% of Variance	Cumulative %	Total	% of Variance	Cumulative %
1	3.520	50.290	50.290	3.520	50.290	50.290	2.527	36.096	36.096
2	1.415	20.217	70.507	1.415	20.217	70.507	1.831	26.162	62.258
3	1.135	16.220	86.727	1.135	16.220	86.727	1.713	24.469	86.727
4	.312	4.450	91.177						
5	.257	3.666	94.844						
6	.208	2.969	97.812						
7	.153	2.188	100.000						

Extraction Method: Principal Component Analysis.

each variable has a variance of 1). The same holds for the third factor whose Eigenvalue lies at 1.135. Factors 4–7, however, only marginally account for the total variance explained, as their Eigenvalues are considerably smaller than 1.

The second set of columns, labeled **Extraction Sums of Squared Loadings**, contains the factor solutions after extraction. Since we chose the default option, SPSS extracts all factors with an Eigenvalue greater than 1 (the Kaiser criterion discussed previously). This leads to a solution in which three factors are extracted, which account for 86.727% of the overall variance. The final part of the table, labeled **Rotation Sums of Squared Loadings**, displays the factors after rotation. Rotation is carried out to optimize the factor structure in order to facilitate the interpretation of the factor solution. Rotation usually alters the factors' Eigenvalues, but will not change the total variance explained. For example, the third factor accounted for 16.220% of the overall variance before rotation; however, after rotation, it accounts for 24.469%.

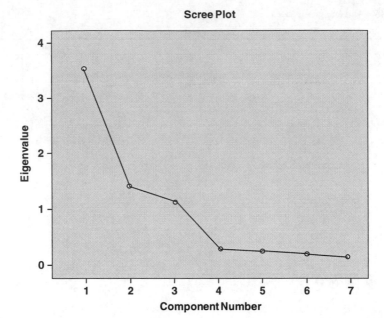

Fig. 8.9 Scree plot

Whereas the Kaiser criterion offers one possibility to determine the number of factors to extract, we can also use the scree plot (Fig. 8.9) to make that decision. In the scree plot, the slope of the curve diminishes and becomes almost horizontal for four factors. Since we always extract one factor less than indicated by the elbow, a three-factor solution is deemed appropriate.[9] As this is in accordance with the Kaiser criterion, we can continue evaluating the results by interpreting the factors.

To do so, take a look at the initial component matrix (Table 8.9), that is, the loadings matrix before factor rotation. In order to interpret the factors, we first "assign" each variable to a certain factor based on its maximum absolute factor loading. After that, we have to find an umbrella term for each factor that best describes the set of variables associated with that factor. Looking at Table 8.9, we see that x_1 through x_5 show the highest loadings for the first factor, whereas the other variables load highly on the second factor. However, what about the third factor? Should it be excluded? It probably should not, as this is a typical example of how an unrotated solution can be misleading. If you take a look at the rotated solution (Table 8.10), a different picture emerges. In this case, only x_1, x_2, and x_3 load highly on the first factor, whereas x_4 and x_5 load on the second, and x_6 and x_7 on the third factor. Comparing the loadings in the unrotated and rotated solution, reveals that the differences in the loadings are quite remarkable. That is why one

---

[9]In the ⌁ Web Appendix (→Chapter 8), we illustrate the use of the parallel analysis and the minimum average partial test for determining the number of factors using this dataset.

Table 8.9 Unrotated factor loadings matrix

Component Matrix[a]

	Component		
	1	2	3
x2	.814	−.369	.230
x3	.813	−.326	.256
x1	.792	−.398	.253
x4	.750	.078	−.586
x5	.680	.135	−.665
x7	.485	.718	.326
x6	.555	.688	.248

Extraction Method: Principal Component
Analysis.
a. 3 components extracted.

Table 8.10 Rotated factor loadings matrix

Rotated Component Matrix[a]

	Component		
	1	2	3
x1	.903	.167	.083
x2	.895	.201	.107
x3	.880	.185	.152
x5	.166	.937	.132
x4	.280	.902	.142
x7	.102	.077	.917
x6	.139	.177	.890

Extraction Method: Principal Component
Analysis.
Rotation Method: Varimax with Kaiser
Normalization.
a. Rotation converged in 4 iterations.

should never use the unrotated solution when interpreting factors! The unrotated solution is only used to determine the number of factors to extract from the dataset. Since the rotation changes the factors' Eigenvalues, the unrotated solution might indicate another number of factors to retain from the data than those indicated by the rotated solution. You see this by comparing the first two and the third set of columns in Table 8.8 (**Initial Eigenvalues** and **Extraction Sums of Squared Loadings** rather than **Rotation Sums of Squared Loadings**).

Having identified which variables load highly on which factor in the rotated solution, we should now try to identify labeling terms for each factor. Variables condition of the stadium (x_1), outer appearance of the stadium (x_2), and interior design of the stadium (x_3) clearly relate to the stadium as such. This seems to be the factor that we mentioned in the introduction of this chapter. Therefore, we can label this *satisfaction with the stadium*. Quality of the team composition (x_4) and number of stars in the team (x_5) describe traits of the soccer team that the respondents evaluated. Even though there are certainly more facets to it, we could label this factor *satisfaction with the team*. The remaining variables, i.e. price of annual season ticket (x_6), and entry fees (x_7) relate to ticket prices. Consequently, we can call the third factor *satisfaction with ticket prices*. Of course, the labeling of factors is subjective and you could provide different descriptions.

The last step involves assessing the analysis's goodness-of-fit. To do so, we first look at the residuals (i.e., the differences between observed and reproduced correlations) in the reproduced correlation matrix (Table 8.11). If we examine the lower part of the table, we see that there are several residuals with absolute values larger than 0.50. Nevertheless, we do not have to count every single value in the matrix (this could be quite exhausting if there are over 100 variables in the dataset). Instead, SPSS counts the proportion of residuals with high residuals, which is reported in the first part of the table. As we can see in point **b.** beneath the table, 23.0% of the residuals have absolute values greater than 0.50. Therefore, we can presume a good model fit. This is also illustrated by the variables' communalities, which are displayed in Table 8.12. Over 80% of each variable's variance is explained by the factors, which is a highly satisfactory result.

Table 8.11 Reproduced correlations and residual matrices

Reproduced Correlations

		x1	x2	x3	x4	x5	x6	x7
Reproduced Correlation	x1	.850[a]	.850	.838	.415	.317	.229	.181
	x2	.850	.852[a]	.841	.447	.351	.255	.205
	x3	.838	.841	.832[a]	.434	.339	.290	.243
	x4	.415	.447	.434	.912[a]	.910	.325	.229
	x5	.317	.351	.339	.910	.923[a]	.306	.210
	x6	.229	.255	.290	.325	.306	.843[a]	.845
	x7	.181	.205	.243	.229	.210	.845	.858[a]
Residual[b]	x1		−.067	-.085	−.020	.021	.017	−.009
	x2	−.067		-.080	−.002	−.001	−.017	.019
	x3	−.085	−.080		.010	−.010	−.003	−.008
	x4	−.020	−.002	.010		−.081	−.014	.012
	x5	.021	−.001	−.010	−.081		−.003	.004
	x6	.017	−.017	−.003	−.014	−.003		−.149
	x7	−.009	.019	−.008	.012	.004	−.149	

Extraction Method: Principal Component Analysis.
a. Reproduced communalities
b. Residuals are computed between observed and reproduced correlations. There are 5 (23,0%) nonredundant residuals with absolute values greater than 0.05.

Table 8.12 Communalities

Communalities

	Initial	Extraction
x1	1.000	.850
x2	1.000	.852
x3	1.000	.832
x4	1.000	.912
x5	1.000	.923
x6	1.000	.843
x7	1.000	.858

Extraction Method: Principal
Component Analysis.

	x6	x7	FAC1_1	FAC2_1	FAC3_1
1	5	5	-.34006	.55130	.16799
2	8	1	.	.	.
3	8	6	.	.	.
4	8	6	.	.	.
5	4	5	.84722	.61924	-.04384
6	4	6	-1.18989	-1.46760	.89205
7	4	4	.83536	.08754	-.35509
8	8	7	.	.	.
9	8	4	.	.	.
10	4	3	-.00081	.34037	-.67535
11	8	4	.	.	.
12	6	4	.73211	.04437	.33035
13	6	6	.64652	1.14657	.95279
14	6	6	.76819	.50151	1.02641

Fig. 8.10 SPSS data view window

At this point, we have completed the principal components analysis. However, if we wish to continue using the analysis results, we should calculate factor scores. We can save factor scores using the **Scores** option; SPSS creates three new variables, one for each factor in the final solution (Fig. 8.10). Using these variables, we could, for example, evaluate whether male and female fans differ significantly with regard to their satisfaction with the stadium (first factor), the team (second factor), or the ticket prices (third factor). SPSS can only calculate these scores if it has information on all the variables included in the factor analysis. If SPSS does not have all the information, it only shows a "." (dot) in the data view window, indicating system-missing values for a certain observation (as it is the case with observations 2, 3, and 4; Fig. 8.10).

Instead of using the factor scores in subsequent analyses, we could use an average score, calculated as the mean of the variables related to the respective factor. This is usually done in cases where the researcher already has an idea which variables relate to which factors, or wants to test a hypothesized factor structure (thus carrying out a confirmatory analysis).

A typical application would be to conduct a follow-up study of fan satisfaction. To ensure the comparability of the results, we could replicate the factor structure from the initial analysis, using summated scores obtained from the follow-up study. However, before doing so, we have to carry out a reliability analysis to assess whether the scale's results are consistent. In other words, we have to ensure that the perception of the constructs did not change significantly over time. To illustrate its usage, let's carry out a reliability analysis of the factor *satisfaction with the stadium* by calculating Cronbach's Alpha as a function of the variables satisfaction with the condition of the stadium, satisfaction with the outer appearance of the stadium, and satisfaction with the interior design of the stadium. To run the reliability analysis, simply click on ▸ Analyze ▸ Scale ▸ Reliability Analysis. Next, enter variables x_1, x_2, and x_3 into the **Items** box and type in the scale's name, namely *satisfaction with the stadium*. Check that **Alpha** is selected in the **Model** drop-down list (Fig. 8.11).

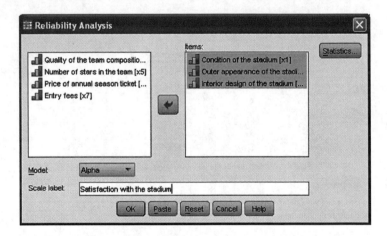

Fig. 8.11 Reliability analysis dialog box

Next, click on **Statistics** and choose **Scale if item deleted** (under **Descriptives for**). If you want, you could also request descriptive statistics for each item and the entire scale or item correlations (submenu **Inter-item**). However, for the sake of simplicity, we will work with the default settings.

The **Reliability Statistics** (Table 8.13) show that the scale exhibits a high degree of reliability. With a value of 0.902, the Cronbach's Alpha coefficient lies well above the commonly suggested threshold of 0.70. This is not surprising, since we are simply testing a scale that has previously been established by means of item correlations. Keep in mind that we usually carry out a reliability analysis to test a scale using a different sample – this example is only for illustration purposes!

Examining the far right column of Table 8.14, we can see how Cronbach's Alpha would develop if a certain item were to be deleted from the scale. When we

Table 8.13 Reliability statistics

Reliability Statistics

Cronbach's Alpha	N of Items
.902	3

Table 8.14 Item-total statistics

Item-Total Statistics

	Scale Mean if Item Deleted	Scale Variance if Item Deleted	Corrected Item-Total Correction	Cronbach's Alpha if them Deleted
x1	10.60	11.082	.808	.860
x2	10.53	11.951	.817	.853
x3	11.00	11.421	.790	.069

compare each of the values to the overall Alpha value, we can see that any change in the scale's set-up would reduce the Alpha value. For example, by removing x_1 from the scale, the Cronbach's Alpha of the new scale comprising only x_2 and x_3 would be reduced to 0.860.

Deleting this item therefore makes little sense. Only if the initial Cronbach's Alpha is below acceptable standards (i.e., below 0.70), we should try to increase it by removing one or more items from the scale. If it is acceptable, we should not attempt to improve it by changing the scale's set-up.

Case Study

Haver & Boecker is one of the world's leading providers of filling and screening systems. The company operates a number of facilities in Germany, as well as production plants in the UK, Belgium, USA, Canada, and Brazil. It is a recognized specialist in the fields of weighing, filling, and material handling technology. Haver & Boecker designs, produces, and markets systems and plants for filling and processing loose bulk materials of every type and, thus, solely operates in industrial markets.

The company's relationships with its customers are usually long-term oriented, and complex. Since the company's philosophy is to assist customers and business partners in solving technical problems and innovating new solutions, their products are often customized to the buyers' needs. Therefore, the customer is no longer a passive buyer, but an active partner. Given this background, the customer's satisfaction plays an important role in establishing, developing, and maintaining successful customer relationships.

http://www.haverboecker.com

Very early on, the company's management realized the importance of customer satisfaction and decided to commission a market research project to identify marketing activities that can positively contribute to the business's overall success. Based on a thorough literature review as well as interviews with experts, the company developed a short survey to explore their customers' satisfaction with specific performance features and their overall satisfaction. All items were measured on 7-point scales with higher scores denoting higher levels of satisfaction. A standardized survey was mailed to customers in 12 countries worldwide, which yielded 281 fully completed questionnaires. The following items (names in parentheses) were listed in the survey:

- Reliability of the machines and systems (s_1)
- Life-time of the machines and systems (s_2)
- Functionality and user-friendliness operation of the machines and systems (s_3)
- Appearance of the machines and systems (s_4)
- Accuracy of the machines and systems (s_5)
- Timely availability of the after-sales service (s_6)
- Local availability of the after-sales service (s_7)
- Fast processing of complaints (s_8)
- Composition of quotations (s_9)
- Transparency of quotations (s_{10})
- Fixed product prize for the machines and systems (s_{11})
- Cost/performance ratio of the machines and systems (s_{12})
- Overall, how satisfied are you with the supplier (*overall*)?

Your task is to analyze the dataset to provide the management of Haver & Boecker with advice for effective customer satisfaction management. The dataset is labeled *haver_and_boecker.sav* (🖰 Web Appendix → Chap. 8).

1. Using regression analysis, locate those variables that best explain the customers' overall satisfaction. Evaluate the model fit and assess the impact of each variable on the criterion variable. Remember to consider collinearity diagnostics.

2. Determine the factors that characterize the respondents by means a factor analysis. Use items s_1–s_{12} for this. Run a principal axis factoring with varimax rotation to facilitate interpretation. Consider the following issues:
   (a) Are all assumptions for carrying out a factor analysis met? Pay special attention to the question whether the data are sufficiently correlated.
   (b) How many factors would you extract?
   (c) Try to find suitable labels for the extracted factors.
   (d) Evaluate the solution's goodness-of-fit.
3. Use the factor scores and regress the customers' overall satisfaction (*overall*) on these. Evaluate the strength of the model and compare it with the initial regression. What should Haver & Boecker's management do to increase their customers' satisfaction?
4. Calculate Cronbach's Alpha over items s_1–s_5 and interpret the results.

For further information on the dataset and the study, compare Festge and Schwaiger (2007) as well as Sarstedt et al. (2009).

Questions

1. What is factor analysis? Try to explain what factor analysis is in your own words.
2. Describe the terms Eigenvalue, communality, and factor loading. How do these concepts relate to one another?
3. What is the difference between principal components analysis and principal axis factoring?
4. Describe three approaches used to determine the number of factors.
5. What are the purpose and the characteristic of a varimax rotation? Does a rotation alter Eigenvalues, factor loadings or communalities?
6. Re-run the analysis on soccer fan satisfaction by carrying out principal axis factoring and compare the results with our example analysis.
7. Explain the similarities and differences between exploratory factor analysis and confirmatory factor analysis.
8. Explain the basic principle of structural equation modeling.

Further Readings

Fornell C, Bookstein FL (1982) Two structural equation models: LISREL and PLS applied to consumer exit-voice theory. J Mark Res 19(4):440–452
   In this seminal article, the authors compare the statistical principles of covariance- and variance-based structural equation modeling. The illustrations are rather technical and more suited for readers with a strong background in statistics and research methodology.

Nunnally JC, Bernstein IH (1993) Psychometric theory, 3rd edn. McGraw-Hill, New York

Psychometric Theory is a classic text and the most comprehensive introduction to the fundamental principles of measurement. Chapter 7 provides an in-depth discussion of the nature of reliability and its assessment.

Stewart DW (1981) The application and misapplication of factor analysis in marketing research. J Mark Res 18(1):51–62

David Stewart discusses procedures for determining when data are appropriate for factor analysis, as well as guidelines for determining the number of factors to extract, and for rotation.

References

Asparouhov T, Muthén B (2009) Exploratory structural equation modeling. Struct Equ Modeling 16(3):397–438

Bronner F, Neijens P (2006) Audience experiences of media context and embedded advertising. Int J Mark Res 48(1):81–100

Chin WW (1998) The partial least squares approach for structural equation modeling. In: Marcoulides GA (ed) Modern methods for business research. Lawrence Erlbaum Associates, London, pp 295–336

Cronbach LJ (1951) Coefficient alpha and the internal structure of tests. Psychometrika 16(3): 297–334

Diamantopoulos A, Siguaw JA (2000) Introducing LISREL: a guide for the uninitiated. Sage, London

Festge F, Schwaiger M (2007) The drivers of customer satisfaction with industrial goods: an international study. Adv Int Mark 18:179–207

Haenlein M, Kaplan AM (2004) A beginner's guide to partial least squares. Underst Stat 3(4): 283–297

Hair JF, Black WC, Babin BJ, Anderson RE (2010) Multivariate data analysis, 7th edn. Pearson Prentice Hall, Upper Saddle River, NJ

Hair, Joe Jr, Ringle CM, Sarstedt M (2011) PLS-SEM. Indeed a Silver Bullet. Journal of Marketing Theory & Practice, forthcoming

Henseler J, Ringle CM, Sinkovic RR (2009) The use of partial least squares path modeling in international marketing. Adv Int Mark 20:277–320

Hulland J (1999) Use of partial least squares (PLS) in strategic management research: a review of four recent studies. Strateg Manage J 20(2):195–204

Janssens W, Wijnen K, de Pelsmacker P, van Kenhove P (2008) Marketing Research with SPSS, Hanlow, UK: Prentice Hall

Kaiser HF (1974) An index of factorial simplicity. Psychometrika 39(1):31–36

Sarstedt M, Schwaiger M, Ringle CM (2009) Do we fully understand the critical success factors of customer satisfaction with industrial goods?–Festge and Schwaiger's model to account for unobserved heterogeneity. J Bus Mark Manage 3(3):185–206

Chapter 9
Cluster Analysis

Learning Objectives

After reading this chapter you should understand:
- The basic concepts of cluster analysis.
- How basic cluster algorithms work.
- How to compute simple clustering results manually.
- The different types of clustering procedures.
- The SPSS clustering outputs.

Keywords Agglomerative and divisive clustering · Chebychev distance · City-block distance · Clustering variables · Dendrogram · Distance matrix · Euclidean distance · Hierarchical and partitioning methods · Icicle diagram · k-means · Matching coefficients · Profiling clusters · Two-step clustering

Are there any market segments where Web-enabled mobile telephony is taking off in different ways? To answer this question, Okazaki (2006) applies a two-step cluster analysis by identifying segments of Internet adopters in Japan. The findings suggest that there are four clusters exhibiting distinct attitudes towards Web-enabled mobile telephony adoption. Interestingly, freelance, and highly educated professionals had the most negative perception of mobile Internet adoption, whereas clerical office workers had the most positive perception. Furthermore, housewives and company executives also exhibited a positive attitude toward mobile Internet usage. Marketing managers can now use these results to better target specific customer segments via mobile Internet services.

Introduction

Grouping similar customers and products is a fundamental marketing activity. It is used, prominently, in market segmentation. As companies cannot connect with all their customers, they have to divide markets into groups of consumers, customers, or clients (called segments) with similar needs and wants. Firms can then target each of these segments by positioning themselves in a unique segment (such as Ferrari in the high-end sports car market). While market researchers often form

E. Mooi and M. Sarstedt, *A Concise Guide to Market Research*,
DOI 10.1007/978-3-642-12541-6_9, © Springer-Verlag Berlin Heidelberg 2011

market segments based on practical grounds, industry practice and wisdom, cluster analysis allows segments to be formed that are based on data that are less dependent on subjectivity.

The segmentation of customers is a standard application of cluster analysis, but it can also be used in different, sometimes rather exotic, contexts such as evaluating typical supermarket shopping paths (Larson et al. 2005) or deriving employers' branding strategies (Moroko and Uncles 2009).

Understanding Cluster Analysis

Cluster analysis is a convenient method for identifying homogenous groups of objects called clusters. Objects (or cases, observations) in a specific cluster share many characteristics, but are very dissimilar to objects not belonging to that cluster.

Let's try to gain a basic understanding of the cluster analysis procedure by looking at a simple example. Imagine that you are interested in segmenting your customer base in order to better target them through, for example, pricing strategies.

The first step is to decide on the characteristics that you will use to segment your customers. In other words, you have to decide which clustering variables will be included in the analysis. For example, you may want to segment a market based on customers' price consciousness (x) and brand loyalty (y). These two variables can be measured on a 7-point scale with higher values denoting a higher degree of price consciousness and brand loyalty. The values of seven respondents are shown in Table 9.1 and the scatter plot in Fig. 9.1.

The objective of cluster analysis is to identify groups of objects (in this case, customers) that are very similar with regard to their price consciousness and brand loyalty and assign them into clusters. After having decided on the clustering variables (brand loyalty and price consciousness), we need to decide on the clustering procedure to form our groups of objects. This step is crucial for the analysis, as different procedures require different decisions prior to analysis. There is an abundance of different approaches and little guidance on which to use in practice. We are going to discuss the most popular approaches in market research, as they can be easily computed using SPSS. These approaches are: *hierarchical methods*, *partitioning methods* (more precisely, *k-means*), and *two-step clustering*, which is largely a combination of the first two methods. Each of these procedures follows a different approach to grouping the most similar objects into a cluster and to determining each object's cluster membership. In other words, whereas an object in a certain cluster should be as similar as possible to all the other objects in the

Table 9.1 Data

Customer	A	B	C	D	E	F	G
x	3	6	5	3	6	4	1
y	7	7	6	5	5	3	2

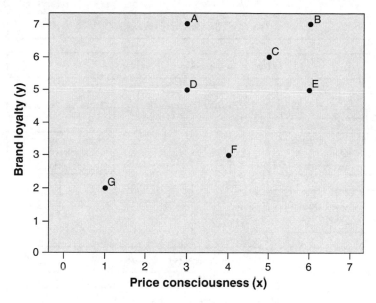

Fig. 9.1 Scatter plot

same cluster, it should likewise be as distinct as possible from objects in different clusters.

But how do we measure similarity? Some approaches – most notably hierarchical methods – require us to specify how similar or different objects are in order to identify different clusters. Most software packages calculate a measure of (dis)similarity by estimating the distance between pairs of objects. Objects with smaller distances between one another are more similar, whereas objects with larger distances are more dissimilar.

An important problem in the application of cluster analysis is the decision regarding how many clusters should be derived from the data. This question is explored in the next step of the analysis. Sometimes, however, we already know the number of segments that have to be derived from the data. For example, if we were asked to ascertain what characteristics distinguish frequent shoppers from infrequent ones, we need to find two different clusters. However, we do not usually know the exact number of clusters and then we face a trade-off. On the one hand, you want as few clusters as possible to make them easy to understand and actionable. On the other hand, having many clusters allows you to identify more segments and more subtle differences between segments. In an extreme case, you can address each individual separately (called one-to-one marketing) to meet consumers' varying needs in the best possible way. Examples of such a micro-marketing strategy are Puma's Mongolian Shoe BBQ (www.mongolianshoebbq.puma.com) and Nike ID (http://nikeid.nike.com), in which customers can fully customize a pair of shoes in a hands-on, tactile, and interactive shoe-making experience. On the other hand, the costs associated with such a strategy may be prohibitively high in many

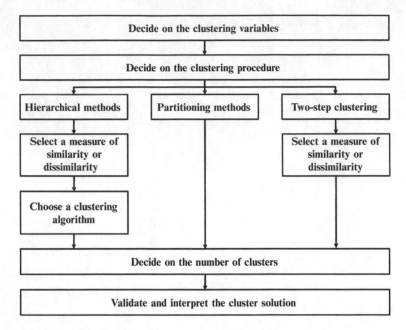

Fig. 9.2 Steps in a cluster analysis

business contexts. Thus, we have to ensure that the segments are large enough to make the targeted marketing programs profitable. Consequently, we have to cope with a certain degree of within-cluster heterogeneity, which makes targeted marketing programs less effective.

In the final step, we need to interpret the solution by defining and labeling the obtained clusters. This can be done by examining the clustering variables' mean values or by identifying explanatory variables to profile the clusters. Ultimately, managers should be able to identify customers in each segment on the basis of easily measurable variables. This final step also requires us to assess the clustering solution's stability and validity. Figure 9.2 illustrates the steps associated with a cluster analysis; we will discuss these in more detail in the following sections.

Conducting a Cluster Analysis

Decide on the Clustering Variables

At the beginning of the clustering process, we have to select appropriate variables for clustering. Even though this choice is of utmost importance, it is rarely treated as such and, instead, a mixture of intuition and data availability guide most analyses in marketing practice. However, faulty assumptions may lead to improper market segments and, consequently, to deficient marketing strategies. Thus, great care should be taken when selecting the clustering variables.

There are several types of clustering variables and these can be classified into *general* (independent of products, services or circumstances) and *specific* (related to both the customer and the product, service and/or particular circumstance), on the one hand, and *observable* (i.e., measured directly) and *unobservable* (i.e., inferred) on the other. Table 9.2 provides several types and examples of clustering variables.

Table 9.2 Types and examples of clustering variables

	General	Specific
Observable (directly measurable)	Cultural, geographic, demographic, socio-economic	User status, usage frequency, store and brand loyalty
Unobservable (inferred)	Psychographics, values, personality, lifestyle	Benefits, perceptions, attitudes, intentions, preferences

Adapted from Wedel and Kamakura (2000)

The types of variables used for cluster analysis provide different segments and, thereby, influence segment-targeting strategies. Over the last decades, attention has shifted from more traditional general clustering variables towards product-specific unobservable variables. The latter generally provide better guidance for decisions on marketing instruments' effective specification. It is generally acknowledged that segments identified by means of specific unobservable variables are usually more homogenous and their consumers respond consistently to marketing actions (see Wedel and Kamakura 2000). However, consumers in these segments are also frequently hard to identify from variables that are easily measured, such as demographics. Conversely, segments determined by means of generally observable variables usually stand out due to their identifiability but often lack a unique response structure.[1] Consequently, researchers often combine different variables (e.g., multiple lifestyle characteristics combined with demographic variables), benefiting from each ones strengths.

In some cases, the choice of clustering variables is apparent from the nature of the task at hand. For example, a managerial problem regarding corporate communications will have a fairly well defined set of clustering variables, including contenders such as awareness, attitudes, perceptions, and media habits. However, this is not always the case and researchers have to choose from a set of candidate variables.

Whichever clustering variables are chosen, it is important to select those that provide a clear-cut differentiation between the segments regarding a specific managerial objective.[2] More precisely, criterion validity is of special interest; that is, the extent to which the "independent" clustering variables are associated with

---

[1]See Wedel and Kamakura (2000).

[2]Tonks (2009) provides a discussion of segment design and the choice of clustering variables in consumer markets.

one or more "dependent" variables not included in the analysis. Given this relationship, there should be significant differences between the "dependent" variable(s) across the clusters. These associations may or may not be causal, but it is essential that the clustering variables distinguish the "dependent" variable(s) significantly. Criterion variables usually relate to some aspect of behavior, such as purchase intention or usage frequency.

Generally, you should avoid using an abundance of clustering variables, as this increases the odds that the variables are no longer dissimilar. If there is a high degree of collinearity between the variables, they are not sufficiently unique to identify distinct market segments. If highly correlated variables are used for cluster analysis, specific aspects covered by these variables will be overrepresented in the clustering solution. In this regard, absolute correlations above 0.90 are always problematic. For example, if we were to add another variable called *brand preference* to our analysis, it would virtually cover the same aspect as *brand loyalty*. Thus, the concept of being attached to a brand would be overrepresented in the analysis because the clustering procedure does not differentiate between the clustering variables in a conceptual sense. Researchers frequently handle this issue by applying cluster analysis to the observations' factor scores derived from a previously carried out factor analysis. However, according to Dolnicar and Grün (2009), this factor-cluster segmentation approach can lead to several problems:

1. The data are pre-processed and the clusters are identified on the basis of transformed values, not on the original information, which leads to different results.
2. In factor analysis, the factor solution does not explain a certain amount of variance; thus, information is discarded before segments have been identified or constructed.
3. Eliminating variables with low loadings on all the extracted factors means that, potentially, the most important pieces of information for the identification of niche segments are discarded, making it impossible to ever identify such groups.
4. The interpretations of clusters based on the original variables become questionable given that the segments have been constructed using factor scores.

Several studies have shown that the factor-cluster segmentation significantly reduces the success of segment recovery.[3] Consequently, you should rather reduce the number of items in the questionnaire's pre-testing phase, retaining a reasonable number of relevant, non-redundant questions that you believe differentiate the segments well. However, if you have your doubts about the data structure, factor-clustering segmentation may still be a better option than discarding items that may conceptually be necessary.

Furthermore, we should keep the sample size in mind. First and foremost, this relates to issues of managerial relevance as segments' sizes need to be substantial to ensure that targeted marketing programs are profitable. From a statistical perspective, every additional variable requires an over-proportional increase in

---

[3]See the studies by Arabie and Hubert (1994), Sheppard (1996), or Dolnicar and Grün (2009).

observations to ensure valid results. Unfortunately, there is no generally accepted rule of thumb regarding minimum sample sizes or the relationship between the objects and the number of clustering variables used.

In a related methodological context, Formann (1984) recommends a sample size of at least 2^m, where m equals the number of clustering variables. This can only provide rough guidance; nevertheless, we should pay attention to the relationship between the objects and clustering variables. It does not, for example, appear logical to cluster ten objects using ten variables. Keep in mind that no matter how many variables are used and no matter how small the sample size, cluster analysis will always render a result!

Ultimately, the choice of clustering variables always depends on contextual influences such as data availability or resources to acquire additional data. Marketing researchers often overlook the fact that the choice of clustering variables is closely connected to data quality. Only those variables that ensure that high quality data can be used should be included in the analysis. This is very important if a segmentation solution has to be managerially useful. Furthermore, data are of high quality if the questions asked have a strong theoretical basis, are not contaminated by respondent fatigue or response styles, are recent, and thus reflect the current market situation (Dolnicar and Lazarevski 2009). Lastly, the requirements of other managerial functions within the organization often play a major role. Sales and distribution may as well have a major influence on the design of market segments. Consequently, we have to be aware that subjectivity and common sense agreement will (and should) always impact the choice of clustering variables.

Decide on the Clustering Procedure

By choosing a specific clustering procedure, we determine how clusters are to be formed. This always involves optimizing some kind of criterion, such as minimizing the within-cluster variance (i.e., the clustering variables' overall variance of objects in a specific cluster), or maximizing the distance between the objects or clusters. The procedure could also address the question of how to determine the (dis)similarity between objects in a newly formed cluster and the remaining objects in the dataset.

There are many different clustering procedures and also many ways of classifying these (e.g., overlapping versus non-overlapping, unimodal versus multimodal, exhaustive versus non-exhaustive).[4] A practical distinction is the differentiation between *hierarchical* and *partitioning methods* (most notably the *k-means* procedure), which we are going to discuss in the next sections. We also introduce *two-step clustering*, which combines the principles of hierarchical and partitioning methods and which has recently gained increasing attention from market research practice.

---

[4]See Wedel and Kamakura (2000), Dolnicar (2003), and Kaufman and Rousseeuw (2005) for a review of clustering techniques.

Hierarchical Methods

Hierarchical clustering procedures are characterized by the tree-like structure established in the course of the analysis. Most hierarchical techniques fall into a category called *agglomerative clustering*. In this category, clusters are consecutively formed from objects. Initially, this type of procedure starts with each object representing an individual cluster. These clusters are then sequentially merged according to their similarity. First, the two most similar clusters (i.e., those with the smallest distance between them) are merged to form a new cluster at the bottom of the hierarchy. In the next step, another pair of clusters is merged and linked to a higher level of the hierarchy, and so on. This allows a hierarchy of clusters to be established from the bottom up. In Fig. 9.3 (left-hand side), we show how agglomerative clustering assigns additional objects to clusters as the cluster size increases.

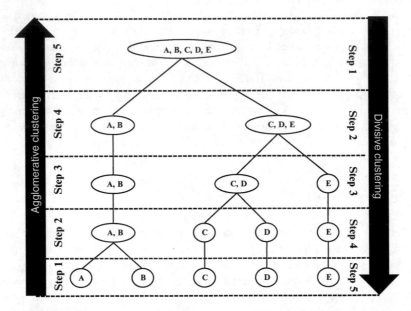

Fig. 9.3 Agglomerative and divisive clustering

A cluster hierarchy can also be generated top-down. In this *divisive clustering*, all objects are initially merged into a single cluster, which is then gradually split up. Figure 9.3 illustrates this concept (right-hand side). As we can see, in both agglomerative and divisive clustering, a cluster on a higher level of the hierarchy always encompasses all clusters from a lower level. This means that if an object is assigned to a certain cluster, there is no possibility of reassigning this object to another cluster. This is an important distinction between these types of clustering and partitioning methods such as k-means, which we will explore in the next section.

Divisive procedures are quite rarely used in market research. We therefore concentrate on the agglomerative clustering procedures. There are various types of agglomerative procedures. However, before we discuss these, we need to define how similarities or dissimilarities are measured between pairs of objects.

Select a Measure of Similarity or Dissimilarity

There are various measures to express (dis)similarity between pairs of objects. A straightforward way to assess two objects' proximity is by drawing a straight line between them. For example, when we look at the scatter plot in Fig. 9.1, we can easily see that the length of the line connecting observations B and C is much shorter than the line connecting B and G. This type of distance is also referred to as *Euclidean distance* (or straight-line distance) and is the most commonly used type when it comes to analyzing ratio or interval-scaled data.[5] In our example, we have ordinal data, but market researchers usually treat ordinal data as metric data to calculate distance metrics by assuming that the scale steps are equidistant (very much like in factor analysis, which we discussed in Chap. 8). To use a hierarchical clustering procedure, we need to express these distances mathematically. By taking the data in Table 9.1 into consideration, we can easily compute the Euclidean distance between customer B and customer C (generally referred to as d(B,C)) with regard to the two variables x and y by using the following formula:

$$d_{Euclidean}(B,C) = \sqrt{(x_B - x_C)^2 + (y_B - y_C)^2}$$

The Euclidean distance is the square root of the sum of the squared differences in the variables' values. Using the data from Table 9.1, we obtain the following:

$$d_{Euclidean}(B,C) = \sqrt{(6-5)^2 + (7-6)^2} = \sqrt{2} = 1.414$$

This distance corresponds to the length of the line that connects objects B and C. In this case, we only used two variables but we can easily add more under the root sign in the formula. However, each additional variable will add a dimension to our research problem (e.g., with six clustering variables, we have to deal with six dimensions), making it impossible to represent the solution graphically. Similarly, we can compute the distance between customer B and G, which yields the following:

$$d_{Euclidean}(B,G) = \sqrt{(6-1)^2 + (7-2)^2} = \sqrt{50} = 7.071$$

Likewise, we can compute the distance between all other pairs of objects. All these distances are usually expressed by means of a *distance matrix*. In this distance matrix, the non-diagonal elements express the distances between pairs of objects

---

[5]Note that researchers also often use the squared Euclidean distance.

and zeros on the diagonal (the distance from each object to itself is, of course, 0). In our example, the distance matrix is an 8×8 table with the lines and rows representing the objects (i.e., customers) under consideration (see Table 9.3). As the distance between objects B and C (in this case 1.414 units) is the same as between C and B, the distance matrix is symmetrical. Furthermore, since the distance between an object and itself is zero, one need only look at either the lower or upper non-diagonal elements.

Table 9.3 Euclidean distance matrix

Objects	A	B	C	D	E	F	G
A	0						
B	3	0					
C	2.236	1.414	0				
D	2	3.606	2.236	0			
E	3.606	2	1.414	3	0		
F	4.123	4.472	3.162	2.236	2.828	0	
G	5.385	7.071	5.657	3.606	5.831	3.162	0

There are also alternative distance measures: The *city-block distance* uses the sum of the variables' absolute differences. This is often called the Manhattan metric as it is akin to the walking distance between two points in a city like New York's Manhattan district, where the distance equals the number of blocks in the directions North-South and East-West. Using the city-block distance to compute the distance between customers B and C (or C and B) yields the following:

$$d_{City-block}(B,C) = |x_B - x_C| + |y_B - y_C| = |6 - 5| + |7 - 6| = 2$$

The resulting distance matrix is in Table 9.4.

Table 9.4 City-block distance matrix

Objects	A	B	C	D	E	F	G
A	0						
B	3	0					
C	3	2	0				
D	2	5	3	0			
E	5	2	2	3	0		
F	5	6	4	3	4	0	
G	7	10	8	5	8	4	0

Lastly, when working with metric (or ordinal) data, researchers frequently use the *Chebychev distance*, which is the maximum of the absolute difference in the clustering variables' values. In respect of customers B and C, this result is:

$$d_{Chebychec}(B,C) = \max(|x_B - x_C|, |y_B - y_C|) = \max(|6 - 5|, |7 - 6|) = 1$$

Figure 9.4 illustrates the interrelation between these three distance measures regarding two objects, C and G, from our example.

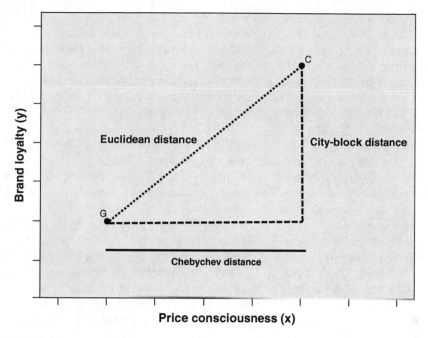

Fig. 9.4 Distance measures

There are other distance measures such as the Angular, Canberra or Mahalanobis distance. In many situations, the latter is desirable as it compensates for collinearity between the clustering variables. However, it is (unfortunately) not menu-accessible in SPSS.

In many analysis tasks, the variables under consideration are measured on different scales or levels. This would be the case if we extended our set of clustering variables by adding another ordinal variable representing the customers' income measured by means of, for example, 15 categories. Since the absolute variation of the income variable would be much greater than the variation of the remaining two variables (remember, that x and y are measured on 7-point scales), this would clearly distort our analysis results. We can resolve this problem by standardizing the data prior to the analysis.

Different standardization methods are available, such as the simple z standardization, which rescales each variable to have a mean of 0 and a standard deviation of 1 (see Chap. 5). In most situations, however, standardization by range (e.g., to a range of 0 to 1 or −1 to 1) performs better.[6] We recommend standardizing the data in general, even though this procedure can reduce or inflate the variables' influence on the clustering solution.

---

[6]See Milligan and Cooper (1988).

Another way of (implicitly) standardizing the data is by using the correlation between the objects instead of distance measures. For example, suppose a respondent rated price consciousness 2 and brand loyalty 3. Now suppose a second respondent indicated 5 and 6, whereas a third rated these variables 3 and 3. Euclidean, city-block, and Chebychev distances would indicate that the first respondent is more similar to the third than to the second. Nevertheless, one could convincingly argue that the first respondent's ratings are more similar to the second's, as both rate brand loyalty higher than price consciousness. This can be accounted for by computing the correlation between two vectors of values as a measure of similarity (i.e., high correlation coefficients indicate a high degree of similarity). Consequently, similarity is no longer defined by means of the difference between the answer categories but by means of the similarity of the answering profiles. Using correlation is also a way of standardizing the data implicitly.

Whether you use correlation or one of the distance measures depends on whether you think the relative magnitude of the variables within an object (which favors correlation) matters more than the relative magnitude of each variable across objects (which favors distance). However, it is generally recommended that one uses correlations when applying clustering procedures that are susceptible to outliers, such as complete linkage, average linkage or centroid (see next section).

Whereas the distance measures presented thus far can be used for metrically and – in general – ordinally scaled data, applying them to nominal or binary data is meaningless. In this type of analysis, you should rather select a similarity measure expressing the degree to which variables' values share the same category. These so-called *matching coefficients* can take different forms but rely on the same allocation scheme shown in Table 9.5.

Table 9.5 Allocation scheme for matching coefficients

		Object 1	
		Number of variables with category 1	Number of variables with category 2
Object 2	Number of variables with category 1	a	b
	Number of variables with category 2	c	d

Based on the allocation scheme in Table 9.5, we can compute different matching coefficients, such as the simple matching coefficient (SM):

$$SM = \frac{a+d}{a+b+c+d}$$

This coefficient is useful when both positive and negative values carry an equal degree of information. For example, gender is a symmetrical attribute because the number of males and females provides an equal degree of information.

Let's take a look at an example by assuming that we have a dataset with three binary variables: gender (male $= 1$, female $= 2$), customer (customer $= 1$, non-customer $= 2$), and disposable income (low $= 1$, high $= 2$). The first object is a male non-customer with a high disposable income, whereas the second object is a female non-customer with a high disposable income. According to the scheme in Table 9.4, $a = b = 0$, $c = 1$ and $d = 2$, with the simple matching coefficient taking a value of 0.667.

Two other types of matching coefficients, which do not equate the joint absence of a characteristic with similarity and may, therefore, be of more value in segmentation studies, are the *Jaccard (JC)* and the *Russel and Rao (RR)* coefficients. They are defined as follows:

$$JC = \frac{a}{a+b+c}$$

$$RR = \frac{a}{a+b+c+d}$$

These matching coefficients are – just like the distance measures – used to determine a cluster solution. There are many other matching coefficients such as Yule's Q, Kulczynski or Ochiai, but since most applications of cluster analysis rely on metric or ordinal data, we will not discuss these in greater detail.[7]

For nominal variables with more than two categories, you should always convert the categorical variable into a set of binary variables in order to use matching coefficients. When you have ordinal data, you should always use distance measures such as Euclidean distance. Even though using matching coefficients would be feasible and – from a strictly statistical standpoint – even more appropriate, you would disregard variable information in the sequence of the categories. In the end, a respondent who indicates that he or she is very loyal to a brand is going to be closer to someone who is somewhat loyal than a respondent who is not loyal at all. Furthermore, distance measures best represent the concept of proximity, which is fundamental to cluster analysis.

Most datasets contain variables that are measured on multiple scales. For example, a market research questionnaire may ask about the respondent's income, product ratings, and last brand purchased. Thus, we have to consider variables measured on a ratio, ordinal, and nominal scale. How can we simultaneously incorporate these variables into one analysis? Unfortunately, this problem cannot be easily resolved and, in fact, many market researchers simply ignore the scale level. Instead, they use one of the distance measures discussed in the context of metric (and ordinal) data. Even though this approach may slightly change the results when compared to those using matching coefficients, it should not be rejected. Cluster analysis is mostly an exploratory technique whose results provide a rough guidance for managerial decisions. Despite this, there are several procedures that allow a simultaneous integration of these variables into one analysis.

---

[7]See Wedel and Kamakura (2000) for more information on alternative matching coefficients.

First, we could compute distinct distance matrices for each group of variables; that is, one distance matrix based on, for example, ordinally scaled variables and another based on nominal variables. Afterwards, we can simply compute the weighted arithmetic mean of the distances and use this average distance matrix as the input for the cluster analysis. However, the weights have to be determined a priori and improper weights may result in a biased treatment of different variable types. Furthermore, the computation and handling of distance matrices are not trivial. Using the SPSS syntax, one has to manually add the MATRIX subcommand, which exports the initial distance matrix into a new data file. Go to the ⫟ Web Appendix (→ Chap. 5) to learn how to modify the SPSS syntax accordingly.

Second, we could dichotomize all variables and apply the matching coefficients discussed above. In the case of metric variables, this would involve specifying categories (e.g., low, medium, and high income) and converting these into sets of binary variables. In most cases, however, the specification of categories would be rather arbitrary and, as mentioned earlier, this procedure could lead to a severe loss of information.

In the light of these issues, you should avoid combining metric and nominal variables in a single cluster analysis, but if this is not feasible, the *two-step clustering procedure* provides a valuable alternative, which we will discuss later. Lastly, the choice of the (dis)similarity measure is not extremely critical to recovering the underlying cluster structure. In this regard, the choice of the clustering algorithm is far more important. We therefore deal with this aspect in the following section.

Select a Clustering Algorithm

After having chosen the distance or similarity measure, we need to decide which clustering algorithm to apply. There are several agglomerative procedures and they can be distinguished by the way they define the distance from a newly formed cluster to a certain object, or to other clusters in the solution. The most popular agglomerative clustering procedures include the following:

- *Single linkage* (nearest neighbor): The distance between two clusters corresponds to the shortest distance between any two members in the two clusters.
- *Complete linkage* (furthest neighbor): The oppositional approach to single linkage assumes that the distance between two clusters is based on the longest distance between any two members in the two clusters.
- *Average linkage*: The distance between two clusters is defined as the average distance between all pairs of the two clusters' members.
- *Centroid*: In this approach, the geometric center (centroid) of each cluster is computed first. The distance between the two clusters equals the distance between the two centroids.

Figures 9.5–9.8 illustrate these linkage procedures for two randomly framed clusters.

Fig. 9.5 Single linkage

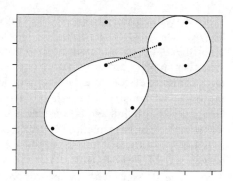

Fig. 9.6 Complete linkage

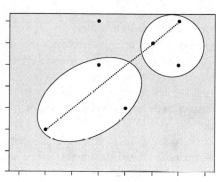

Fig. 9.7 Average linkage

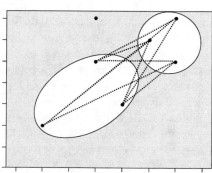

Fig. 9.8 Centroid

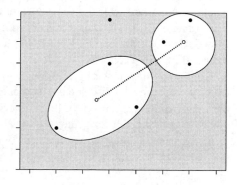

Each of these linkage algorithms can yield totally different results when used on the same dataset, as each has its specific properties. As the single linkage algorithm is based on minimum distances, it tends to form one large cluster with the other clusters containing only one or few objects each. We can make use of this "chaining effect" to detect outliers, as these will be merged with the remaining objects – usually at very large distances – in the last steps of the analysis. Generally, single linkage is considered the most versatile algorithm. Conversely, the complete linkage method is strongly affected by outliers, as it is based on maximum distances. Clusters produced by this method are likely to be rather compact and tightly clustered. The average linkage and centroid algorithms tend to produce clusters with rather low within-cluster variance and similar sizes. However, both procedures are affected by outliers, though not as much as complete linkage.

Another commonly used approach in hierarchical clustering is *Ward's method*. This approach does not combine the two most similar objects successively. Instead, those objects whose merger increases the overall within-cluster variance to the smallest possible degree, are combined. If you expect somewhat equally sized clusters and the dataset does not include outliers, you should always use Ward's method.

To better understand how a clustering algorithm works, let's manually examine some of the single linkage procedure's calculation steps. We start off by looking at the initial (Euclidean) distance matrix in Table 9.3. In the very first step, the two objects exhibiting the smallest distance in the matrix are merged. Note that we always merge those objects with the smallest distance, regardless of the clustering procedure (e.g., single or complete linkage). As we can see, this happens to two pairs of objects, namely B and C ($d(B, C) = 1.414$), as well as C and E ($d(C, E) = 1.414$). In the next step, we will see that it does not make any difference whether we first merge the one or the other, so let's proceed by forming a new cluster, using objects B and C.

Having made this decision, we then form a new distance matrix by considering the single linkage decision rule as discussed above. According to this rule, the distance from, for example, object A to the newly formed cluster is the minimum of $d(A, B)$ and $d(A, C)$. As $d(A, C)$ is smaller than $d(A, B)$, the distance from A to the newly formed cluster is equal to $d(A, C)$; that is, 2.236. We also compute the distances from cluster [B,C] (clusters are indicated by means of squared brackets) to all other objects (i.e. D, E, F, G) and simply copy the remaining distances – such as $d(E, F)$ – that the previous clustering has not affected. This yields the distance matrix shown in Table 9.6.

Continuing the clustering procedure, we simply repeat the last step by merging the objects in the new distance matrix that exhibit the smallest distance (in this case, the newly formed cluster [B, C] and object E) and calculate the distance from this cluster to all other objects. The result of this step is described in Table 9.7.

Try to calculate the remaining steps yourself and compare your solution with the distance matrices in the following Tables 9.8–9.10.

Table 9.6 Distance matrix after first clustering step (single linkage)

Objects	A	B, C	D	E	F	G
A	0					
B, C	2.236	0				
D	2	2.236	0			
E	3.606	1.414	3	0		
F	4.123	3.162	2.236	2.828	0	
G	5.385	5.657	3.606	5.831	3.162	0

Table 9.7 Distance matrix after second clustering step (single linkage)

Objects	A	B, C, E	D	F	G
A	0				
B, C, E	2.236	0			
D	2	2.236	0		
F	4.123	2.828	2.236	0	
G	5.385	5.657	3.606	3.162	0

Table 9.8 Distance matrix after third clustering step (single linkage)

Objects	A, D	B, C, E	F	G
A, D	0			
B, C, E	2.236	0		
F	2.236	2.828	0	
G	3.606	5.657	3.162	0

Table 9.9 Distance matrix after fourth clustering step (single linkage)

Objects	A, B, C, D, E	F	G
A, B, C, D, E	0		
F	2.236	0	
G	3.606	3.162	0

Table 9.10 Distance matrix after fifth clustering step (single linkage)

Objects	A, B, C, D, E, F	G
A, B, C, D, E, F	0	
G	3.162	0

By following the single linkage procedure, the last steps involve the merger of cluster [A,B,C,D,E,F] and object G at a distance of 3.162. Do you get the same results? As you can see, conducting a basic cluster analysis manually is not that hard at all – not if there are only a few objects in the dataset.

A common way to visualize the cluster analysis's progress is by drawing a *dendrogram*, which displays the distance level at which there was a combination of objects and clusters (Fig. 9.9).

We read the dendrogram from left to right to see at which distance objects have been combined. For example, according to our calculations above, objects B, C, and E are combined at a distance level of 1.414.

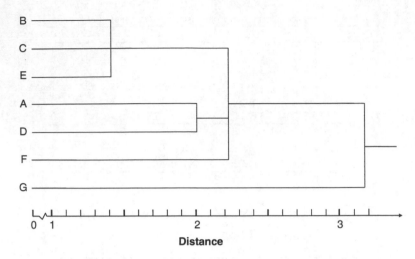

Fig. 9.9 Dendrogram

Decide on the Number of Clusters

An important question we haven't yet addressed is how to decide on the number of clusters to retain from the data. Unfortunately, hierarchical methods provide only very limited guidance for making this decision. The only meaningful indicator relates to the distances at which the objects are combined. Similar to factor analysis's scree plot, we can seek a solution in which an additional combination of clusters or objects would occur at a greatly increased distance. This raises the issue of what a great distance is, of course.

One potential way to solve this problem is to plot the number of clusters on the x-axis (starting with the one-cluster solution at the very left) against the distance at which objects or clusters are combined on the y-axis. Using this plot, we then search for the distinctive break (*elbow*). SPSS does not produce this plot automatically – you have to use the distances provided by SPSS to draw a line chart by using a common spreadsheet program such as Microsoft Excel.

Alternatively, we can make use of the dendrogram which essentially carries the same information. SPSS provides a dendrogram; however, this differs slightly from the one presented in Fig. 9.9. Specifically, SPSS rescales the distances to a range of 0–25; that is, the last merging step to a one-cluster solution takes place at a (rescaled) distance of 25. The rescaling often lengthens the merging steps, thus making breaks occurring at a greatly increased distance level more obvious.

Despite this, this distance-based decision rule does not work very well in all cases. It is often difficult to identify where the break actually occurs. This is also the case in our example above. By looking at the dendrogram, we could justify a two-cluster solution ([A,B,C,D,E,F] and [G]), as well as a five-cluster solution ([B,C,E], [A], [D], [F], [G]).

Research has suggested several other procedures for determining the number of clusters in a dataset. Most notably, the *variance ratio criterion* (VRC) by Calinski and Harabasz (1974) has proven to work well in many situations.[8] For a solution with n objects and k segments, the criterion is given by:

$$VRC_k = (SS_B/(k-1))/(SS_W/(n-k)),$$

where SS_B is the sum of the squares between the segments and SS_W is the sum of the squares within the segments. The criterion should seem familiar, as this is nothing but the F-value of a one-way ANOVA, with k representing the factor levels. Consequently, the VRC can easily be computed using SPSS, even though it is not readily available in the clustering procedures' outputs.

To finally determine the appropriate number of segments, we compute ω_k for each segment solution as follows:

$$\omega_k = (VRC_{k+1} - VRC_k) - (VRC_k - VRC_{k-1}).$$

In the next step, we choose the number of segments k that minimizes the value in ω_k. Owing to the term VRC_{k-1}, the minimum number of clusters that can be selected is three, which is a clear disadvantage of the criterion, thus limiting its application in practice.

Overall, the data can often only provide rough guidance regarding the number of clusters you should select; consequently, you should rather revert to practical considerations. Occasionally, you might have a priori knowledge, or a theory on which you can base your choice. However, first and foremost, you should ensure that your results are interpretable and meaningful. Not only must the number of clusters be small enough to ensure manageability, but each segment should also be large enough to warrant strategic attention.

Partitioning Methods: k-means

Another important group of clustering procedures are partitioning methods. As with hierarchical clustering, there is a wide array of different algorithms; of these, the *k-means procedure* is the most important one for market research.[9] The k-means algorithm follows an entirely different concept than the hierarchical methods discussed before. This algorithm is not based on distance measures such as Euclidean distance or city-block distance, but uses the within-cluster variation as a

---

[8]Milligan and Cooper (1985) compare various criteria.

[9]Note that the k-means algorithm is one of the simplest non-hierarchical clustering methods. Several extensions, such as k-medoids (Kaufman and Rousseeuw 2005) have been proposed to handle problematic aspects of the procedure. More advanced methods include finite mixture models (McLachlan and Peel 2000), neural networks (Bishop 2006), and self-organizing maps (Kohonen 1982). Andrews and Currim (2003) discuss the validity of some of these approaches.

measure to form homogenous clusters. Specifically, the procedure aims at segmenting the data in such a way that the within-cluster variation is minimized. Consequently, we do not need to decide on a distance measure in the first step of the analysis.

The clustering process starts by randomly assigning objects to a number of clusters.[10] The objects are then successively reassigned to other clusters to minimize the within-cluster variation, which is basically the (squared) distance from each observation to the center of the associated cluster. If the reallocation of an object to another cluster decreases the within-cluster variation, this object is reassigned to that cluster.

With the hierarchical methods, an object remains in a cluster once it is assigned to it, but with k-means, cluster affiliations can change in the course of the clustering process. Consequently, k-means does not build a hierarchy as described before (Fig. 9.3), which is why the approach is also frequently labeled as non-hierarchical.

For a better understanding of the approach, let's take a look at how it works in practice. Figs. 9.10–9.13 illustrate the k-means clustering process.

Prior to analysis, we have to decide on the number of clusters. Our client could, for example, tell us how many segments are needed, or we may know from previous research what to look for. Based on this information, the algorithm randomly selects a center for each cluster (step 1). In our example, two cluster centers are randomly initiated, which CC1 (first cluster) and CC2 (second cluster) in Fig. 9.10

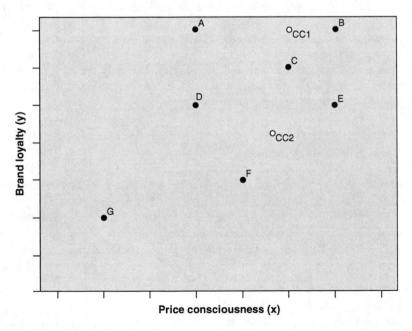

Fig. 9.10 k-means procedure (step 1)

---

[10]Note this holds for the algorithms original design. SPSS does not choose centers randomly.

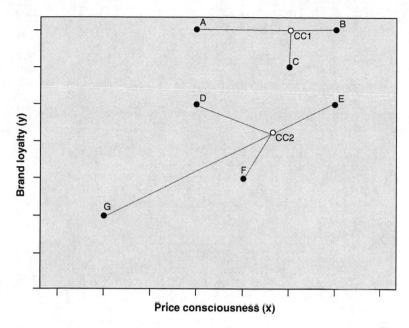

Fig. 9.11 k-means procedure (step 2)

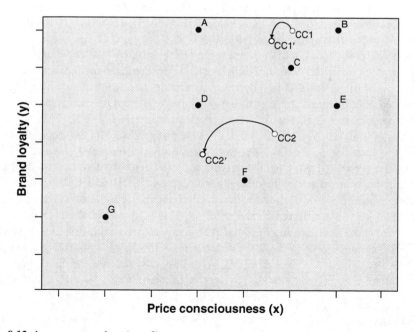

Fig. 9.12 k-means procedure (step 3)

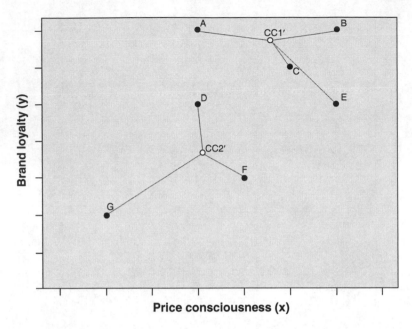

Fig. 9.13 k-means procedure (step 4)

represent.[11] After this (step 2), Euclidean distances are computed from the cluster centers to every single object. Each object is then assigned to the cluster center with the shortest distance to it. In our example (Fig. 9.11), objects A, B, and C are assigned to the first cluster, whereas objects D, E, F, and G are assigned to the second. We now have our initial partitioning of the objects into two clusters.

Based on this initial partition, each cluster's geometric center (i.e., its centroid) is computed (third step). This is done by computing the mean values of the objects contained in the cluster (e.g., A, B, C in the first cluster) regarding each of the variables (price consciousness and brand loyalty). As we can see in Fig. 9.12, both clusters' centers now shift into new positions (CC1' for the first and CC2' for the second cluster).

In the fourth step, the distances from each object to the newly located cluster centers are computed and objects are again assigned to a certain cluster on the basis of their minimum distance to other cluster centers (CC1' and CC2'). Since the cluster centers' position changed with respect to the initial situation in the first step, this could lead to a different cluster solution. This is also true of our example, as object E is now – unlike in the initial partition – closer to the first cluster center (CC1') than to the second (CC2'). Consequently, this object is now assigned to the first cluster (Fig. 9.13). The k-means procedure now repeats the third step and re-computes the cluster centers of the newly formed clusters, and so on. In other

---

[11]Conversely, SPSS always sets one observation as the cluster center instead of picking some random point in the dataset.

words, steps 3 and 4 are repeated until a predetermined number of iterations are reached, or convergence is achieved (i.e., there is no change in the cluster affiliations).

Generally, k-means is superior to hierarchical methods as it is less affected by outliers and the presence of irrelevant clustering variables. Furthermore, k-means can be applied to very large datasets, as the procedure is less computationally demanding than hierarchical methods. In fact, we suggest definitely using k-means for sample sizes above 500, especially if many clustering variables are used. From a strictly statistical viewpoint, k-means should only be used on interval or ratio-scaled data as the procedure relies on Euclidean distances. However, the procedure is routinely used on ordinal data as well, even though there might be some distortions.

One problem associated with the application of k-means relates to the fact that the researcher has to pre-specify the number of clusters to retain from the data. This makes k-means less attractive to some and still hinders its routine application in practice. However, the VRC discussed above can likewise be used for k-means clustering (an application of this index can be found in the 🖱 Web Appendix → Chap. 9). Another workaround that many market researchers routinely use is to apply a hierarchical procedure to determine the number of clusters and k-means afterwards.[12] This also enables the user to find starting values for the initial cluster centers to handle a second problem, which relates to the procedure's sensitivity to the initial classification (we will follow this approach in the example application).

Two-Step Clustering

We have already discussed the issue of analyzing mixed variables measured on different scale levels in this chapter. The *two-step cluster analysis* developed by Chiu et al. (2001) has been specifically designed to handle this problem. Like k-means, the procedure can also effectively cope with very large datasets.

The name two-step clustering is already an indication that the algorithm is based on a two-stage approach: In the first stage, the algorithm undertakes a procedure that is very similar to the k-means algorithm. Based on these results, the two-step procedure conducts a modified hierarchical agglomerative clustering procedure that combines the objects sequentially to form homogenous clusters. This is done by building a so-called cluster feature tree whose "leaves" represent distinct objects in the dataset. The procedure can handle categorical and continuous variables simultaneously and offers the user the flexibility to specify the cluster numbers as well as the maximum number of clusters, or to allow the technique to automatically choose the number of clusters on the basis of statistical evaluation criteria. Likewise, the procedure guides the decision of how many clusters to retain from the data by calculating measures-of-fit such as *Akaike's Information Criterion (AIC)* or *Bayes*

---

[12]See Punji and Stewart (1983) for additional information on this sequential approach.

Information Criterion (BIC). Furthermore, the procedure indicates each variable's importance for the construction of a specific cluster. These desirable features make the somewhat less popular two-step clustering a viable alternative to the traditional methods. You can find a more detailed discussion of the two-step clustering procedure in the ⏎ Web Appendix (→ Chap. 9), but we will also apply this method in the subsequent example.

Validate and Interpret the Cluster Solution

Before interpreting the cluster solution, we have to assess the solution's stability and validity. Stability is evaluated by using different clustering procedures on the same data and testing whether these yield the same results. In hierarchical clustering, you can likewise use different distance measures. However, please note that it is common for results to change even when your solution is adequate. How much variation you should allow before questioning the stability of your solution is a matter of taste. Another common approach is to split the dataset into two halves and to thereafter analyze the two subsets separately using the same parameter settings. You then compare the two solutions' cluster centroids. If these do not differ significantly, you can presume that the overall solution has a high degree of stability. When using hierarchical clustering, it is also worthwhile changing the order of the objects in your dataset and re-running the analysis to check the results' stability. The results should not, of course, depend on the order of the dataset. If they do, you should try to ascertain if any obvious outliers may influence the results of the change in order.

Assessing the solution's reliability is closely related to the above, as reliability refers to the degree to which the solution is stable over time. If segments quickly change their composition, or its members their behavior, targeting strategies are likely not to succeed. Therefore, a certain degree of stability is necessary to ensure that marketing strategies can be implemented and produce adequate results. This can be evaluated by critically revisiting and replicating the clustering results at a later point in time.

To validate the clustering solution, we need to assess its criterion validity. In research, we could focus on criterion variables that have a theoretically based relationship with the clustering variables, but were not included in the analysis. In market research, criterion variables usually relate to managerial outcomes such as the sales per person, or satisfaction. If these criterion variables differ significantly, we can conclude that the clusters are distinct groups with criterion validity.

To judge validity, you should also assess face validity and, if possible, expert validity. While we primarily consider criterion validity when choosing clustering variables, as well as in this final step of the analysis procedure, the assessment of face validity is a process rather than a single event. The key to successful segmentation is to critically revisit the results of different cluster analysis set-ups (e.g., by using different algorithms on the same data) in terms of managerial relevance. This underlines the exploratory character of the method. The following criteria will help you make an evaluation choice for a clustering solution (Dibb 1999; Tonks 2009; Kotler and Keller 2009).

- *Substantial*: The segments are large and profitable enough to serve.
- *Accessible*: The segments can be effectively reached and served, which requires them to be characterized by means of observable variables.
- *Differentiable*: The segments can be distinguished conceptually and respond differently to different marketing-mix elements and programs.
- *Actionable*: Effective programs can be formulated to attract and serve the segments.
- *Stable*: Only segments that are stable over time can provide the necessary grounds for a successful marketing strategy.
- *Parsimonious*: To be managerially meaningful, only a small set of substantial clusters should be identified.
- *Familiar*: To ensure management acceptance, the segments composition should be comprehensible.
- *Relevant*: Segments should be relevant in respect of the company's competencies and objectives.
- *Compactness*: Segments exhibit a high degree of within-segment homogeneity and between-segment heterogeneity.
- *Compatibility*: Segmentation results meet other managerial functions' requirements.

The final step of any cluster analysis is the interpretation of the clusters.

Interpreting clusters always involves examining the cluster centroids, which are the clustering variables' average values of all objects in a certain cluster. This step is of the utmost importance, as the analysis sheds light on whether the segments are conceptually distinguishable. Only if certain clusters exhibit significantly different means in these variables are they distinguishable – from a data perspective, at least. This can easily be ascertained by comparing the clusters with independent t-tests samples or ANOVA (see Chap. 6).

By using this information, we can also try to come up with a meaningful name or label for each cluster; that is, one which adequately reflects the objects in the cluster. This is usually a very challenging task. Furthermore, clustering variables are frequently unobservable, which poses another problem. How can we decide to which segment a new object should be assigned if its unobservable characteristics, such as personality traits, personal values or lifestyles, are unknown? We could obviously try to survey these attributes and make a decision based on the clustering variables. However, this will not be feasible in most situations and researchers therefore try to identify observable variables that best mirror the partition of the objects. If it is possible to identify, for example, demographic variables leading to a very similar partition as that obtained through the segmentation, then it is easy to assign a new object to a certain segment on the basis of these demographic characteristics. These variables can then also be used to characterize specific segments, an action commonly called *profiling*.

For example, imagine that we used a set of items to assess the respondents' values and learned that a certain segment comprises respondents who appreciate self-fulfillment, enjoyment of life, and a sense of accomplishment, whereas this is not the case in another segment. If we were able to identify explanatory variables such as gender or age, which adequately distinguish these segments, then we could partition a new person based on the modalities of these observable variables whose traits may still be unknown.

Table 9.11 summarizes the steps involved in a hierarchical and k-means clustering.

While companies often develop their own market segments, they frequently use standardized segments, which are based on established buying trends, habits, and customers' needs and have been specifically designed for use by many products in mature markets. One of the most popular approaches is the PRIZM lifestyle segmentation system developed by Claritas Inc., a leading market research company. PRIZM defines every US household in terms of 66 demographically and behaviorally distinct segments to help marketers discern those consumers' likes, dislikes, lifestyles, and purchase behaviors.

Visit the Claritas website and flip through the various segment profiles. By entering a 5-digit US ZIP code, you can also find a specific neighborhood's top five lifestyle groups.

One example of a segment is "Gray Power," containing middle-class, home-owning suburbanites who are aging in place rather than moving to retirement communities. Gray Power reflects this trend, a segment of older, midscale singles and couples who live in quiet comfort.

http://www.claritas.com/MyBestSegments/Default.jsp

We also introduce steps related to two-step clustering which we will further introduce in the subsequent example.

Table 9.11 Steps involved in carrying out a factor analysis in SPSS

Theory	Action
Research problem	
Identification of homogenous groups of objects in a population	
Select clustering variables that should be used to form segments	Select relevant variables that potentially exhibit high degrees of criterion validity with regard to a specific managerial objective.
Requirements	
Sufficient sample size	Make sure that the relationship between objects and clustering variables is reasonable (rough guideline: number of observations should be at least 2^m, where m is the number of clustering variables). Ensure that the sample size is large enough to guarantee substantial segments.
Low levels of collinearity among the variables	► Analyze ► Correlate ► Bivariate
	Eliminate or replace highly correlated variables (correlation coefficients > 0.90).
Specification	
Choose the clustering procedure	If there is a limited number of objects in your dataset or you do not know the number of clusters:
	► Analyze ► Classify ► Hierarchical Cluster
	If there are many observations (> 500) in your dataset and you have a priori knowledge regarding the number of clusters:
	► Analyze ► Classify ► K-Means Cluster
	If there are many observations in your dataset and the clustering variables are measured on different scale levels:
	► Analyze ► Classify ► Two-Step Cluster
Select a measure of similarity or dissimilarity (only hierarchical and two-step clustering)	*Hierarchical methods*:
	► Analyze ► Classify ► Hierarchical Cluster ► Method ► Measure
	Depending on the scale level, select the measure; convert variables with multiple categories into a set of binary variables and use matching coefficients; standardize variables if necessary (on a range of 0 to 1 or −1 to 1).
	Two-step clustering:
	► Analyze ► Classify ► Two-Step Cluster ► Distance Measure
	Use Euclidean distances when all variables are continuous; for mixed variables, use log-likelihood.
Choose clustering algorithm (only hierarchical clustering)	► Analyze ► Classify ► Hierarchical Cluster ► Method ► Cluster Method
	Use Ward's method if equally sized clusters are expected and no outliers are present. Preferably use single linkage, also to detect outliers.
Decide on the number of clusters	*Hierarchical clustering*:
	Examine the dendrogram:
	► Analyze ► Classify ► Hierarchical Cluster ► Plots ► Dendrogram

(*continued*)

Table 9.11 (continued)

Theory	Action
	Draw a scree plot (e.g., using Microsoft Excel) based on the coefficients in the agglomeration schedule.
	Compute the VRC using the ANOVA procedure: ▶ Analyze ▶ Compare Means ▶ One-Way ANOVA
	Move the cluster membership variable in the **Factor** box and the clustering variables in the **Dependent List** box.
	Compute VRC for each segment solution and compare values.
	k-means:
	Run a hierarchical cluster analysis and decide on the number of segments based on a dendrogram or scree plot; use this information to run k-means with k clusters.
	Compute the VRC using the ANOVA procedure: ▶ Analyze ▶ Classify ▶ K-Means Cluster ▶ Options ▶ ANOVA table; Compute VRC for each segment solution and compare values.
	Two-step clustering:
	Specify the maximum number of clusters: ▶ Analyze ▶ Classify ▶ Two-Step Cluster ▶ Number of Clusters
	Run separate analyses using AIC and, alternatively, BIC as clustering criterion: ▶ Analyze ▶ Classify ▶ Two-Step Cluster ▶ Clustering Criterion
	Examine the auto-clustering output.
Validate and interpret the cluster solution	
Assess the solution's stability	Re-run the analysis using different clustering procedures, algorithms or distance measures.
	Split the datasets into two halves and compute the clustering variables' centroids; compare centroids for significant differences (e.g., independent-samples t-test or one-way ANOVA).
	Change the ordering of objects in the dataset (hierarchical clustering only).
Assess the solution's reliability	Replicate the analysis using a separate, newly collected dataset.
Assess the solution's validity	*Criterion validity*:
	Evaluate whether there are significant differences between the segments with regard to one or more criterion variables.
	Face and expert validity:
	Segments should be substantial, accessible, differentiable, actionable, stable, parsimonious, familiar and relevant. Segments should exhibit high degrees of within-segment homogeneity and between-segment heterogeneity. The segmentation results should meet the requirements of other managerial functions.

(*continued*)

Example   265

Table 9.11 (continued)

Theory	Action
Interpret the cluster solution	Examine cluster centroids and assess whether these differ significantly from each other (e.g., by means of t-tests or ANOVA; see Chap. 6). Identify names or labels for each cluster and characterize each cluster by means of observable variables, if necessary (cluster profiling).

Example

Silicon-Valley-based Tesla Motors Inc. (http://www.teslamotors.com) is an automobile startup company focusing on the production of high performance electrical vehicles with exceptional design, technology, performance, and efficiency. Having reported the 500th delivery of its roadster in June 2009, the company decided to focus more strongly on the European market. However, as the company has only limited experience in the European market, which has different characteristics than that of the US, it asked a market research firm to provide a segmentation concept. Consequently, the market research firm gathered data from major car manufacturers on the following car characteristics, all of which have been measured on a ratio scale (variable names in parentheses):

- Engine displacement (*displacement*)
- Turning moment in Nm (*moment*)
- Horsepower (*horsepower*)
- Length in mm (*length*)
- Width in mm (*width*)
- Net weight in kg (*weight*)
- Trunk volume in liters (*trunk*)
- Maximum speed in km/h (*speed*)
- Acceleration 0–100 km/h in seconds (*acceleration*)

http://www.teslamotors.com

The pretest sample of 15, randomly taken, cars is shown in Fig. 9.14. In practice, clustering is done on much larger samples but we use a small sample size to illustrate the clustering process. Keep in mind that in this example, the ratio between the objects and clustering variables is much too small. The dataset used is *cars.sav* ($\circlearrowleft$ Web Appendix → Chap. 9).

	Name	displacement	moment	horsepower	length	width	weight	trunk	speed	acceleration
1	Kia Picanto 1.1 Start	1086	97	65	3535	1595	929	127	154	15.10
2	Suzuki Splash 1.0	996	90	65	3715	1680	1050	178	160	14.70
3	Renault Clio 1.2	1149	105	75	3986	1719	1155	288	167	13.40
4	Dacia Sandero 1.6	1598	128	87	4020	1746	1111	320	174	11.50
5	Fiat Grande Punto 1.4	1598	140	88	3986	1719	1215	288	177	11.90
6	Peugot 207 1.4	1360	133	88	4030	1748	1214	270	180	12.70
7	Renault Clio 1.6	1368	125	95	4030	1687	1135	275	178	11.40
8	Porsche Cayman	3386	340	295	4341	1801	1340	410	275	5.40
9	Nissan 350Z	3498	353	301	4315	1815	1610	235	250	5.80
10	Mercedes C 200 CDI	2148	270	136	4595	1770	1605	485	208	10.80
11	VWPassat Variant 2.0	1968	320	140	4774	1820	1596	588	201	10.50
12	Skoda Octavia 2.0	1968	320	140	4572	1769	1425	580	207	9.70
13	Mercedes E 280	2996	300	231	4852	1822	1660	540	250	7.30
14	Audi A6 2.4	2393	230	177	4916	1855	1525	546	231	8.90
15	BMW 525i	2497	250	218	4841	1846	1550	520	245	7.50

Fig. 9.14 Data

In the next step, we will run several different clustering procedures on the basis of these nine variables. We first apply a hierarchical cluster analysis based on Euclidean distances, using the single linkage method. This will help us determine a suitable number of segments, which we will use as input for a subsequent k-means clustering. Finally, we will run a two-step cluster analysis using SPSS.

Before we start with the clustering process, we have to examine the variables for substantial collinearity. Just by looking at the variable set, we suspect that there are some highly correlated variables in our dataset. For example, we expect rather high correlations between *speed* and *acceleration*. To determine this, we run a bivariate correlation analysis by clicking ▸ Analyze ▸ Correlate ▸ Bivariate, which will open a dialog box similar to that in Fig. 9.15. Enter all variables into the **Variables** box and select the box **Pearson** (under **Correlation Coefficients**) because these are continuous variables.

The correlation matrix in Table 9.12 supports our expectations – there are several variables that have high correlations. *Displacement* exhibits high (absolute) correlation coefficients with *horsepower*, *speed*, and *acceleration*, with values well above 0.90, indicating possible collinearity issues. Similarly, *horsepower* is highly correlated with *speed* and *acceleration*. Likewise, *length* shows a high degree of correlation with *width*, *weight*, and *trunk*.

A potential solution to this problem would be to run a factor analysis and perform a cluster analysis on the resulting factor scores. Since the factors obtained are, by definition, independent, this would allow for an effective handling of the collinearity issue. However, as this approach is associated with several problems (see discussion above) and as there are only several variables in our data set, we should reduce the variables, for example, by omitting *displacement*, *horsepower*,

Example   267

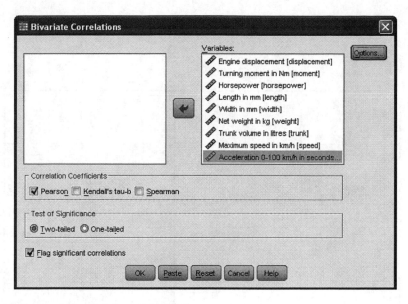

Fig. 9.15 Bivariate correlations dialog box

and *length* from the subsequent analyses. The remaining variables still provide a sound basis for carrying out cluster analysis.

To run the hierarchical clustering procedure, click on ▸ Analyze ▸ Classify ▸ Hierarchical Cluster, which opens a dialog box similar to Fig. 9.16.

Move the variables *moment*, *width*, *weight*, *trunk*, *speed*, and *acceleration* into the **Variable(s)** box and specify *name* as the labeling variable (box **Label Cases by**). The **Statistics** option gives us the opportunity to request the distance matrix (labeled proximity matrix in this case) and the agglomeration schedule, which provides information on the objects being combined at each stage of the clustering process. Furthermore, we can specify the number or range of clusters to retain from the data. As we do not yet know how many clusters to retain, just check the box **Agglomeration schedule** and continue.

Under **Plots**, we choose to display a dendrogram, which graphically displays the distances at which objects and clusters are joined. Also ensure you select the icicle diagram (for all clusters), which is yet another graph for displaying clustering solutions.

The option **Method** allows us to specify the cluster method (e.g., single linkage or Ward's method), the distance measure (e.g., Chebychev distance or the Jaccard coefficient), and the type of standardization of values. In this example, we use the single linkage method (**Nearest neighbor**) based on **Euclidean distances**. Since the variables are measured on different levels (e.g., speed versus weight), make sure to standardize the variables, using, for example, the **Range −1 to 1 (by variable)** in the **Transform Values** drop-down list.

Table 9.12 Correlation matrix

Correlations

		displacement	moment	horsepower	length	width	weight	trunk	speed	acceleration
displacement	Pearson Correlation	1	.875**	.983**	.657**	.764**	.768**	.470	.967**	-.969**
	Sig. (2-tailed)		.000	.000	.008	.001	.001	.077	.000	.000
	N	15	15	15	15	15	15	15	15	15
moment	Pearson Correlation	.875**	1	.847**	.767**	.766**	.862**	.691**	.859**	-.861**
	Sig. (2-tailed)	.000		.000	.001	.001	.000	.004	.000	.000
	N	15	15	15	15	15	15	15	15	15
horsepower	Pearson Correlation	.983**	.847**	1	.608*	.732**	.714**	.408	.968**	-.961**
	Sig. (2-tailed)	.000	.000		.016	.002	.003	.131	.000	.000
	N	15	15	15	15	15	15	15	15	15
length	Pearson Correlation	.657**	.767**	.608*	1	.912**	.921**	.934**	.741**	-.714**
	Sig. (2-tailed)	.008	.001	.016		.000	.000	.000	.002	.003
	N	15	15	15	15	15	15	15	15	15
width	Pearson Correlation	.764**	.766**	.732**	.912**	1	.884**	.783**	.819**	-.818**
	Sig. (2-tailed)	.001	.001	.002	.000		.000	.001	.000	.000
	N	15	15	15	15	15	15	15	15	15
weight	Pearson Correlation	.768**	.862**	.714**	.921**	.884**	1	.785**	.778**	-.763**
	Sig. (2-tailed)	.001	.000	.003	.000	.000		.001	.001	.001
	N	15	15	15	15	15	15	15	15	15
trunk	Pearson Correlation	.470	.691**	.408	.934**	.783**	.785**	1	.579*	-.552*
	Sig. (2-tailed)	.077	.004	.131	.000	.001	.001		.024	.033
	N	15	15	15	15	15	15	15	15	15
speed	Pearson Correlation	.967**	.859**	.968**	.741**	.819**	.778**	.579*	1	-.971**
	Sig. (2-tailed)	.000	.000	.000	.002	.000	.001	.024		.000
	N	15	15	15	15	15	15	15	15	15
acceleration	Pearson Correlation	-.969**	-.861**	-.961**	-.714**	-.818**	-.763**	-.552*	-.971**	1
	Sig. (2-tailed)	.000	.000	.000	.003	.000	.001	.033	.000	
	N	15	15	15	15	15	15	15	15	15

**. Correlation is significant at the 0.01 level (2-tailed).

*. Correlation is significant at the 0.05 level (2-tailed).

Example   269

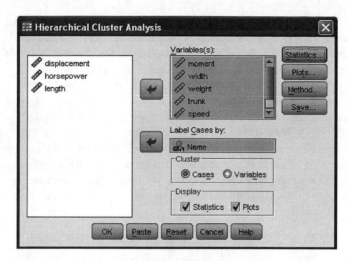

Fig. 9.16 Hierarchical cluster analysis dialog box

Lastly, the **Save** option enables us to save cluster memberships for a single solution or a range of solutions. Saved variables can then be used in subsequent analyses to explore differences between groups. As a start, we will skip this option, so continue and click on **OK** in the main menu.

Table 9.13 Agglomeration schedule

Agglomeration Schedule

Stage	Cluster Combined		Coefficients	Stage Cluster First Appears		Next Stage
	Cluster 1	Cluster 2		Cluster 1	Cluster 2	
1	5	6	.149	0	0	2
2	5	7	.184	1	0	3
3	4	5	.201	0	2	5
4	14	15	.213	0	0	6
5	3	4	.220	0	3	8
6	13	14	.267	0	4	11
7	11	12	.321	0	0	9
8	2	3	.353	0	5	10
9	10	11	.357	0	7	11
10	1	2	.389	0	8	14
11	10	13	.484	9	6	13
12	8	9	.575	0	0	13
13	8	10	.618	12	11	14
14	1	8	.910	10	13	0

First, we take a closer look at the agglomeration schedule (Table 9.13), which displays the objects or clusters combined at each stage (second and third column) and the distances at which this merger takes place. For example, in the first stage, objects 5 and 6 are merged at a distance of 0.149. From here onward, the resulting cluster is labeled as indicated by the first object involved in this merger, which is object 5. The last column on the very right tells you in which stage of the algorithm this cluster will appear next. In this case, this happens in the second step, where it is merged with object 7 at a distance of 0.184. The resulting cluster is still labeled 5, and so on. Similar information is provided by the icicle diagram shown in Fig. 9.17. Its name stems from the analogy to rows of icicles hanging from the eaves of a house. The diagram is read from the bottom to the top, therefore the columns correspond to the objects being clustered, and the rows represent the number of clusters.

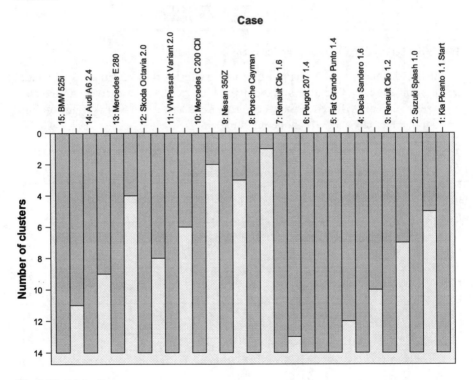

Fig. 9.17 Icicle diagram

As described earlier, we can use the agglomeration schedule to determine the number of segments to retain from the data. By plotting the distances (**Coefficients** column in Table 9.13) against the number of clusters, using a spreadsheet program, we can generate a scree plot. The distinct break (elbow) generally indicates the solution regarding where an additional combination of two objects or clusters would occur at a greatly increased distance. Thus, the number of clusters prior to this merger is the most probable solution. The scree plot - which we made

Example   271

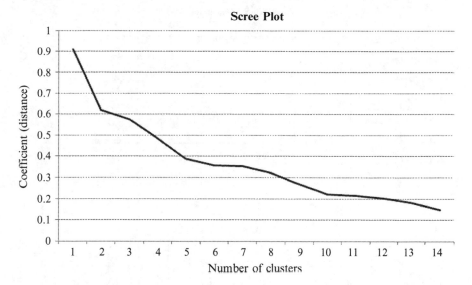

Fig. 9.18 Scree plot

separately using Microsoft Excel - (Fig. 9.18) does not show such a distinct break. Note that – unlike in the factor analysis – we do not pick the solution with one cluster less than indicated by the elbow. The sharp increase in distance when switching from a one to a two-cluster solution occurs in almost all analyses and must not be viewed as a reliable indicator for the decision regarding the number of segments.

The scree plot in Fig. 9.18 shows that there is no clear elbow indicating a suitable number of clusters to retain. Based on the results, one could argue for a five-segment or six-segment solution. However, considering that there are merely 15 objects in the dataset, this seems too many, as we then have very small (and, most probably, meaningless) clusters. Consequently, a two, three or four-segment solution is deemed more appropriate.

Let's take a look at the dendrogram shown in Fig. 9.19. We read the dendrogram from left to right. Vertical lines are objects and clusters joined together – their position indicates the distance at which this merger takes place. When creating a dendrogram, SPSS rescales the distances to a range of 0–25; that is, the last merging step to a one-cluster solution takes place at a (rescaled) distance of 25. Note that this differs from our manual calculation shown in Fig. 9.9, where we did not do any rescaling! Again, the analysis only provides a rough guidance regarding the number of segments to retain. The change in distances between the mergers indicates that (besides a two-segment solution) both a three and four-segment solution are appropriate.

To clarify this issue, let's re-run the analysis, but this time we pre-specify different segment numbers to compare these with regard to content validity. To do so, just re-run the analysis using hierarchical clustering. Now switch to the **Save** option, specify a range of solutions from 2 to 4 and run the analysis. SPSS generates

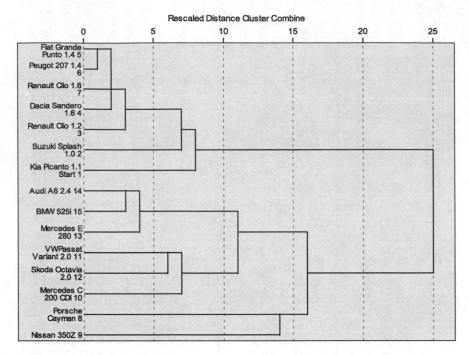

Fig. 9.19 Dendrogram

the same output but also adds three additional variables to your dataset (*CLU4_1*, *CLU3_1*, and *CLU2_1*), which reflect each object's cluster membership for the respective analysis. SPSS automatically places *CLU* in front, followed by the number of clusters (4, 3, or 2), to identify each object's cluster membership. The results are

Table 9.14 Cluster memberships

Name	Four clusters, observation member of cluster	Three clusters, observation member of cluster	Two clusters, observation member of cluster
Kia Picanto 1.1 Start	1	1	1
Suzuki Splash 1.0	1	1	1
Renault Clio 1.2	1	1	1
Dacia Sandero 1.6	1	1	1
Fiat Grande Punto 1.4	1	1	1
Peugot 207 1.4	1	1	1
Renault Clio 1.6	1	1	1
Porsche Cayman	2	2	2
Nissan 350Z	3	2	2
Mercedes C 200 CDI	4	3	2
VW Passat Variant 2.0	4	3	2
Skoda Octavia 2.0	4	3	2
Mercedes E 280	4	3	2
Audi A6 2.4	4	3	2
BMW 525i	4	3	2

Example   273

illustrated in Table 9.14. SPSS does not produce this table for us, so we need to enter these cluster memberships ourselves in a table or spreadsheet.

When we view the results, a three-segment solution appears promising. In this solution, the first segment comprises compact cars, whereas the second segment contains sports cars, and the third limousines. Increasing the solution by one segment would further split up the sports cars segment into two sub-segments. This does not appear to be very helpful, as now two of the four segments comprise only one object. This underlines the single linkage method's tendency to identify outlier objects – in this case the Nissan 350Z and Porsche Cayman. In this specific example, the Nissan 350Z and Porsche Cayman should not be regarded as outliers in a classical sense but rather as those cars which may be Tesla's main competitors in the sports car market.

In contrast, the two-segment solution appears to be rather imprecise considering the vast differences in the mix of sports and middle-sized cars in this solution.

To get a better overview of the results, let's examine the cluster centroids; that is, the mean values of the objects contained in the cluster on selected variables. To do so, we split up the dataset using the **Split File** command (▸ Data ▸ Split File) (see Chap. 5). This enables us to analyze the data on the basis of a grouping variable's values. In this case, we choose *CLU3_1* as the grouping variable and select the option **Compare groups**. Subsequently, we calculate descriptive statistics (▸ Analyze ▸ Descriptive Statistics ▸ Descriptives, also see Chap. 5) and calculate the mean, minimum and maximum values, as well as the standard deviations of the clustering variables. Table 9.15 shows the results for the variables *weight*, *speed*, and *acceleration*.

Table 9.15 Cluster centroids

Descriptive Statistics

CLU3_1		N	Minimum	Maximum	Mean	Std. Deviation
1	weight	7	929	1215	1115.57	100.528
	speed	7	154	180	170.00	9.950
	acceleration	7	11.40	15.10	12.9571	1.50317
	Valid N (listwise)	7				
2	weight	2	1340	1610	1475.00	190.919
	speed	2	250	275	262.50	17.678
	acceleration	2	5.40	5.80	5.6000	.28284
	Valid N (listwise)	2				
3	weight	6	1425	1660	1560.17	81.081
	speed	6	201	250	223.67	21.163
	acceleration	6	7.30	10.80	9.1167	1.48649
	Valid N (listwise)	6				

From the descriptive statistics, it seems that the first segment contains light-weight compact cars (with a lower maximum speed and acceleration). In contrast, the second segment comprises two sports cars with greater speed and acceleration, whereas the third contains limousines with an increased weight and intermediate speed and acceleration. Since the descriptives do not tell us if these differences are significant, we could have used a one-way ANOVA (menu ▸ Analyze ▸ Compare Means ▸ One-Way ANOVA) to calculate the cluster centroids and compare the differences formally.

In the next step, we want to use the *k-means* method on the data. We have previously seen that we need to specify the number of segments when conducting k-means clustering. SPSS then initiates cluster centers and assigns objects to the clusters based on their minimum distance to these centers. Instead of letting SPSS choose the centers, we can also save the centroids (cluster centers) from our previous analysis as input for the k-means procedure. To do this, we need to do some data management in SPSS, as the cluster centers have to be supplied in a specific format. Consequently, we need to aggregate the data first (briefly introduced in Chap. 5). By selecting ▸ Data ▸ Aggregate, a dialog box similar to Fig. 9.20 opens up.

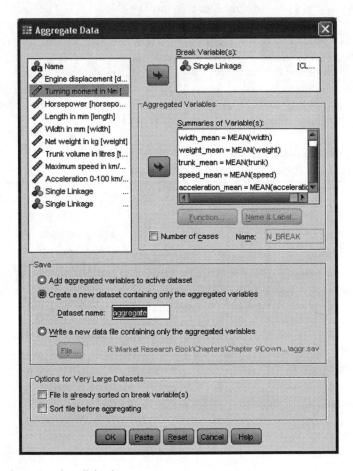

Fig. 9.20 Aggregate data dialog box

Example   275

Note that we choose **Display Variable Names** instead of **Display Variable Labels** by clicking the right mouse button on the left box showing the variables in the dataset. Now we proceed by choosing the cluster membership variable (*CLU3_1*) as a break variable and move the *moment, width, weight, trunk, speed,* and *acceleration* variables into the **Summaries of Variable(s)** box. When using the default settings, SPSS computes the variables' mean values along the lines of the break variable (indicated by the postfix *_mean*, which is added to each aggregate variable's name), which corresponds to the cluster centers that we need for the k-means analysis. You can change each aggregate variable's name from the original one by removing the postfix *_mean* – using the **Name & Label** option – if you want to. Lastly, we do not want to add the aggregated variables to the active dataset, but rather need to create a new dataset comprising only the aggregated variables. You must therefore check this under **SAVE** and specify a dataset label such as *aggregate*. When clicking on **OK**, a new dataset labeled *aggregate* is created and opened automatically.

The new dataset is almost in the right format – but we still need to change the break variable's name from *CLU3_1* to *cluster_* (SPSS will issue a warning but this can be safely ignored). The final dataset should have the form shown in Fig. 9.21.

Now let's proceed by using k means clustering. Make sure that you open the original dataset and go to Analyze ▸ Classify ▸ K-Means Cluster, which brings up a new dialog box (Fig. 9.22).

	cluster_	moment	width	weight	trunk	speed	acceleration
1	1	116.86	1699.14	1115.57	249.43	170.00	12.96
2	2	346.50	1808.00	1475.00	322.50	262.50	5.60
3	3	281.67	1813.67	1560.17	543.17	223.67	9.12

Fig. 9.21 Aggregated data file

As you did in the hierarchical clustering analysis, move the six clustering variables to the **Variables** box and specify the case labels (variable name). To use the cluster centers from our previous analysis, check the box **Read initial** and click on **Open dataset**. You can now choose the dataset labeled *aggregate*. Specify 3, which corresponds to the result of the hierarchical clustering analysis, in the **Number of Clusters** box. The **Iterate** option is of less interest to us. Instead, click on **Save** and check the box **Cluster Membership**. This creates a new variable indicating each object's final cluster membership. SPSS indicates whether each observation is a member of cluster 1, 2, or 3. Under **Options**, you can request several statistics and specify how missing values should be treated. Ensure that you request the initial cluster centers as well as the ANOVA table and that you exclude the missing values listwise (default). Now start the analysis.

The k-means procedure generates Tables 9.16 and 9.17, which show the initial and final cluster centers. As you can see, these are identical (also compare Fig. 9.21), which indicates that the initial partitioning of the objects in the first step of the k-means procedure was retained during the analysis. This means that it

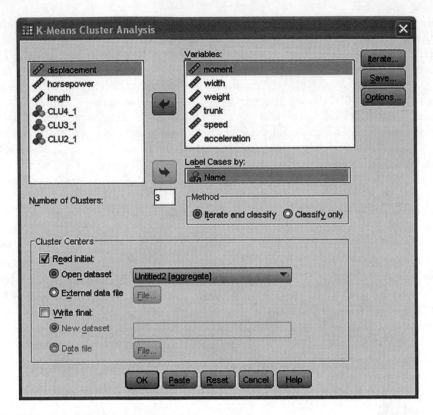

Fig. 9.22 K-means cluster analysis dialog box

Table 9.16 Initial cluster centers

Initial Cluster Centers

	Cluster		
	1	2	3
moment	117	347	282
width	1699	1808	1814
weight	1116	1475	1560
trunk	249	323	543
speed	170	263	224
acceleration	12.96	5.60	9.12

Input from FILE Subcommand

Example   277

Table 9.17 Final cluster centers

Final Cluster Centers

	Cluster		
	1	2	3
moment	117	347	282
width	1699	1808	1814
weight	1116	1475	1560
trunk	249	323	543
speed	170	263	224
acceleration	12.96	5.60	9.12

was not possible to reduce the overall within-cluster variation by re-assigning objects to different clusters.

Likewise, the output **Iteration History** shows that there is no change in the cluster centers. Similarly, if you compare the partitioning of objects into the three clusters by examining the newly generated variable QCL_1, you see that there is no change in the clusters' composition. At first sight, this does not look like a very exciting result, but this in fact signals that the initial clustering solution is stable. In other words, the fact that two different clustering methods yield the same outcomes provides some evidence of the results' stability.

In contrast to hierarchical clustering, the k-means outputs provide us with an ANOVA of the cluster centers (Table 9.18). As you can see, all the clustering variables' means differ significantly across at least two of the three segments, because the null hypothesis is rejected in every case (**Sig.** ≤ 0.05).

Table 9.18 ANOVA output

ANOVA

	Cluster		Error			
	Mean Square	df	Mean Square	df	F	Sig.
moment	64318.455	2	784.224	12	82.015	.000
width	23904.771	2	1966.183	12	12.158	.001
weight	339920.393	2	10829.712	12	31.388	.000
trunk	142764.143	2	4311.754	12	33.110	.000
speed	8628.283	2	262.153	12	32.913	.000
acceleration	50.855	2	2.057	12	24.722	.000

Since we used the prior analysis results from hierarchical clustering as an input for the k-means procedure, the problem of selecting the "correct" number of segments is not problematic in this example. As discussed above, we could have also used the VRC to make that decision. In the ⏀ Web Appendix (→ Chap. 9), we present a VRC application to this example.

As a last step of the analysis, we conduct a two-step clustering approach. First, go to Analyze ▸ Classify ▸ Two-Step Cluster. A new dialog box is opened, similar to that shown in Fig. 9.23.

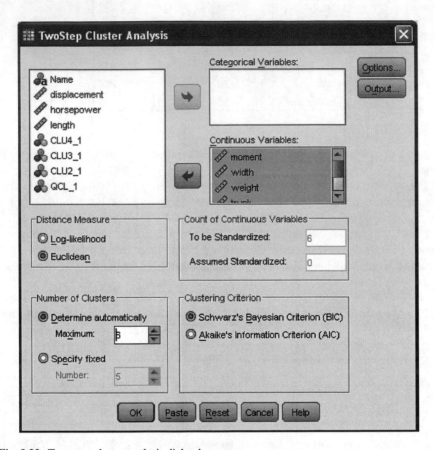

Fig. 9.23 Two-step cluster analysis dialog box

Move the variables we used in the previous analyses to the **Continuous Variables** box.

The **Distance Measure** box determines how the distance between two objects or clusters is computed. While **Log-likelihood** can be used for categorical and continuous variables, the **Euclidean** distance can only be applied when all of the variables are continuous. Unless your dataset contains categorical variables (e.g., gender) you should choose the Euclidean distance measure, as this generally provides better results. If you use ordinal variables and therefore use the **Log-likelihood** procedure, check that the answer categories are equidistant. In our dataset, all variables are continuous, therefore select the second option, namely **Euclidean**.

Example   279

Under **Number of Clusters**, you can specify a fixed number or a maximum number of segments to retain from the data. One of two-step clustering's major advantages is that it allows the automatic selection of the number of clusters. To make use of this advantage, you should specify a maximum number of clusters, for example, 6. Next to this box, in which the number of clusters is specified, you can choose between two criteria (also referred to as model selection or information criteria) which SPSS can use to pick an appropriate number of segments, namely **Akaike's information criterion (AIC)** and **Bayes information criterion (BIC)**. These are relative measures of goodness-of-fit and are used to compare different solutions with different numbers of segments. "Relative" means that these criteria are not scaled on a range of, for example, 0 to 1 but can generally take any value. Compared to an alternative solution with a different number of segments, smaller values in AIC or BIC indicate an increased fit. SPSS computes solutions for different segment numbers (up to the maximum number of segments specified before) and chooses the appropriate solution by looking for the smallest value in the chosen criterion. However, which criterion should we choose? AIC is well-known for overestimating the "correct" number of segments, while BIC has a slight tendency to underestimate this number. Thus, it is worthwhile comparing the clustering outcomes of both criteria and selecting a smaller number of segments than actually indicated by AIC. Nevertheless, when running two separate analyses, one based on AIC and the other based on BIC, SPSS usually renders the same results. But what do we do if the two criteria indicate different numbers of clusters? In such a situation, we should evaluate each solution on practical grounds as well as in light of the solution's interpretability. Do not solely rely on the automatic model selection, especially when there is a combination of continuous and categorical variables, as this does not always work well. Examine the results very carefully!

Under **Options**, you can specify issues related to outlier treatment, memory allocation, and variable standardization. Variables that are already standardized have to be assigned as such, but since this is not the case in our analysis, you can simply proceed.

Lastly, under the option **Output**, we can specify additional variables for describing the obtained clusters. However, let's stick to the default option for now. Make sure that you click the box **Create cluster membership variable** before clicking **Continue**. Note that the menu options as well as the outputs in SPSS 18 are no longer the same as in prior SPSS versions. Here, we discuss the menus and outputs as provided in SPSS 18, but if you want to learn what the analysis looks like in SPSS 17 (and prior versions), go to the ⌑ Web Appendix (→ Chap. 9).

SPSS produces a very simple output, as shown in Fig. 9.24. The upper part of the output describes the algorithm applied, the number of variables used (labeled input features) and the final number of clusters retained from the data. In our case, the number of clusters is chosen according to BIC, which indicates a two-segment solution (the same holds when using AIC instead of BIC). Note that this result differs from our previous analysis!

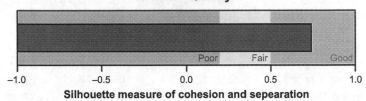

Fig. 9.24 Two-step clustering output

The lower part of the output (Fig. 9.24) indicates the quality of the cluster solution. The *silhouette measure of cohesion and separation* is a measure of the clustering solution's overall goodness-of-fit. It is essentially based on the average distances between the objects and can vary between −1 and +1. Specifically, a silhouette measure of less than 0.20 indicates a poor solution quality, a measure between 0.20 and 0.50 a fair solution, whereas values of more than 0.50 indicate a good solution (this is also indicated under the horizontal bar in Fig. 9.24). In our case, the measure indicates a satisfactory cluster quality. Consequently, you can proceed with the analysis by double-clicking on the output. This will open up the model viewer (Fig. 9.25), an evaluation tool that graphically presents the structure of the revealed clusters.

The model viewer provides us with two windows: the main view, which initially shows a model summary (left-hand side), and an auxiliary view, which initially features the cluster sizes (right-hand side). At the bottom of each window, you can request different information, such as an overview of the cluster structure and the overall variable importance as shown in Fig. 9.25.

In the main view, we can see a description of the two clusters, including their (relative) sizes. Furthermore, the output shows each clustering variables' mean values across the two clusters as well as their relative importance. Darker shades (i.e., higher values in feature importance) denote the variable's greater importance for the clustering solution. Comparing the results, we can see that *moment* is the most important variable for each of the clusters, followed by *weight, speed, width, acceleration,* and *trunk*. Clicking on one of the boxes will show a graph with the frequency distribution of each cluster. The auxiliary view shows an overview

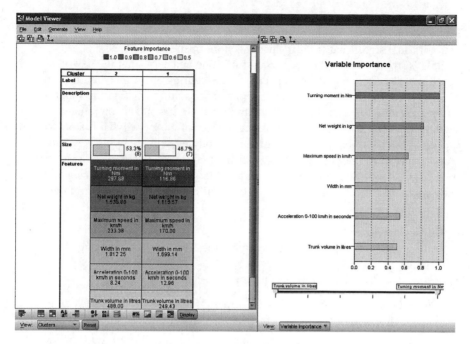

Fig. 9.25 Additional options in the model viewer

of the variables' overall importance for the clustering solution, which provides the same result as the cluster-specific analysis. The model viewer provides us with additional options for visualizing the results or comparing clustering solutions. It is worthwhile to simply play around with the different self-explanatory options. So go ahead and explore the model viewer's features yourself!

Case Study

Facing dramatically declining sales and decreased turnover, retailers such as Saks Fifth Avenue and JCPenney are rethinking their pricing strategies, scaling back inventories, and improving the fashion content. Men's accessories are one of the bright spots and Saks Fifth Avenue has jumped on the trend with three recently opened shops prominently featuring this category. The largest men's store opened in Beverly Hills in the late 2008 and stocks top brands in jewelry, watches, sunglasses, and leather goods. By providing a better showcase for men's accessories, Saks aims at strengthening its position in a market that is often neglected in the larger department store arena. This is because the men's accessories business generally requires expertise in buying since this typically involves small, artisan vendors – an investment many department stores are not willing to make.

The Beverly Hills store was chosen to spearhead the accessories program because it is considered the company's West Coast flagship and the department had not had a significant facelift since the store opened in 1995.[13]

Saks's strategy seemed to be successful if one considers that the newly opened boutiques already exerted an impact on sales during their first holiday season. However, before opening accessories shops in any other existing Saks stores, the company wanted to gain further insights into their customers' preferences. Consequently, a survey was conducted among visitors of the Beverly Hills store to gain a deeper understanding of their attitudes to buying and shopping. Overall, 180 respondents were interviewed using mall-intercept interviewing. The respondents were asked to indicate the importance of the following factors when buying products and services using a 5-point scale (1 = not at all important, 5 = very important):

- Saving time (x_1)
- Getting bargains (x_2)
- Getting products that aren't on the high street (x_3)
- Trying new things (x_4)
- Being aware of what companies have to offer (x_5)

The resulting dataset *Buying Attitudes.sav* (⌀ Web Appendix → Chap. 9) also includes each respondent's gender and monthly disposable income.[14]

1. Given the levels of measurement, which clustering method would you prefer? Carry out a cluster analysis using this procedure.
2. Interpret and profile the obtained clusters by examining cluster centroids. Compare differences across clusters on observed variables using ANOVA and post-hoc tests (see Chap. 6).
3. Use a different clustering method to test the stability of your results. If necessary, omit or rescale certain variables.
4. Based on your evaluation of the dataset, make recommendations to the management of Saks's Beverly Hills store.

Questions

1. In your own words, explain the objective and basic concept of cluster analysis.
2. What are the differences between hierarchical and partitioning methods? When do we use hierarchical or partitioning methods?
3. Run the k-means analysis again from the example application (*Cars.sav*, ⌀ Web Appendix → Chap. 9). Compute a three-segment solution and compare the results with those obtained by the initial hierarchical clustering.

---

[13]For further information, see Palmieri JE (2008). "Saks Adds Men's Accessories Shops," *Women's Wear Daily*, 196 (128), 14.

[14]Note that the data are artificial.

4. Run the k-means analysis again from the example application (*Cars.sav*, ✧ Web Appendix → Chap. 9). Use a factor analysis considering all nine variables and perform a cluster analysis on the resulting factor scores (factor-cluster segmentation). Interpret the results and compare these with the initial analysis.
5. Repeat the manual calculations of the hierarchical clustering procedure from the beginning of the chapter, but use complete or average linkage as clustering method. Compare the results with those of the single linkage method.
6. Make a list of the market segments to which you belong! What clustering variables did you take into consideration when you placed yourself in those segments?

Further Readings

Bottomley P, Nairn A (2004) Blinded by science: The managerial consequences of inadequately validated cluster analysis solutions. Int J Mark Res 46(2):171–187

In this article, the authors investigate if managers could distinguish between cluster analysis outputs derived from real-world and random data. They show that some managers feel able to assign meaning to random data devoid of a meaningful structure, and even feel confident formulating entire marketing strategies from cluster analysis solutions generated from such data. As such, the authors provide a reminder of the importance of validating clustering solutions with caution.

Everitt BS, Landau S, Leese M (2001) Cluster analysis, 4th edn. Arnold, London

This book is comprehensive yet relatively non-mathematical, focusing on the practical aspects of cluster analysis. The authors discuss classical approaches as well as more recent methods such as finite mixture modeling and neural networks.

Journal of Classification. New York, NY: Springer, available at:

http://www.springer.com/statistics/statistical+theory+and+methods/journal/357

If you are interested in the most recent advances in clustering techniques and have a strong background in statistics, you should check out this journal. Among the disciplines represented are statistics, psychology, biology, anthropology, archeology, astronomy, business, marketing, and linguistics.

Punj G, Stewart DW (1983) Cluster analysis in marketing research: review and suggestions for application. J Mark Res 20(2):134–148

In this seminal article, the authors discuss several issues in applications of cluster analysis and provide further theoretical discussion of the concepts and rules of thumb that we included in this chapter.

Romesburg C (2004) Cluster analysis for researchers. Lulu Press, Morrisville, NC

Charles Romesburg nicely illustrates the most frequently used methods of hierarchical cluster analysis for readers with limited backgrounds in mathematics and statistics.

Wedel M, Kamakura WA (2000) Market segmentation: conceptual and methodological foundations, 2nd edn. Kluwer Academic, Boston, NE

This book is a clear, readable, and interesting presentation of applied market segmentation techniques. The authors explain the theoretical concepts of recent

analysis techniques and provide sample applications. Probably the most comprehensive text in the market.

References

Andrews RL, Currim IS (2003) Recovering and profiling the true segmentation structure in markets: an empirical investigation. Int J Res Mark 20(2):177–192

Arabie P, Hubert L (1994) Cluster analysis in marketing research. In: Bagozzi RP (ed) Advanced methods in marketing research. Blackwell, Cambridge, pp 160–189

Bishop CM (2006) Pattern recognition and machine learning. Springer, Berlin

Calinski, T, Harabasz J (1974) A dendrite method for cluster analysis. Commun Stat Theory Methods 3(1):1–27

Chiu T, Fang D, Chen J, Wang Y, Jeris C (2001) A robust and scalable clustering algorithm for mixed type attributes in large database environment. In: Proceedings of the 7th ACM SIGKDD international conference in knowledge discovery and data mining, Association for Computing Machinery, San Francisco, CA, pp 263–268

Dibb S (1999) Criteria guiding segmentation implementation: reviewing the evidence. J Strateg Mark 7(2):107–129

Dolnicar S (2003) Using cluster analysis for market segmentation – typical misconceptions, established methodological weaknesses and some recommendations for improvement. Australas J Mark Res 11(2):5–12

Dolnicar S, Grün B (2009) Challenging "factor-cluster segmentation". J Travel Res 47(1):63–71

Dolnicar S, Lazarevski K (2009) Methodological reasons for the theory/practice divide in market segmentation. J Mark Manage 25(3–4):357–373

Formann AK (1984) Die Latent-Class-Analyse: Einführung in die Theorie und Anwendung. Beltz, Weinheim

Kaufman L, Rousseeuw PJ (2005) Finding groups in data. An introduction to cluster analysis. Wiley, Hoboken, NY

Kohonen T (1982) Self-organized formation of topologically correct feature maps. Biol Cybern 43 (1):59–69

Kotler P, Keller KL (2009) Marketing management, 13th edn. Pearson Prentice Hall, Upper Saddle River, NJ

Larson JS, Bradlow ET, Fader PS (2005) An exploratory look at supermarket shopping paths. Int J Res Mark 22(4):395–414

McLachlan GJ, Peel D (2000) Finite mixture models. Wiley, New York, NY

Milligan GW, Cooper M (1985) An examination of procedures for determining the number of clusters in a data set. Psychometrika 50(2):159–179

Milligan GW, Cooper M (1988) A study of variable standardization. J Classification 5(2):181–204

Moroko L, Uncles MD (2009) Employer branding and market segmentation. J Brand Manage 17(3):181–196

Okazaki S (2006) What do we know about Mobile Internet Adopters? A Cluster Analysis. Inf Manage 43(2):127–141

Punji G Stewart DW (1983) Cluster analysis in marketing research: review and suggestions for application. J Mark Res 20(2):134–148

Sheppard A (1996) The sequence of factor analysis and cluster analysis: differences in segmentation and dimensionality through the use of raw and factor scores," tourism analysis. Tourism Anal 1(Inaugural Volume):49–57

Tonks DG (2009) Validity and the design of market segments. J Mark Manage 25(3–4):341–356

Wedel M, Kamakura WA (2000) Market segmentation: conceptual and methodological foundations, 2nd edn. Kluwer, Boston, NE

Chapter 10
Communicating the Results

Learning Objectives

After reading this chapter you should understand:
- Why communicating the results is a crucial element of every market research study.
- Which elements should be included in a written research report and how these elements can be structured.
- How to communicate the findings in an oral presentation.
- Ethical issues regarding the communication of the report findings to the client.

Keywords Ethics · Follow-up · Identify and understand the audience · Minto principle · Oral presentation · Pyramid structure for presentations · Report structure · Visual aids · Written report

---

To discuss the significance and future development of information and communication technologies (ICT), TNS Infratest have published the International Delphi Study 2030 in May 2010. 551 international experts from business, academia and politics assessed 144 future scenarios in two consecutive survey waves by mid 2009. The development and use of ICT and media up to 2030 were assessed under four focal issues:
- Social implications of ICT development
- ICT innovation policy
- Infrastructure development and key technologies
- ICT drivers of innovation in central areas of application

The final 300-page report provides a comprehensive overview over the survey method, survey period, sample structure, study's results and includes recommendations for public policy and companies. The authors also included an executive summary which highlights the main findings by means of five core messages.

(continued)

E. Mooi and M. Sarstedt, *A Concise Guide to Market Research*,
DOI 10.1007/978-3-642-12541-6_10, © Springer-Verlag Berlin Heidelberg 2011

http://tinyurl.com/delphi2030

Introduction

Communicating results is a critical step in a market research project. This includes giving clear answers to the research questions and recommending a course of action, where appropriate. The importance of communicating marketing research results should not be underestimated. Even if the research has been carefully conducted, spending too little time and energy on communication makes it difficult for clients to understand the implications of the results and to appreciate the study's quality. To communicate the findings effectively, these need to be comprehensible to clients who may know little about market research and who may even be unfamiliar with the specific market research project. Hence, the communication must provide a clear picture of the whole project and should be relevant for the audience.

Usually, market researchers provide clients with a written report summarizing the key findings. This report is the written evidence of the research effort and is often the only record of the full results. In addition, market researchers frequently present findings to company management, which requires specific communication skills. Identifying the audience is critical, as this determines how the findings are best communicated. In this chapter, we discuss guidelines on how to communicate research findings effectively in written and oral form. We first discuss written reports before listing some cornerstones of oral presentations. We also provide some hints for research follow-up. At the end of the chapter, ethical issues related to market research are briefly reviewed.

Identify the Audience

When providing written reports (as well as oral presentations), you should keep the audience's characteristics and specific needs in mind and should tailor the report to their objectives. In market research, we have two audiences who need to be treated differently: academics and practitioners.

While academics are generally experienced in reading statistical data and interested in the underlying theory and methodological details, managers may wish to know how to solve a specific marketing problem and are thus primarily interested in the recommendations. In this chapter, we focus on this second important group of practitioners.

Imagine the marketing department of a company planning to launch a new product and therefore needing to learn more about potential customers' buying behavior. The knowledge and level of interest in the study might greatly differ within the department. While managers who commissioned the study generally know its objective and design, others, who are unfamiliar with its background (e.g., the marketing director or the sales staff) must also be made familiar with the research so that they can understand the research findings. When preparing the report, you should consider the following questions:

- Who will read the report?
- Why will they read the report?
- Which parts of the report are of specific interest to them?
- What do they already know about the study?
- What information will be new to them?
- What is the most important point for them to know after having read the report?

These questions help you determine the level of detail that has to be included in your report. Furthermore, they reveal information that requires specific focus during the project. Remember that a successful report is one that meets its audience's needs! However, not everything that you consider appropriate for your audience might actually be. Nothing is worse than suggesting an idea that is unpalatable to the audience, (e.g., saying that a specific behavior or attitude of the senior management is a major obstacle to success), or to propose a course of action that has been attempted before. Thus, informal talks with the client before results are presented are vital – never formally present findings without discussing them with the client first!

Further, ask clients early in the project what their expectations are and what recommendations they think will be made. A good market research company can then go beyond these anticipated findings and offer recommendations that clients do not expect. It increases the chances of obtaining truly new insights. Furthermore, this avoids presenting research findings that clients already know. Essentially, why spend, say, 50,000 USD if the answers are at hand? Asking clients what they anticipate can avoid this issue.

Structure the Written Report

When preparing a written report – besides the difficulty of satisfying several audiences – you also face the trade-off between discussing the study in too much detail, which risks boring the audience and perhaps even garbling the message, and providing too little information, leaving the readers unsure of the research quality. A clear structure can help readers navigate through the report to quickly and easily find those elements in which they are interested.

Although reports differ regarding the researcher, the client, the topic, and the nature of the project itself (just think of the introductory example on the International Delphi Study 2030), the outline presented in Table 10.1 is the suggested format for writing a research report.

Table 10.1 Suggested format for a written research report

TITLE PAGE
EXECUTIVE SUMMARY
TABLE OF CONTENTS
1. INTRODUCTION
1.1 Problem definition
1.2 Research objectives
1.3 Research questions and/or hypotheses[a]
2. METHODOLOGY
2.1 Population, sampling method and sample description
2.2 Quantitative and qualitative methods used for data analysis
3. RESULTS
4. CONCLUSIONS AND RECOMMENDATIONS
5. LIMITATIONS
6. APPENDIX

[a]In practice, the word hypotheses may not be used but terms such as research question(s) or proposition(s)

Title Page

The title page should state the title of the report, the name of the client who commissioned the report, the organization or researcher submitting it, and the date of release. The heading should clearly state the nature of the report. It may simply describe the research (e.g., "Survey of Mobile Phone Usage") or may outline the objectives of the study (e.g., "Increasing Adaption of Wireless Internet").

Executive Summary

The summary is the heart and core of the report because it is often the only part that executives read. But even those who read more will be influenced in their expectations by the summary. Hence, this section must be short enough so that busy executives are willing to read it, but should enable them to grasp the essence of the research.

The executive summary should contain key findings and recommendations and should stimulate interest in the full study. Furthermore, it should help the readers remember the key points of the entire report by providing the necessary background information on the study (research problem, approach, and design). Since the executive summary is very important, you should pay special attention to its structure. A common way of doing this is to follow the classic narrative pattern of story-telling. Begin with a description of the situation, then introduce a complication, which gives rise to a number of questions; lead the reader through your line of reasoning to the answer:

- *Situation*: background information that the reader already knows.
- *Complication*: a change from a formerly stable situation or a new business opportunity (i.e., the reason for your research study).
- *Question*: the scope and goal of your research study.
- *Answer*: your findings, conclusions, and recommendations.

Table of Contents

The table of contents helps the reader locate specific aspects of the report. Listings in the table of contents should correspond to the main headings of the report. It should also include lists of tables and figures with page references.

Introduction

This section must provide the reader with the project context. Questions to be answered include: Why was the study undertaken? What were the objectives and key questions? Is the study related to other studies and, if so, what findings did they produce?

Besides introducing the background and purpose of the research, this part should also shortly explain how the problem was addressed. In particular, theoretical foundations or analytical models on which the study was based are presented in this section. Hypotheses or propositions that will be tested during the research should be mentioned. Furthermore, unfamiliar terms used in the report have to be defined. For example, in the airline industry, terms such as CASM (cost per available seat mile) are used, which need explanation. As a rule, the following three questions regarding the research should be answered in the introduction, but should be neither too detailed nor too technical:

- What was done?
- How was it done?
- Why was it done?

Keep in mind that the introduction should set the stage for the body of the report and presentation of the results, but no more than that. A detailed description of how the data were collected and analyzed is provided in the next section of the report.

Methodology

In this section, you should describe the procedure of the research and the different statistical methods used for the data analysis. Although not everyone will be interested in the details, these must be presented precisely and coherently, allowing the reader to understand the process and basic principles of the analyses. Always consider your audience! If the audience has a strong interest in research methodology, you should describe the procedures in detail, but skip the basics. If the client has little knowledge of the analyses, you could introduce the methodology briefly. Should the explanations be extensive, integrate these in the appendix.

If not already stated in the previous section, you should define whether the study is exploratory, descriptive or causal in nature and whether the results are based on secondary or primary data. If primary data are used, their source should be specified (observation vs. questionnaire). If a questionnaire was used, you should state whether it was administered through face-to-face interviews, telephone interviews or web or mailed surveys. Explain why this particular method was chosen.

The reader should also know the demographic or other relevant characteristics of the target population. This includes the geographical area, age group, and gender. While it is usually sufficient to describe the population in a few sentences, the sampling method needs more explanation: How was the sample selected? Which sampling units were chosen? In addition, information on the sample size, response rate, and sample characteristics are essential as they indicate the results' reliability and validity.

A copy of the actual instruments used, such as the questionnaire or the interview guide, as well as detailed statistical analyses of the results should be included in the appendix or even as a separate report. Although these are important to fully understand the characteristics of the research project, their inclusion in the main text would make reading the report more difficult.

Results

This section is usually the longest in the report. Here, the researcher presents the findings and describes how these relate to a possible solution to the research problem and to the recommendations. There are several ways to logically present the results. You could, for instance, use the different research objectives as a guideline to structure this section and then analyze them one by one.

Another way is to first summarize the overall findings and then analyze them according to the relevant subgroups, such as gender or geographical regions. If several research methods were used, it is also possible to classify the findings correspondingly. For example, you could first present the conclusions of the secondary data collection and then those derived from an analysis of the questionnaire.

When presenting statistical data, tables and graphs should be used to bring life to the report and make it more interesting. Furthermore, tables and graphs structure information, thereby facilitating its understanding. Both allow the researcher to visually represent very complex data in a way which is not fully feasible when using tables. However, graphs can also be misleading as they can be adjusted to favor a specific viewpoint (see Box 10.1 for examples).

Box 10.1 Window-dressing with graphs

While graphs have the obvious advantage of presenting complex information in an accessible manner, they can be used to mislead the reader by promoting an idea or favoring a specific viewpoint. Experience in generating and interpreting graphs will help you spot these issues. In this box, examples are shown of how graphs can be presented in a misleading way.

By simply shortening the x-axis in Fig. 10.1 (i.e., removing the years 2003–2007), we convey a potentially misleading idea of the growth in units sold (Fig. 10.2). Likewise, we can "adjust" the y-axis by modifying the scale range (Fig. 10.3 vs. Fig. 10.4). By simply reducing the axis to a range from 98 to 114 units, the situation is made to look much more positive. Another typical example is the "floating" y-axis (Fig. 10.5 vs. Fig. 10.6) which increases the scale range along the y-axis, thus making the drop in number of units sold less pronounced visually.

Data are often presented using three-dimensional figures such as in Fig. 10.7. While these can be visually appealing, they are also subject to window-dressing. In this example, the lengths of all the edges were doubled to correspond to the 100% increase in turnover. However, the resulting area is not twice but four times as large as the original image, thus presenting a false picture of the increase.

These are just some common examples; Huff's (1993) classical text offers more on this topic.

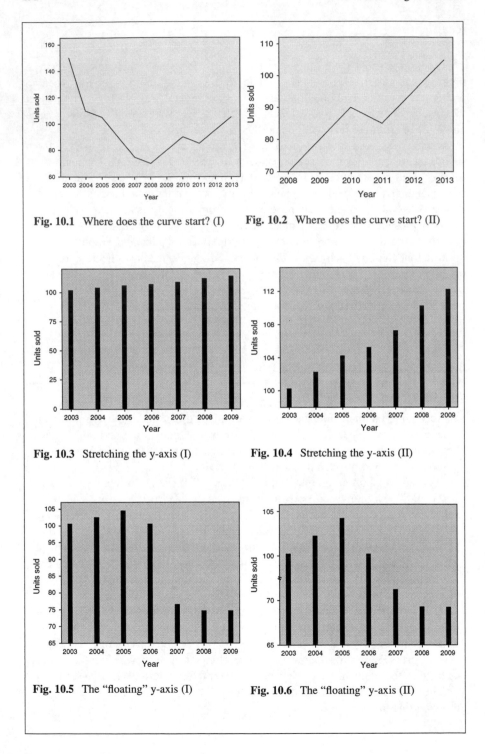

Fig. 10.1 Where does the curve start? (I)   **Fig. 10.2** Where does the curve start? (II)

Fig. 10.3 Stretching the y-axis (I)   **Fig. 10.4** Stretching the y-axis (II)

Fig. 10.5 The "floating" y-axis (I)   **Fig. 10.6** The "floating" y-axis (II)

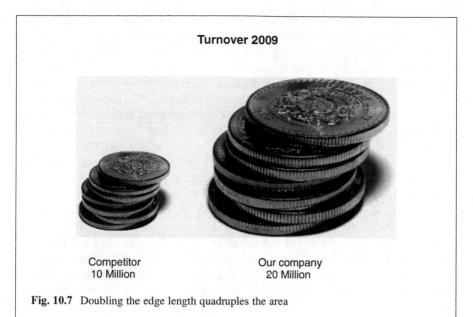

Turnover 2009

Competitor
10 Million

Our company
20 Million

Fig. 10.7 Doubling the edge length quadruples the area

On the other hand, tables are less susceptible to manipulation as they contain more detail. Tables present exact figures and thus enable the reader to accurately retrieve specific facts. As a rule, every table or graph in the report should be numbered sequentially and have a meaningful title, which briefly describes the information provided. Alternatively, you could use a representative quotation from an interview as the title, giving the graph or table a personal touch.

Note that executives need to grasp the message presented in the table or graph at a glance, because most readers first turn their attention to these before reading the accompanying text. Furthermore, units of measurement must be clearly stated. If the reader cannot easily determine whether a figure quoting "2 million" refers to the number of units sold or to turnover realized, the information cannot be interpreted correctly.

There are many different kinds of graphs and each type has its advantages and disadvantages. Please review Chap. 5 where we discussed the most commonly used graphs in marketing research studies.

Conclusion and Recommendations

Having presented the findings, the next step is to summarize the most relevant points and interpret them in light of the research objectives. You should write the conclusions in such a way that they present information relevant to managerial decision-making. Keep in mind that, for the client, the quality of the marketing research depends heavily on how well decision makers can use the information! The research must provide the client with clear benefits, which could lead to further research assignments.

Researchers are increasingly asked to go beyond merely stating facts and interpreting them, but to also provide recommendations or to advise on management decisions. Whereas conclusions that are purely based on the research have to be unbiased and impersonal, specific recommendations are grounded in a personal and (at least partially) subjective opinion on how the results can be most favorably used in the clients' interest. Thus, you have to make sure that recommendations are recognizable as such. The extent to which a research report should include recommendations is determined by the client during negotiations prior to the start of the project. This will also depend on the researcher's expertise in the area of concern.

In this respect, the researcher should be aware of all factors that influence the marketing issue. Researchers may provide logical recommendations based upon the findings of their work, yet these might be unrealistic or impossible for the client to implement due to issues such as insufficient budgets, fixed operation methods, or specific policies and regulations.

Consider the following example. A candy producing company wishes to know how it can increase sales and has commissioned a research organization to gain insights into its different customer segments. The researchers find that teenagers are the most important target for the given brand and suggest that vending machines within schools would increase the company's revenue. Although this could indeed boost sales, the recommendation does not help the company if vending machines are not allowed in schools. To avoid such issues, make sure that you or another member of your research team is familiar with the overall context, including regulatory and legal issues. Also consider whether the research is merely a part of a larger project. Furthermore, before making recommendations, review them with the client to determine whether these are acceptable and actionable.

Limitations

Finally, you should explain the extent to which the findings can be generalized. All research studies have limitations due to time, budget, and other constraints. Furthermore, errors might have occurred during the data collection. Not mentioning potential weaknesses, such as the utilization of a convenience sample, or a small sample size, for whatever reason, reduces the credibility of the research. Taking all factors into regard, the results of the research should always be discussed in a balanced and objective way. You should neither overly diminish the importance and validity of the research, nor try to conceal sources of errors and, hence, potentially mislead managers regarding the results you present.

Appendix

All material not directly necessary for an understanding of the project, but still related to the study should be included in the appendix. This includes questionnaires, interview guides, detailed data analyses or other types of data or material.

Guidelines for Written Reports

As already mentioned, you should always keep in mind who is being addressed in the report. Decision makers are typically less familiar with statistical details, but they wish to know how the findings relate to practice. Research jargon should be avoided, while keeping to the point, stating points clearly and not omitting any important facts or factors.

According to Churchill and Iacobucci (2009), there are four major rules to consider when writing a report:

1. The report must be *complete*, that is, it must contain all information that the reader needs to fully understand and appreciate the research. This also means that technical or ambiguous terms should be defined and illustrated. Not all readers understand terms like heteroskedasticity or Eigenvalue.

2. The report must be *accurate*. The readers will base their assessment of the entire research project's quality on the report. Consequently, the report must be well written. For example, the grammar must be correct, no slang should be used, tables must be labeled correctly, and page numbers should be included. Furthermore, objectivity is an important attribute of any report. This means that personal beliefs or feelings should influence the interpretation of the findings to the smallest possible degree.

3. The report must be *clear*. The art of writing a research report is to keep the language simple and concise. Try to use:

   - Short sentences instead of a complex sentence structure.
   - Simple and unambiguous words which are not likely to be misunderstood.
   - Concrete examples to illustrate difficult aspects of the research.
   - Active instead of passive voice to bring life to the report and to facilitate understanding.
   - Use the present tense as far as possible – avoid passive forms.

   Depending on your audience, try to present statistical data in a way that is easy to follow: for example, instead of saying "53% of the respondents are familiar with the brand," you could say "more than half of the respondents know the brand."

4. The report must be *concise*. As the report should be action-driven, the reader must immediately understand its purpose as well as its results. This means that you should not describe all the details, but should select important and interesting points. This rule also applies to the appendix, which should not be

overloaded with irrelevant material. In addition, keep in mind that the first sentences of each section are the most important ones: they should summarize the main idea you want to express in this section.

Guidelines for Oral Presentations

Most clients want a presentation in addition to the written report. This could be given during the research in the form of an interim report or at the end to explain the findings to the management. However, note that members of the client staff often present research findings to the management and not the market research company as such. Specifically, an internal market researcher or business analyst, who knows the context and business processes inside out, often delivers the presentation. Market research firms that are perceived as not familiar with the industry instantly lose their credibility when presenting to senior management. By letting the client deliver the presentation of the report, this may be avoided.

If asked to deliver an oral presentation, you should keep the principles of a written report in mind which are similar to those of oral presentations. It is especially important to identify and understand your audience and to prepare the presentation thoroughly. A disorganized presentation will have a negative impact on the managers' overall impression of the project. Similarly, a professional and interesting presentation might increase interest in the written report! Furthermore, since the oral presentation allows for interaction, interesting points can be highlighted and discussed in more detail. Conversely, if you are not well prepared for the presentation nor understand the expectations, needs, and wants of your audience, you could face an unpleasant situation. Finally, you should always keep the following golden rule in mind:

Never deliver a presentation you wouldn't want to sit through!

Structure the Oral Presentation

Be aware that an oral presentation cannot cover the same amount of information as in a written report. You must be selective and structure the presentation content clearly and logically. A good way of starting your presentation is by structuring the introduction in the classic narrative pattern of story-telling (situation → complication → question → answer) introduced earlier in the context of written reports. Limit the introduction to what the audience can accept. Nothing would be worse than triggering repudiation of what is presented right at the beginning of your oral presentation.

Next, move on to the main part of your presentation. Based on a brief description of your major findings, capture the audience's attention by presenting answers to the logical questions that arise from the project, such as "How were these results achieved?" or "How did we reach this conclusion?"

Essentially, you follow a pyramid structure: at any point you raise a question in the audience's mind that has to be answered in this pyramid's subsequently lower level. Figure 10.8 illustrates this concept using an example of a mobile phone study which found that a novel smartphone should be introduced in white.

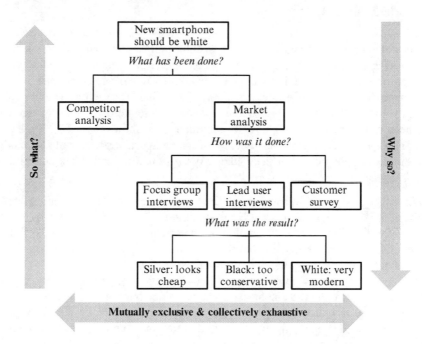

Fig. 10.8 Pyramid structure for presentations

You begin by introducing the result of the study (i.e., the smartphone should be introduced in white) and then work your way down. Begin by explaining that a comprehensive market analysis was carried out, after which you discuss the elements of the analysis (i.e., focus group interviews, lead user interviews, and a customer survey). Finally, present the results of each element in the report (e.g., that lead users perceived the black color as too conservative, silver as too cheap, while white was perceived as modern). Once at the bottom of the pyramid, it is time to pause and to provide a summary, before moving from the first key line which you have just presented to the next key line, and so on.

This process forces you to only provide the information relevant to the question under consideration. By moving from top to bottom and then bottom to top, helps you answer the questions: "Why so?" and "So what?," while being collectively exhaustive and mutually exclusive regarding the results and concepts you have presented. Ensure you never provide findings that do not lead to specific conclusions and do not offer conclusions that are not based on findings.

Ultimately, this pyramid approach helps the audience grasp the line of reasoning better.

This technique is also frequently called the *Minto principle* or *Minto pyramid*, called after its founder Barbara Minto. To learn more about this principle, we recommend Minto (2008).

Provide Visual Aids

It is useful to provide the audience with a written summary or a handout so that they do not have to note everything but can focus on the presentation. If focus group interviews were conducted, for example, you could show excerpts from the recordings to provide concrete examples in support of a finding. The saying "a picture says more than a thousand words" is also true of the oral presentation. Visual aids such as overhead transparencies, flip charts or computer slide shows (e.g., Powerpoint or Prezi at www.prezi.com) not only help emphasize important points, but also facilitate the communication of difficult ideas. We summarize some hints concerning slide shows:

- When using PowerPoint, use a simple master slide and avoid fancy animations.
- Use a sufficiently large font size (as a rule of thumb, 16pt. or higher and never less than 12pt.) so that everyone attending the presentation can read the slides.
- Do not have too much information on one slide (as a general rule, one key issue per slide). Never put a block of text on a page.
- Use simple graphs, diagrams or short sentences rather than tables.
- Use contrasting colors to emphasize specific points, but not too many.
- If you intend to use media elements in your presentation, make sure the equipment to be used supports them (e.g., that that the sound equipment is working or that your video formats are supported).
- Use a small number of slides relative to the time available for the presentation. The focus should be on the presenter and not on the slides. Having more slides than minutes available is not a good idea. Good presenters often use between 3 and 5 minutes to discuss a slide.
- Prepare colored handouts (e.g., print two slides per page) for all members of the audience.

Follow-Up

After having delivered the written report and oral presentation, two tasks remain: First, you need to help the client in implementing the findings. This includes answering questions that may arise from the written report and oral presentation, providing assistance in selecting a product, advertising agency, marketing actions etc., or incorporating information from the report into the firm's marketing information system or decision support system (see Chap. 3). This provides an opportunity for discussing further research projects. For example, you might agree on repeating the study after one year to see whether the marketing actions were effective. Second, you need to evaluate the market research project, both internally, and with the client. Only (critical) feedback can help disclosing potential problems that may have occurred and, thus, provide the necessary grounds for improving your work. Using uniform questionnaires for the evaluation of different projects helps to compare the feedback across different projects conducted simultaneously or different at points in time.

Ethics in Research Reports

Ethics is an important topic in marketing research, because research interacts with human beings at several stages (e.g., data collection and the communication of findings). There are two "problematic" relations that can ultimately lead to ethical dilemma.

First, ethical issues arise when the researcher's interests conflict with those of the participants. For instance, the researcher's interest is to gather as much information as possible from respondents but respondents often request confidentiality and privacy. Second, in addition to the legal and professional responsibilities that researchers have regarding their respondents, they also have reporting responsibilities. The Council of American Research Organizations (CASRO) sets clear guidelines in its "Code of Standards and Ethics for Survey Research":

It is the obligation of the Research Organization to insure that the findings they release are an accurate portrayal of the survey data, and careful checks on the accuracy of all figures are mandatory. (CASRO 2008, p. 16)

Similarly, the European Society for Opinion and Marketing Research (ESOMAR) has established a code which sets minimum standards of ethical conduct to be followed by all researchers:

- *Market researchers shall conform to all relevant national and international laws.*
- *Market researchers shall behave ethically and shall not do anything which might damage the reputation of market research.*
- *Market researchers shall take special care when carrying out research among children and young people.*
- *Respondents' cooperation is voluntary and must be based on adequate, and not misleading, information about the general purpose and nature of the project when their agreement to participate is being obtained and all such statements shall be honoured.*
- *The rights of respondents as private individuals shall be respected by market researchers and they shall not be harmed or adversely affected as the direct result of cooperating in a market research project.*

- *Market researchers shall never allow personal data they collect in a market research project to be used for any purpose other than market research.*
- *Market researchers shall ensure that projects and activities are designed, carried out, reported and documented accurately, transparently and objectively.*
- *Market researchers shall conform to the accepted principles of fair competition. (ESOMAR 2007, p. 4)*

In practice, though, researchers generally face an ethical dilemma. They are paid by the client and feel forced to deliver "good" results. In this sense, they might be tempted to interpret results in a way that fits the client's perspective or the client's presumed interests. For instance, researchers might ignore data because they would reveal an inconvenient truth (e.g., the client's brand has low awareness or customers do not like the product design). Similarly, if no statistically significant data could be found, researchers might try to over-interpret the findings.

Remember that researchers should never mislead the audience! For instance, it would be ethically questionable to modify the scales of a graph so that the results look more impressive, as shown in Fig. 10.1–10.4. Furthermore, researchers have a duty to treat information and research results confidentially. However, if a researcher works for various companies operating in the same industry, can using this knowledge for later research projects commissioned by another company really be avoided?

Above all, you should keep in mind that marketing research is based on trust. Thus, when writing the report, you should respect the profession's ethical standards in order to maintain this trust.

Questions

1. Why is the report such an important element of the research project?
2. What are the basic elements of any written research report?
3. Revisit the case study on Haver & Boecker in Chap. 8 and prepare an outline for a written research report.
4. Consider the following situations. Do you think they confront the market researcher with ethical issues?
   (a) The client asks the researcher to make a list of respondents available to target selling activities at these people.
   (b) The client asks the researcher not to disclose part of the research to his organization.
   (c) The client asks the researcher to present other recommendations.
   (d) The client asks the researcher to re-consider the analysis because the findings seem implausible to him/her.
   (e) The client wishes to know the name of a particular customer who was very negative about the quality of service provided.

Further Readings

Huff D (1993) How to lie with statistics. Norton & Company, New York, NY

First published in 1954, this book remains relevant as a wake-up call for people unaccustomed to the slippery world of means, correlations, and graphs. Although many of the examples used in the book are dated, the conclusions are timeless.

Durate N (2008) Slideology. The art and science of crafting great presentations. O'Reilly Media, Sebastopol, CA

In this book, the author presents a rich source for effective visual expression in presentations. It is full of practical approaches to visual story development that can be used to connect with your audience. The text provides good hints to fulfill the golden rule to never deliver a presentation you wouldn't want to sit through.

Market Research Society at http://www.mrs.org.uk/standards/guidelines.htm

Under this link you find the (ethical) guidelines of the Market Research Society. The guidelines discuss for example the ethical issues surrounding research using children or elderly as participants.

References

Churchill GA Jr, Iacobucci D (2009) Marketing research: methodological foundations, 10th edn. South-Western College Publishers, Mason, OH

Council of American Survey Research Organizations (CASRO) (2008) Codes of standards and ethics for survey research, http://www.casro.org/codeofstandards.cfm

European Society for Opinion and Marketing Research (ESOMAR) (2007) ICC/ESOMAR international code on market and social research, http://www.esomar.org/uploads/pdf/professional-standards/ICCESOMAR_Code_English_.pdf

Huff D (1993) How to lie with statistics. W. W. Norton & Company, New York, NY

Minto B (2008) The pyramid principle: logic in writing and thinking, 3rd edn. Pearson, Harlow

Index

E. Mooi and M. Sarstedt, *A Concise Guide to Market Research*,
DOI 10.1007/978-3-642-12541-6, © Springer-Verlag Berlin Heidelberg 2011